To Dad

With best wishes on your
80th. birthday, from Luchey &
Brian, with love.

TO SIR COMPTON MACKENZIE

On the High C's

(A LIGHT-HEARTED JOURNEY)

An Autobiography by

Father Sydney MacEwan

GLASGOW:
JOHN S. BURNS & SONS
1973

ILLUSTRATIONS

Foreword

Canon Sydney MacEwan has asked me to write a foreword to his remarkable autobiography, which he has so
generously dedicated to myself.

I first met Sydney MacEwan when he was a student at
Glasgow University and a member of the Committee of the
Glasgow University Scottish Nationalist Association which
secured my election as Rector in 1931. I was much impressed by the quality of his voice and the potential style
of his singing. I asked my old friend John McCormack to
give him a hearing—I wrote, " I would not be bothering
you with him if I didn't believe him to have the makings
of a really great tenor." McCormack's verdict was, "Go
ahead—make it your career." So the young singer went to
the R.A.M. I was also able to give him an introduction to
another old friend of mine, Plunkett Greene, who helped
his pupil to develop that wonderful clarity of enunciation
which has been a hallmark of all his work.

As early as 1934, the young singer was making records
for Parlophone and it was clear that a new star had arisen.
Then in 1936, after leaving the Academy, he made his first
world tour. His success in Australia was immediate and
outstanding, and success is not lightly won there among
audiences who really do know what good singing is.

Another world tour followed two years later, but by now
Sydney MacEwan knew that he had a vocation for the
Priesthood. He had a worldly career that the most ambitious artist might envy; the higher call summoned him to
reject that career. He entered Scots College in Rome as a
student and in 1944 he was ordained Priest.

7

Through the years he continued to make records and he was not lost to the concert platform. Thanks to the wisdom of his ecclesiastical superiors, Canon Sydney MacEwan was able to tour Australia in 1948 to earn precious money for the work of Almighty God, and with even greater success he was allowed to tour Australia again in 1951 to help raise some of the money necessary to finish the beautiful Cathedral in Oban. The U.S.A. was reconquered in 1954, 1955 and 1956. At this time, in my opinion, he was the greatest living interpreter of Celtic music. Sydney MacEwan's achievement is indeed heartening. I know of no other instance in which piety, art, romance and success have been so happily mingled.

It is a privilege for me to write this brief foreword because there is no greater pleasure for any artist than to see his own belief in another artist confirmed by the public. I only wish that John McCormack and Plunkett Greene were still alive to share that pleasure with me.

Compton Mackenzie

(COMPTON MACKENZIE)

CHAPTER

I

I am looking down a well again, like the one in the place where we trained to be priests.

A great, ancient, cool, oceanic well into which you could drop a stone and count the seconds till it reached the base.

At the bottom of the well I am looking in now is a little boy who thinks that his days are the happiest days of his life.

He is sixty years away, but I think he was right.

I was most of the time a kind of orphan in that I lived with only one parent. I certainly never felt like an orphan. I was never deprived. I was never aware of an emptiness in growing up without a father.

I was born on the 19th October, 1908, in a tenement house at 198 Keppochhill Road, Springburn.

Springburn is a sector of Glasgow, and we were on its fringe. Our block was a pleasant building, not long built, and Sighthill Cemetery was opposite, and the rail-road snaked away to Edinburgh.

My mother was a small, fragile woman, whose greatness was in her personality. She was skilled at portrait-painting, and she knew how to laugh at life. She was Irish and had a soldier-father, and their roots were deep in a little place not far from Portadown in Northern Ireland.

He was a sergeant in the Royal Irish Regiment and lies buried in Clonmel Barracks.

I had a great-uncle who was a bandmaster in the British Army, and another whose instrument was the anvil. As a sergeant-blacksmith, he hammered his way through Mons and enjoyed the miracle of emerging from that horrific experience intact.

With my granny, I used to go across to Portadown on a cattle boat from the Broomielaw, keeping close to the funnel to keep out the cold, because sometimes we travelled on nights that were bitter and wet. But warm with excitement for a seven-year-old.

We went to visit my mother's Uncle George and Aunt Lettie. There was an Aunt Mary who lived with them, and she was all that spoiled my jaunts to Ireland.

She was what you might call quaint. Night and day she always wore a hat—a black affair embellished with feathers. She wore it inside the house and out, and it must have been as old as Aunt Mary. She may have slept in it for all I know.

I never discovered whether her hair was weak, or she may have been completely bald. Certainly I wouldn't have dared to ask. In many ways she had a heart of gold. But to a little boy, she was an awesome figure. She used to be always in my nightmares.

One of our trips was to Aunt Lettie's funeral. Because I was small, the family thought the preliminaries of the funeral might be distasteful. So it was decided I should go for a walk with Charlie, my mother's cousin.

I liked Charlie. He was truly a magnificent man—probably the handsomest man I've known. But, as with all of us, Charlie had a weakness.

Our walk before the funeral was more of a pub crawl than a stroll. And when eventually he took me home, the mourners were beginning to move out of the house.

It was Charlie's distinction that he almost missed his own mother's funeral.

And it wasn't just black looks he got from the rest of the family—especially Aunt Mary.

Charlie Montgomery had a number of sisters, and they were all just as handsome. They were in fact the beauties of Portadown. Theirs was a pure, porcelain type of beauty. Perhaps they were too near perfection.

I've been back to the little churchyard there, and the Montgomery grave is the biggest of all. The Montgomery girls all died when young, each a victim of T.B.

It's reputed to be a bigoted town, although I never found it so. But they say the Pope's a bad word in Portadown. Yet I remember giving a recital there on 12th July, and the reception was warm and enthusiastic.

So much for the Irish part of me. My father was a Scot. He left my mother when I was very, very young. I have only the memory of a large man in a jaunty straw hat.

Long years after, I learned from an uncle that he once showed considerable athletic talent and ran at Powderhall. But the sporting instincts of the father I never knew didn't stop at athletics. I have the image of a punter at the races, a boxing fan and an exuberant supporter of fitba'. That is my picture of my father, whom my mother never once miscalled and who never darkened our door.

I have vague, young recollections of attempts at reconciliation. There was the priest who sought to bring them together again, and was shown to the door in no uncertain fashion by my grandmother with whom we lived.

My father was older than my mother, and she was into her ninetieth year when she died. She was round about 86 when a newspaper article reported that "Sydney MacEwan's mother is still alive, but his father is dead."

Two days later, I got a note which bore no sign of origin and said simply: "Tell that newspaperman I'm still very much alive!"

It was the only communication we ever had. He must have been a tremendous age, this sporting man with the strawbasher hat.

Looking back now, I am aware of just a tinge of sadness that we were never buddies. I have a feeling that, despite his neglect of his family, he was probably a jolly, companionable man, someone I think I'd like to have known.

We weren't long in Keppochhill when we moved to a room and kitchen in Gourlay Street. 248 was the number —I remember it well. What youngster could forget such days as those!

So far as a healthy boy was concerned, this humble row of humble homes could well have been termed Paradise Road. For consider its location.

We are still in Springburn, but green fields stretch right to the horizon. And almost as if for my special benefit, wonderful things began to happen in the green fields of Springburn. The tennis courts came, and the bowling greens, and most exciting of all, twelve football pitches!

In addition, what did this boy that was me look out on from his kitchen window? The Cowlairs railway engine yards. Not any old railway engine yards, but Cowlairs! I was thereby a constant surveyor of the locomotive centre for the world. Not for me mere dreams of driving one of these great steam giants. They were there every day at our kitchen window.

And my world was filled with engine-men—quiet, honest, hard-working, God-fearing fitters and turners and boiler-makers and coach-painters and carriage trimmers.

Sometimes they quarrelled, but never with knives or jagged bottles, and the policeman's lot in Gourlay Street was indeed a happy one.

Flanagan's Field, among the corn, was where feuds were settled on a Sunday morning—and no expensive Monday morning magistrates as their sequel. The bare-knuckle fighting in Flanagan's Field, with the combatants invariably stripped to the waist, was always fair and manly and finished with the handshake of peace.

We were a Co-operative family, and we called it " The Co." Indeed, in those far-off, unpretentious, kail-and-mince days, I should imagine the greater part of the whole of Springburn did its shopping at " The Co " as a matter of necessity.

Friday was my day for going the messages, and I looked upon it as a considerable bore. It was such a waste of good football time.

Our number on the book was 367. We had a share number also—6528. And the bottom of our book bore a red ink mark. There were always queues on Friday, and the books were stacked on one counter and you patiently waited your turn. I put the red ink mark on ours so that I could watch it getting closer to the top of the pile.

For a wee lad it was quite a walk with a heavy grocery basket—all the way up Gourlay Street, a distance of half a mile.

The daft thing was, " The Co " had a branch right opposite our home—just a few easy steps across the street. But we always shopped at the far-away store—at my matriarchal Irish granny's specific request.

The neighbours all shopped across the way, and she wasn't running the risk of their prying into her personal financial affairs!

Football in my early boyhood was more important than food and drink. These were what are loosely called the tanner-ba' days, but our soccer standard was even more humble. Some lucky lad with an American uncle might turn up one day with a tanner ba', and that was heaven indeed.

Come Christmas time, there might even appear a size 3 " blether," and that was the real Mackay, near enough the same as the ones kicked around by those wonderful men of Rangers and Celtic. We called it a blether because it contained a bladder. It was a real football, a man's football, the kind that needed blowing up.

But most of the year our dreams of playing at Hampden centred on a modest tuppenny ba'. We even made do sometimes with one that cost a penny.

The demand for access to such an apparently paltry plaything was so great that you had to be picked—usually by one of a number of mysterious rites.

The captain, for instance, might turn his back and spit on the palm of one hand. Then he held out his fists, knuckles up, and you had to guess, " Wet or dry?".

Some of my hygienic pals settled for the simple selection method of " Cock or hen?". And sometimes the choice was one that must have been peculiar to this area that lived by the locomotive—" Puggy or engine?".

We played youthful games like " buckety-buck," which the posher kids called " kick-the-can." There were other improvised activities, such as " leave-o " and " larky " and " run a mile " and " fit an' a hauf." But always we came back to football. It had a strange magic about it that made it virtually a way of life.

Yet one thing could stop even fitba' in Springburn. The tuppenny ba' game could be at its most critical stage and excitement at its peak. Then this sound could bring everything to an immediate halt—a distant roar not unlike approaching thunder.

That was " The Borderer " snorting its way up the incline from Queen Street, eager to be on its way to Edinburgh.

Suddenly there was a great mob of boys, kicking up their heels down Alford Street and lining the fence at its bottom in order to wave to a train.

You'd think we'd never seen a train before! But the thrill of a roaring engine was always new—something to do with its size and its strength and its cleverness, and the fact that we Springburn boys felt subconsciously it belonged to us.

The driver always gave us a wave. He was probably the father of one of the kids—or an uncle, or the man who lived upstairs.

We made engines in Springburn for far-away places. And when word got round that a loco was being loaded at the docks for Africa or India, what an excitement there was.

Hundreds of people lined the wharf, and no human emigrant got a greater send-off than a Cowlairs engine. There was great pride in work in those distant days—not just among the men themselves, but with their wives and mothers and families as well.

In that kind of environment Scotland built wonderful engines, reliable, lasting, the best in the world. And the engine yards were something more than a place to grab a pay-poke. They were a Springburn institution, a way of life, a great, noisy, trustworthy friend, a psychological umbrella. And sometimes a broadcasting station.

I remember the time of the big fight for the heavyweight championship of the world—Jack Dempsey, the American, versus Georges Carpentier—Gorgeous George, the pride of France, with a punch to beat them all.

Twice the handsome Frenchman had humiliated our own Joe Beckett. Some customers didn't even see the British champ when they met for the very first time. He was horizontal by the time they got into their seats—knocked cold in precisely ten seconds.

In their second match, Carpentier was either more sympathetic or more sluggish to get going. This time he gave poor old Joe two minutes before sending him into fairyland.

And now it was Dempsey, the tough but kindly hobo who'd " ridden the rods " and for whom the business of living had been a continual fifteen rounds.

The excitement in Springburn was like a fever. For days it was fed on newspaper stories of each gladiator's history and the very circumference of his thighs to a fraction of an inch. The suspense became almost a personal thing, and there wasn't the wireless to bring relief. So we turned again to the engine-works, that consistent friend in time of need.

The arrangement was made that the horn would blow as soon as the fight result came through—two hoots to announce a Carpentier win, three hoots if the winner was Dempsey.

All over the district a silence fell as if war was being declared. Then, reliable as ever, the siren blew—one blast, two blasts—three!

Dempsey was still the champ, and Springburn, that didn't even know him from Adam, went wild with delight. As a little boy I was caught up in the long-range adulation. Little did I know that one day I would dine with Dempsey—and shake hands with Carpentier also!

If we were proud of our engines, we were equally proud of our fitba'. And with just about every young man intent on kicking a ball around, our reputation for football was similarly worldwide.

There were no coffee bars to sit around in and become the companion of boredom.

Sometimes wee Sydney felt out of it slightly, with no father to be proud of in the engine yards. And I was one of the last to get a gird.

Now the gird was something of a status symbol among the boys of Springburn. You just weren't "with it" without a gird. The English called them hoops, but theirs were paltry devices made of wood. In this man's world of locomotives, Springburn girds were solid iron, with their steering device made of iron also and known as a cleek. Our marbles, or " bools," were steel ball bearings.

I had no one to bring me home the almost traditional gird and cleek. Then one of our neighbours said one day, " How is it you've nae gird?" He added, " Be at the gate at half-past five, an' I'll see what I can dae."

I got my gird at half-past five—polished and shining, and round to perfection. This man to me has always been something of an angel—despite his blackened face and oily cap. All these years I've even treasured his name. He was called Mr. Meechie.

How that common domestic fitment, the window, has come down in the world, so to speak. Nowadays it does nothing more than let in light and make a nuisance of itself when it needs cleaning. But the tenement window of my boyhood days was a multi-purpose device indeed.

Glasgow called it a " windy," but sometimes it served as the equivalent of a box at the opera. Arms akimbo, the women of Springburn used the window as a look-out on to the most exciting show in the world—the daily parade of real, live people.

Sometimes their show achieved a musical content. The performance was usually solo—in the shape of a raggy, shabby, unshaven, back-court character with a singing voice to match.

These nomadic artistes were proud of their art—so much so that they showed repeated willingness to sacrifice even religious conviction on its altar.

In Glasgow there were distinct Protestant and Catholic sectors. And a favourite with the minstrel of the Protestant back-court was " The Old Rugged Cross." Or it might be " Abide with me."

What a dedicated disciple of John Knox! Thus might the naive observer react.

But when the audience for this same unkempt performer was a Catholic tenement, the highlight of his repertoire was inevitably, " Hail, glorious St. Patrick, dear saint of our isle!"

Glasgow was a kindly place, even in its threadbare days. Sometimes the two-faced, unmusical but astute vocalist sang for more than his supper by way of compassionate donations from the multi-purpose windies—humble coins rolled in protective bits of newsprint.

The windows were a means of communication—however great their height from the ground. Ma to the weans in one direction—the weans to Ma in another.

It was strenuous work the fitba', and nobody had the money for the endless variety of sweetmeats and goodies that are nowadays alleged to magically plug the energy gap.

" Maw!" would go up the hungry howl to the window line of communication. " Maw!—throw us ower a jeely piece!"

This is when the window became a remarkable, high-level cafeteria. Out over its sill would come flying a newspaper-wrapped missile. Its newspaper was its hygiene-seal—its protection against an unfortunate landing on something unpleasant! For even with skill born out of experience, an accurate aim with a jeely piece was well-nigh impossible—especially from the topmost windows.

Some of these air-borne packages were complete high-calorie meals in themselves. When unwrapped, they looked not unlike a used bandage, with the blood-red jam seeping into the half-inch wads of soggy, steamed flour.

If that sounds off-putting, let me point out that the jeely piece that seemed to descend like the buskers' pennies from heaven, had a heavenly taste as well. Especially for a hungry, football-playing boy. And the fact that the bread soon became a pale grey with the imprint of dirty young fingers only seemed to add to its savour.

Girls played peever. It's hard to describe peever to a modern audience. But the basic idea was to inscribe the pavement with a series of squares or beds—sometimes as many as twelve. And there was a semi-circle for turning in at the end of the beds.

There was something of the grace of the ballet the way those wee lassies hopped and skipped their way from one bed to another, all the while controlling with their dancing feet the stone or peever.

Mind you, in Springburn this was one case where they had the very best to play with. The Springburn peever might be made of real Italian marble no less.

Remember, I mentioned Sighthill cemetery. That's where the marble peevers came from. Not that we went around chipping bits off the gravestones—that kind of vandalism had not yet reached the dictionary.

The marble peevers came from off-cuts from the stone-mason's yard in the far corner of Sighthill.

A similar game was played by the girls—only this time with a ball. So its title was " Ba' beds," and this time all the ballet sequences had to be performed while bouncing the ball from box to box. Only, bouncing was called " stottin'."

There was an aspect of this refined form of peever which remained for me forever a mystery. Some of the girls had golf balls. Old ones, of course, but nevertheless golf balls. And the point is, no one in our street played golf—the game was almost unheard of. It needed money for golf. Golf was exclusive to the wealthy.

Never would I have asked a girl how she came by her exotic plaything. Boys of my time didn't speak to girls. And there were certain aspects of childhood living which were clearly defined according to sex—like peever and jumps.

Most of the Springburn lassies were brilliant jumpers—especially when they indulged in that sophisticated development of skipping known as " Belgium," during which two ropes were in action simultaneously.

An extrovert boy might run through the ropes and leave behind a trail of indignant feminine abuse. But that was as far as his skipping went. Skipping was for girls. And you looked at girls from a distance. If you'd been seen talking to girls up to a certain age, you'd have been ostracised completely.

I walk by playgrounds now and remarkable are the things I see. Wee tots holding hands and ogling each other like film stars. Weeny boppers, I think, they're called.

If these romantic babies of the present age have eyes for anything other than each other, they may get the impression that the passing priest is viewing the " winchin' " with disapproval.

Let me say it is not so. If I give them a second glance, it's one of curious wonderment, that the air is clear of the sound of abuse and never is a cat-call heard.

If a boy in Springburn had held hands with a lassie, there would have been one public reaction and one reaction only: " Awa', ye cissy!"

Sometimes our street would form a team and we little chaps would go round the houses chanting a rhyme that went like this: "We have the best team, the best team of all—please help to buy our team a ball."

None of the good folk of Springburn even questioned how we could be all that good if we didn't have anything to play with. Instead, they usually gave us a penny.

It needed long and patient canvassing to reach the ten bob needed for a full-size ball. But we were all that poor and we liked it that way. The football that costs weeks and months of slogging up and down tenement stairs—that ball's a pretty precious thing once you get it.

We were organised into street teams, and our street somehow or other managed to acquire eleven jerseys as well. They were green and red horizontal stripes. We must have looked like mangled-out strawberries.

We never rose to such affluence as white pants—not like the boys at the other end of Gourlay Street. Their jerseys were white with a blue band, and we called them the Marjies, which was short for Blue Band Margarine.

The Marjies had magnificent white shorts—and most wondrous of all, their very own goal posts which they carried around from pitch to pitch. We were green as the bands in our jerseys with envy.

It was jackets for us—two separate heaps at each end and frequent were the arguments on the lines of "Yer no' gettin' that ane—that wus miles too high!"

We played also, of course, without a referee. And here's a remarkable thing—there weren't many fights. Argument maybe, but always eventual agreement. I wonder if the very lack of a ref. was the reason. For want of a neutral observer, we had to settle our own disputes or there wouldn't be a game. And that was the last thing any of us wanted to happen.

CHAPTER

2

I should have gone at the age of five to St. Aloysius' School. It was the Roman Catholic school for our parish in Springburn. But my mother taught at St. Saviour's, Govan, and we were given permission to go together.

It meant a two and a half mile trek every morning, to Cowcaddens, for the Underground train that took us to Copland Road—a long way for little, five-year-old legs. Mother always walked.

It was also a journey into poverty—stark, abject, humiliating poverty, of which we in Springburn were completely unaware, secure in the comparative prosperity of our engine works.

St. Saviour's was the school where I heard the strange classroom cry of: " Please, miss, vermin!"

It was a call I heard often, because we were instructed to report thus publicly whenever we saw " Beasties " in another child's head. And the unfortunate child was removed from the classroom—sometimes to have his head shaved and washed in paraffin.

Many children of Govan could not afford shoes. Their trousers were patches, patched with patches. And what charity there was debased itself by declaring its virtues from the rooftops.

In extreme, necessitous cases, the School Board fitted children out with suits and boots. But the boots were clogs, and charity clothes were always uniform Norfolk suits in the same pattern of the same course material. No boy could ever hide the fact that he was in receipt of relief.

There were free meals, too, for the very poor. But all youngsters on the list had to wear a brass medal. Their meal ticket had to be public.

Our headmaster was named O'Connor. He had a large, bristling moustache that he ill could afford. For of hair his head was completely devoid. It was obviously a source of pique to the poor man's ego. He never removed his hat in class.

It was pre the 1918 Education (Scotland) Act, and Roman Catholic schools were governed by the local parish priest—in the case of St. Saviour's, a Belgian called Canon De Backer.

The Canon made frequent unexpected visits of inspection, and Mr. O'Connor had every member of his staff warned that immediate word of the governor's approach must be passed on to him. He wanted the time to discard his hat—by lodging it on the hat-stand in the corner of the room. There were so many such emergencies that Mr. O'Connor became quite expert at hooking his headpiece at considerable range.

My infant mistress's name was Price. I can still sense the awe I felt the first time I saw her. She was a magnificent woman. Against the background of all those puny, half-starved, ragged Govan bairns, she seemed to tower like a radiant Amazon from some other planet. The remarkable fact is that Miss Price, my very first teacher, is still alive. I saw her only yesterday, and we talked of the long ago.

" I remember the rocking horse in the corner," I told her. " You let me on it the very first day."

" I remember," said she, " I was talking about heaven where all of you would go and how lovely it would be. And I noticed your little head was down on the desk, and you weren't far from tears.

" I remember I asked you what was wrong, and you said you didn't want to go to heaven. ' I don't want to leave my Mammy,' you said."

She is 93 and the grace and the dignity and the goodness are still there.

Her class was First Infants, only Govan called it the Penny Buff. Second Infants was the Tuppenny Buff—and similarly with the others up to Number 5.

Our reading books had buff-coloured covers. And each year the book got slightly bigger and therefore more expensive. But most of our early scribbling was pencil on slate and we rubbed out with sleeves charged with spit. It may not have been hygienic, but it was quite effective and cheap. And in under-nourished Govan in the early years of the century cheapness was of paramount importance.

It was probably this daily contact with the awful results of not having two ha'pennies to rub together that made me something of a mercenary youngster. I appreciated early the value of money.

It was therefore a red-letter day in my life when the offer came from one of my pals whose name was Sanny Seton. " I'm gie'in' up the milk—dae ye wahnt the joab? I could put in a word wi' Grace at the dairy."

Sanny was no ordinary milk-boy. He worked with the Co—and a Co-operative milk-boy had considerable status. There were only half a dozen attached to our Cowlairs branch, and they were a respected elite—the cream of milk-boys in fact.

Looking back, I realise that as a family we were a snobbish lot—not in a nasty, objectionable sense, but granny, mother and, I suppose, myself, had this built-in notion that we were maybe just a cut above the neighbours in the block in Gourlay Street. I think it was something to do with the military connections. After all, it wasn't every family in Gourlay Street that had an army bandmaster for an uncle and a grandfather who was a sergeant in the Royal Irish Regiment! And mother being a teacher, too—that gave us our ridiculous smugness of being that bit superior to the others.

Mother's reaction to my milk-boy suggestion was therefore initially chill. I told her the wage was three shillings a week—a fortune for a 12-year-old. We needed the money as much as the next one—but if the financial aspect impressed her at all, she certainly managed to conceal her enthusiasm. Remember, teachers in Catholic schools were paid very little before the 1918 Education Act—they were paid by the Church.

It was only with a grudge that I got permission for Sanny to make the approach. Granny made the philosophical observation: " Sure, he'll not likely get the job."

But Grace, the woman in charge of the dairy, had known me for years and approved immediately of Sanny's nominated successor.

Not that such an appointment was filled as simply as that. Mother and I had to travel up to the Cowlairs head office of the Co-operative and fill in and sign all sorts of forms. No wonder there was pride in my heart when I set out into the grey of the dawn with my arms weighed down with radiant tin-cans on my very first rake for the Co.

A rake was a round, and the milk bottle hadn't been invented. I was allocated our own tenement, and five times between six and eight a.m. I had to run clattering back to the dairy for Grace to refill my cans.

Up and down stairs in every close I stopped and gave each customer a can. And always it was a completely faceless operation. The can reappeared round the partly-opened door, sometimes on the end of a pale, naked arm. Even in Springburn, there was too much pride to be seen face to face at that early hour when the pallor and the wrinkles and the stubble of the night before had not yet been erased. Modesty forbade that even a wee milk-boy should see a man in his night-shirt.

I gave the three bob to my mother intact. That still left me in pocket. Every Saturday, for all their comparative lack of riches, some of the good folk of Springburn gave me a ha'penny or a penny to myself. My average weekly take from tips was usually round about tenpence. I felt like a millionaire!

I was always an imaginative boy when it came to making money. There was a time when the great enthusiasm was for coloured cards of football players.

We devised all sorts of schemes for swapping and adding to our collections. One of the techniques was to cover the bottom of the card with one hand so that the other boy had to guess the name of the player. If he guessed right, he won the card. A wrong guess and he had to pay with one from his collection.

Eventually my young brain devised a much more profitable scheme. I got a board of wood and fitted it all over with nails. At its bottom I hammered in a little circle of nails, and this was inscribed in crayon, " Goal."

It was one football card to play the game, and I always insisted on at least five players. They each chose one of the collection of coloured bools or marbles contained at the top of the board behind a ruler.

When the ruler was removed, the bools rolled down the improvised pin-table and I paid out three cards for the one that scored a goal in the circle of nails.

I could never make less than a profit of two cards. Eventually, I had to put away my lucrative board. But not until I'd skint every boy in the street.

Sometimes I went holidays with my cousin Charlie and his family. Their destination was always Largs. These were the golden days of the Clyde resorts. Glaswegians hadn't yet found their wings to such far-away places as Costa del Sol. Their summer-time trek was inevitably " doon the watter," and the watter was always the wonderful Clyde.

They trooped out of such railway stations as Largs with their battered cases and hampers and bags. And a cocky wee boy would be there to meet them with the invitation : " Kerry yer bag, missus?"

The wee boy was me—earning quite a bit of pocket-money by way of transport fees of a penny and tuppence according to the distance and the weight of the baggage. Working class folks didn't hire taxis.

I was aged about 12. Already I was something of an actor. I had my two accents—the posh one I'd been taught at home, and the vernacular of the Glasgow streets. It was the latter that always took a trick when a 12-year-old touted for casual labour.

Our own favourite holiday place was Dunoon where my granny had a modest cottage. It was at Dunoon that I got the love for boats that has been with me all my life.

At Kirn pier there was always a pierrot show, and once a week the professional entertainers augmented their own song and dance by way of a Grand Talent Contest.

The season was coming close to its end, and this was the day of the cream of the talent—the day when the finalists of the fading summer reassembled in competition for the championship of champions.

My brother it was who had entered my name. He'd heard my soprano at school and sometimes in the parish hall. He knew I was good. And he had his eye on the prize that he knew would be shared.

I was at the age of indifference. I had my boats, and that was enough—paltry, moored cobles that developed in my child's imagination into pirate ships and handsome, salt-sprayed brigantines, edging their way through the seven seas.

I still was busy at the business of ships when my brother shouted: " The concert's started!"

And I came running to the pier where the pierrots had their stage. There were lots of other ambitious youngsters there. The girls had on their Sunday-best frocks and their heads were dressed with ribbons. The boys looked uncomfortably clean, with their hair slicked down and their boots reflecting the sun.

I bore the mark of my boats. Their tar had rubbed off on my hands and knees, and the jersey I'd started the day with was sadly the worse for wear.

I sang without effort or nervous concern. I suppose my main idea was to get the thing over and back to my sailing of the seas.

But even at this early age the Lord had blessed me with an exceptional voice. None of the embellishments of silk and lace could alter the fact that I was the obvious winner. Its confirmation was the audience applause that echoed along the pier.

The prize was a five-shilling piece and a shining half-crown. Such wealth! We were off to spend that half-a-crown—the five-shilling piece was for taking home.

We spent it, of course, on the hire of a boat, and my notions of piracy became more real. We were out there rowing when my mother turned up on the beach, and she yelled and waved and looked anxious—not for our safety, but as to how we'd come by the money for the hire.

We ran up the shingle, and my brother dropped out the words excitedly as he ran: " Sydney won the talent competition! "

By the time I reached her, I'd worked up a certain sense of pride and confidently held out the five-shilling piece.

I was assaulted with abuse. My brother got it also. Imagine her son appearing on a public stage in the sort of state that West Coasters sum up picturesquely as " having the erse hangin' oot o' his breeks "!

I suppose that day was really one for the history books. This was my official, if impromptu, debut as a professional. And my reward was the severest of dressing-downs. Looking back, perhaps I was lucky. I really must have looked a tink. With some mothers it would have been a thorough belting. The measure of my mother's later remorse was to let me keep the five shillings.

In the latter months of the First War, what was known as Spanish 'flu swept across Europe and did almost as thorough a mission for Death as the four years of bloody battle. When it came to Springburn, it wiped people out like flies. We were undernourished from the wartime years and our resistance was low.

Young men played football at three o'clock in the afternoon and were dead by three next morning.

It was all so sudden and ruthless. When a hearse trundled over the cobbles, it carried not one coffin but four—or sometimes even five. And the grown-ups said this fashion for the mass transport of corpses was one of the antidotes to panic—an attempt to make the awful results of the plague less obvious.

We were still singing the war song that went like this:

> " Good-bye-ee, don't sigh-ee,
> There's a silver lining in the sky-ee,
> Napoo, toodle-oo, good-bye-ee."

But we kids of Springburn had our own variation:

> " Good-bye-ee, don't sigh-ee,
> There's a silver lining in the sky-ee,
> Napoo, take the 'flu and die-ee!"

CHAPTER

3

I was twelve when my mother insisted that I take steps to ensure my further education. I sought entry to St. Aloysius' College—the Jesuit establishment in Garnethill.

It's amazing that for all the teeming Catholics in Glasgow and the West, there were then only two secondary schools —the Jesuit St. Aloysius' College and the Marist St. Mungo's Academy—for Catholics.

A great mass of the believers, however, were simple folk —the progeny of the thousands who'd fled from potatoes and poverty in their native Ireland. There was Highland stock also—the descendants of folk who'd been starved out of their magnificent mountains and been treated as inferior to sheep.

The Catholics of the West were predominantly the hewers of wood and the drawers of water. They dug roads and railways, canals and ditches. They were good, honest, God-fearing people who frequently had little reading or writing. They were destined to fill the menial roles, to earn their humble daily bread by way of muscle rather than brain.

Yet so many had the ambition that their children would somehow drag themselves out of the slough of poverty by acquiring the education that had passed them by.

My mother took me to be interviewed by Fr. Hanson, S.J., the Headmaster—a convert and Oxford graduate— the greatest Headmaster the College has ever had.

He was grey and professional, a kindly but unintentionally pompous man. He had this polished Oxford accent which made communication difficult with a wee boy from Springburn.

But we made it. I shall always remember his words to my mother: "I think we might find a place for your boy."

Later, I discovered that my acceptance was not because of any possible fame and credit I might bring to the school. I got into St. Aloysius' because my brother was there before me and was doing very well.

That was a joyous day. Off to Sauchiehall Street we went to equip me with the mark of my latest distinction. St. Aloysius' had not yet acquired its own blazer or such distinctive trappings as special school jerseys or stockings.

Its sole item of uniform was a cap. It was green with a golden eagle for its badge—a reproduction of the arms of the Gonzaga family to which St. Aloysius belonged.

I got a golden eagle for my head and something else for my feet. As a token of this notable milestone, my mother took me into Copeland and Lye's and let me have my choice of scooters—not the motorised kind on which youngsters nowadays race around the countryside.

My scooter was a simple device which you propelled with one foot. But it had wheels with rubber tyres! And shining, silver handle-bars like a bike!

I was more thrilled by my silver scooter than I was with my golden eagle.

It cost me three ha'pence a day at St. Aloysius'. I walked all the way in the morning—about $2\frac{1}{2}$ miles—and the halfpenny was the tram-fare home. With the penny I was supposed to buy my mid-day glass of milk. I confess I spent it always on lemonade. This washed down my bread and cheese.

There were no school meals in my schooldays. But you could get a lunch for sixpence at the nearby Convent of the Sisters of Mercy.

Most of the boys, like myself, carried sandwiches or pieces of bread and jam. Sixpence a day was big money, and few of us could afford it.

The year I started at St. Aloysius', I made what could be called my first religious move. From quite an early age I was in awe of the local priest. When he came to our house, we hung on his every word.

It was the same with every Catholic youngster. The priest was for admiring. If not a halo, he certainly carried with him an aura of greatness, an air of mystique and authority. Film stars we worshipped not. The doctor and teacher might have our respect. But the priest—he was the greatest. His was all the glamour.

I cannot claim therefore at this early age to have had any great spiritual bond with the Church. I wanted to get involved simply because I was dazzled by the priesthood. I wanted one day to share its glamour.

So I took a tram-ride to St. Joseph's, North Woodside Road, deep in the heart of Glasgow's slumland. And there I met Brother Cragg—a Jesuit lay brother.

How inaptly named he was. There was no cragginess, no hardness, no flint in this man. A dear, old, gentle Jesuit, whose great love was music and especially the human voice.

When I asked him if I could join his altar boys, his first question was significant: " Can you sing?"

There was not much shyness in me at twelve—that came later. Without a trace of inhibition, I said: " Yes, I can!"

He raised a grey eyebrow at my self-assurance, and said in that quiet way of his: " Ah, well, we'll see."

I have never forgotten his test-piece. After all, this was really my very first audition, although little did I know to what it would lead. I wasn't even all that interested in the singing. I wanted simply to get on the altar to be part of the beautiful pomp and ceremony—the only glamour poor congregations had in their drab lives.

I'm afraid my choice of song in that boys' sacristy at St. Joseph's, North Woodside Road, was particularly lacking in religious significance. " Sound the slogan," I piped in my best young soprano. " Fire the heather, spring to arms, ye sons of Gaul. Strike for freedom and Prince Charlie, let your foes before you fall!"

He seemed to be impressed with my warlike chant. Anyhow, I was in. Not that I got close to the altar. That took months of waiting—with some boys as long as a year.

I see altar boys now and am amazed at their indifference. They think nothing even of going absent for no particular good reason. We were trained and disciplined, and disciplined again, and we stuck it for month after month without demur for the prize that would be our eventual lot—the thrill of " getting inside " and serving at Mass.

Even this early, I must have been blessed with a somewhat outstanding voice. I was always being asked to sing solo—at all sorts of functions throughout the parish. Mine was the early distinction of singing at the opening of the Crib at Christmas—before a church packed with hundreds of people.

I was only a boy, and never a single twinge of nerves.

CHAPTER

4

Brother Cragg ran a football team, and when I was about 16 years of age my world was a remarkable Jekyll and Hyde affair. My Sundays were polite and solemn and clean. But my Saturdays! Oh, those fantastic, rough and tumble Saturdays!

We played in the Glasgow Juvenile League, and don't be foxed by the juvenile bit. A juvenile could be any age from 17 to 30. This was not so much a grade of football, rather more like a course in unarmed combat. Those who suggest that ice-hockey is tough, or shinty is tough, or boxing is tough, never knew the Glasgow juveniles.

It was not uncommon for referees to go home in the hamper made for the strips. It was their only way of leaving the ground and escaping the wrath of supporters they'd " disappointed." To make his escape, one actually had to swim the Clyde, at Glasgow Green.

Our team was known as Woodside Rovers, and we had a player called Shangie MacGuire. Shangie was not exactly a George Best, but Shangie could run like a whippet. There was not a faster man in Garscube Road or the whole of the Cowcaddens.

We were playing at Temple in Anniesland, and Shangie fouled the home team's centre, who was something of a local god. It was almost as if he'd pressed a button for the complete release of all Hell's furies.

This great, dark mob of angry supporters was suddenly pouring across the field. Shangie was as brave as the best of them, but in this kind of situation he decided that courage was for fools. Shangie decided to run. And he ran and ran in his bright striped jersey and white pants—despite the handicap of mud-caked football boots. What a sight that must have been in the Great Western Road on a peaceful Saturday afternoon!

They never got near him, of course. Shangie showed them a clean pair of heels all the miles to Glasgow and the three stairs up to the safety of his room-and-kitchen with the door banged shut and the door then locked.

One Saturday we were playing at Possilpark and I got involved with one of the opposing half-backs. I won't go into the details of the physical consequences so far as he was concerned. But the net result of the barney for me was a considerable black eye—a real king of a keeker!

It was more the worry than the pain that bothered. What was I going to tell mother? I think I may have walked into the kitchen with some sort of naive impression that the disfigurement might escape her notice.

" What have you done to your face?" were her very first words.

I knew I was in trouble. We'd had frequent disagreements about the football company I kept, and this latest development might make things difficult.

I put on my innocent look. " You know those big branch candlesticks on the altar?" I said. " I was carrying one of them and it swung round and hit me right there!"

She accepted the religious explanation and sympathetically told me to come and have the thing bathed.

There are crises in life when even potential priests must perforce resort to little white lies—if one could thus describe a black eye.

My most memorable game with Woodside Rovers was the day the referee lost the place. The sequel was the closest I've ever come to appearing in a criminal court.

The ref. did have an off-day. Maybe it was a hang-over or something from Friday night. Certainly the abuse that was heaped upon his head was more than normally justified. But verbal assault for one of our admirers—a hotheaded little character—provided insufficient relief. When a decision was given that was precisely the opposite of what it should have been, he ran off to the little shed that we used for changing. He was out again like a lightning streak, this time carrying a kettle.

It was kept in the shed for making tea, and it was none of your modern, aluminium, lightweight appliances. It was black and made of iron, and the next thing we knew, its considerable weight was descending on the referee's head!

I have heard all sorts of suggestions as to what should happen to referees, but never physical violence with a kettle.

Anyhow, it turned out to be most effective. The poor man went down like a stone and the match was immediately abandoned.

The police, of course, had to be involved, and the spectator was charged with assault.

There was that terrible day when the sergeant turned up with a constable from the Maitland Street police station and announced to my mother that they were inquiring into the case.

As I've said, we had only a humble room-and-kitchen, but the polis came in and looked around and the sergeant said: " Y'know, missus, this is the only decent hoose we've been in since we started!"

Then he added with a mixture of puzzlement and concern: " How d'ye let yer laddie play in an awful team like that?"

My mother said something about this being the last time, but chose to add that I was fitba' daft and what was she to do with me on a Saturday afternoon?

" Don't worry, missus," the sergeant said. " I'll get him into a team in the Churches League."

It was my mother's impression for weeks thereafter that her laddie went off each Saturday to play in the comparatively safe and disciplined atmosphere of Churches football. But my team was still good old Woodside Rovers!

We got word that there was to be an identity parade, and most of the lads when we met wore bunnets. The bunnet was the thing in this sector of Glasgow. But I owned a hat —the type known as a snap-brim or down-the-river.

We were much the same for size and I suggested that for the purpose of the parade the accused should wear my snap-brim. I also let him borrow my coat.

I remember thinking when I donned his faded bunnet: "My God, what'll happen if I get picked out!"

But, despite the disguise, the referee chose the culprit all right. I'm afraid I've forgotten the statutory penalty in Glasgow at the time for assault with cast-iron kettle!

We actually won the league that season, but we didn't get any medals. There wasn't the money to buy them, because the league treasurer, who came from Lyon Street, had done a bunk with the funds.

It was that kind of street that this team represented—a scruffy, smelly, dilapidated alley no more than a hundred yards long.

Its young men lived not only for football; they were ostensibly footballers all through the week.

Their studded boots were sometimes their only footwear. They might rise to an aged, cast-off jacket and a pair of stained and crumpled trousers. But underneath were their Saturday clothes—their bright-striped jerseys and faded shorts.

They stood at the corners and seemed to be waiting. They weren't dressed for the sudden emergency match. What they waited for was work. And their underwear was a football strip for the want of anything else.

Yet what a record this slum had in World War I. Every single house had at least one man at the front—nearly all of them with the H.L.I. And just about every one who came back brought with him a medal.

In Lyon Street, D.S.M.s were ten a penny. There was even a V.C. The street had such fame at the H.L.I.'s Maryhill Barracks that every Armistice Day the regiment sent down two buglers, and on the 11th hour of the 11th day of the 11th month, they played their tribute to this warrior row.

That was the kind of football team I played in. The bhoys from Lyon Street. The lion-hearted bhoys. They lacked for just about everything but courage.

CHAPTER

5

I was pretty unhappy at St. Aloysius' College. Looking back, I sense that the fault may in part have been my own. Temperamentally, we MacEwans were not cut out for the Jesuit type of training.

What was irksome was the rigidity of the rules. After some time I was put in the Science section, which meant I got no Latin.

I came to an age when my notions of joining the priest-hood were beginning to crystallise, and Latin was essential. Yet it was insisted that I remain with the Science section.

There were three of us in this predicament—Chandler, who is now a priest, Dillon, who became a chemist, and myself.

We were compelled to make the ridiculous move of taking Latin by way of night classes at Glasgow High School. Twice a week I had Latin. I was also studying violin. And singing still took up a lot of my time.

It was really far too much for a youngster to cope with. At the end of term I told my mother I wanted to go to Hillhead High. I could see the look approaching alarm that crossed her face.

Hillhead High was a Protestant school.

As a teacher she realised that at St. Aloysius' I was not progressing as well as I should. As a Catholic, she was aware of the frightening implications of my wanting to change.

By sending me to a Protestant school she ran the risk of being denied the sacraments—especially since I was already on a course of Catholic education.

This was one of the occasions when her strength of character showed itself.

She got me into Hillhead High without seeking episcopal permission. And she made no change in her own way of life. She still went to Mass, and no questions were asked.

It was one of the happiest moves of my life.

The Hillhead Rector was Dr. McGillivray, a man of impressive dignity in top hat and morning coat. He also had a well-trimmed beard. He was a small man, but a giant in education. And his staff were similarly outstanding. I felt a new sense of vocation from the very first days.

At St. Aloysius' it seemed to be homework, homework all the time, with so very little to show for it. At Hillhead you were scarcely aware of homework, yet all the time you seemed to be learning fast.

Hillhead was predominantly for the sons and daughters of upper middle-class, business types. Its pupils in the main were probably the social superior of their teachers. But the English-trained Jesuits of St. Aloysius', many of them from the great English Recusant families such as the de Traffords, Vaughans, Vavasours, etc., were the social superiors of the boys. I suppose we Glesca' laddies irritated such men enormously.

Discipline at Hillhead wasn't nearly so tough and I suppose if truth were told these Jesuit scholars would have much preferred to have been working in a parish.

At this stage I do not wish to enter into debate on the subject of segregated schools. I will simply point out that my experience of Protestant Hillhead was pleasant and rewarding.

This early in life I made many Protestant friends. This friendship with non-Catholics continued during my university days. I can now claim friendship with scores of Church of Scotland ministers.

At Hillhead, where I was one of only two Catholics in the entire school, I gained tremendously from the scholastic point of view. Of that I have no doubt. The built-in bonus was that I learned understanding and toleration, also.

The other Catholic, by the way, was my brother Harold. I'm sure his reactions to his change of school would be very similar to my own.

I have always been saddened by religious intolerance.

Will we ever find a solution to the centuries-old feuding between Orange and Green—at least could we forget about the Battle of the Boyne.

Many a drum-beating Protestant and just as many a breast-beating Catholic have been rudely shaken by my telling them the true historical facts.

King James was King William's son-in-law. That knocks them back for a start. Their eyebrows go up when I point out also that the Battle of the Boyne was not in fact on July 12, 1690—the date on which all the drum-bashing happens.

But what makes both groups really uncomfortable—Orangeman and Catholic—is my explaining that King Billy in this historic contest had the backing of the Pope!

This is absolute truth. What seems to have been forgotten is that the Pope was a king in his own right. He was a complete monarch, head of all the Papal States.

The battle was part of a great international struggle for power. The Pope's support was for King William and his Austro-German army against James, whose soldiers were predominantly French and supporters of the excommunicated Louis XIV.

If it is in any way related to the Battle of the Boyne, all this persistent Orange and Green hatred is so much nonsense. For when news of King Billy's victory was announced the dome of St. Peter's was lit up in celebration and a Te Deum was sung!

At Hillhead, I certainly felt no shyness, no sense of being among strangers. On my very first day I joined the school's

My mother.

Gourlay Street, Springburn,
Glasgow,
where I was brought
up as a child.

Uncle Tom and
myself at
Dunoon, 1940.

Brother Cragg, S.J.

officers' training corps, and by the end of term I was awarded the prize for the best recruit of the year.

At Hillhead, I started to play rugby, I who had been such a soccer addict from almost the day I could toddle. What the lads of Lyon Street thought of this double life I led, I don't know.

My rugby was played on Saturday mornings. And in the afternoon I was still the right-winger of Woodside Rovers.

The year we won the league championship from all those juvenile teams in Glasgow—and not a medal to show for it—my scoring record from the wing was 35 goals, which everyone considered pretty good going.

The team's performance in general and that of the right wing in particular attracted even the attention of the great and mighty Celtic. They sent a scout to watch us in action.

Looking back now, I suppose this could have been a turning point in my career. Celtic were such a schoolboys' dream, there was such an awe among us all for the very turf of Parkhead, that I doubt if I could have resisted any invitation that might have been made to don the envied green and white.

But the man who caught the eye of the scout was my inside-right named Jerry Solis. It was really a case of justice being done.

For a winger I certainly had an impressive scoring record. But so many of my goals had been Jerry-built. He was the man who created the moves, who provided the inch-perfect passes.

I saw him as a football genius. I have watched a great deal of soccer since, and he still remains one of the most brilliant ball-players I have ever seen.

And when he signed for Celtic we all of us thought that an international star was in the making. Jerry played one game for Celtic first eleven, and was scarcely heard of again.

I adjusted to rugger sufficiently well to achieve the Hillhead XV. From my years of soccer I had the edge on most of the rugger-trained types when it came to kicking a ball. But I still played my morning's rugby with my eye on the afternoon's fitba'. If there's sport in heaven, I will opt for soccer.

Yet, what a game is rugby for character building. When a great giant of a forward comes at you like one of those Cowlairs steam engines, it needs guts to get in his path at all. To throw yourself at his piston-like ankles calls for something approaching self-sacrifice.

I have no regrets at this rugby phase in my life. As a 17-year-old, I was involved in soccer, rugby, cricket, tennis and cross-country running. If I achieved any capacity for taking the knocks in life without complaint, it was possibly born out of contact, sometimes literally, with the rugger field more than the playing of any of the other games.

For me it had none of the spectator appeal of soccer— unless at international level. But I would agree that sometimes at Murrayfield the atmosphere of excitement and entertainment has achieved a pitch that even a cup-final at Hampden could not equal.

CHAPTER

6

I was a regular theatre-goer at the age of 14. I still had my milk round and my tenpence in tips. I could sit with the stars for ninepence a time, and a penny left over for the tram.

Govan had its Lyceum and George's Cross its Play-house. Bridgeton had its Olympia and the Queen's as well. There was still no show like a live show at the Pavilion, the Princess, the Empire, the King's, the Coliseum, the Alhambra, the Met, the Royal Palacium. The music-hall was still the thing in places like Greenock and Paisley and Ayr.

What a dream world of entertainment good old Glasgow used to be.

And soon it cost me not a penny. My weekly milk money remained intact despite my regular theatre indulgence.

I suppose you could describe my Uncle Tom as being in the business. His connection, mind you, was tenuous. He ran a barber's shop in North Woodside Road and every week he did his bit for show business by sticking a poster for next week's Pavilion behind the glass of his barber's shop door.

For this contribution to the world of entertainment he received the weekly reward of two free seats. And when he learned of my young enthusiasm for the footlights, he passed on the tickets to me and my cousin Charlie.

I watched G. H. Elliot over a span of 20 years, and never once tired of his artistry. I still put on his records and shut my eyes as he sighs again for the silvery moon. And I'm captured again by the magic of his Chocolate Coloured Coon and his yodelling and his inimitable soft-shoe shuffle.

But the impact he made on a 14-year-old was unique. For a time he was the idol of Glasgow. To me he was something of a god.

I was fascinated weekly by the Will Fyffes and the Tommy Lornes and the Florrie Fords. And suddenly there was a threat to this regular excitement. Edith and Evelyn objected that the boys got all the jam.

They were my cousins, Charlie's sisters. And quite rightly they argued that why should the boys get all the free shows? Weren't girls entitled to a night out as well?

Contrary to the popular image, I have always found bookmakers the kindest, most generous and most gentle of men. I am not put off this opinion by the nature of their profession.

My Church's attitude to gambling is that the sinner is the man who neglects his wife and family. But the man who is attentive to their welfare and still finds he has a bob or two in his pocket, can throw what's left over into the Clyde if he so chooses. Or have a flutter on a horse.

My uncle Tom was certainly one of the finest men I ever knew. He was passionately fond of good music. He was not averse to dispensing free haircuts to men who were on the dole.

And Uncle Tom had a side-line. His hairdressing establishment in North Woodside Road was the facade for his other business. With a man called Gormley, who later ran a most respectable jeweller's business in Sauchiehall Street, he acted as a receiver of poor men's bets. Uncle Tom was a bookie.

Rich men were not among his clients. They could use the telephone or run up what was called a turf account.

Only the less well-off were obliged to pursue their hobby in a furtive, sinister manner with bet collectors called runners, biting their nails and sucking their fag-ends up closes and in back-greens and down in public toilets.

The gambling laws were a nonsense of course, and even the polis agreed. That's why Uncle Tom and the local policemen used to organise its part-evasion between them.

"Look, Tom," they would tell him, "we'll be doing your place on Monday. Sorry again—but we've got to go through the motions."

And be sure that Uncle Tom, who was the kindest of men, never once allowed the thoughtfulness of his friends in blue to pass without reward.

I know he didn't. Because for a time I was what you might call associated with his bookmaking activities in a minor capacity. In my lunch break from school, I used to run with bets.

It was Uncle Tom again who turned out to be my good fairy when Charlie's sisters started to get their share of the theatre tickets.

One of the features of being a bookie is that it gives you a tremendous circle of contacts. Uncle Tom explained that he knew a man called Frankie, who was actually in the theatre business. He helped to operate the Pavilion lights. And Charlie and I were welcome to be his guests whenever we chose.

Not only were we back on the free-seat basis, we sat in the circle each side of Frankie, while he directed on to the stage his various limes or coloured lights. We felt more than ever part of the show.

Coming up to my fifteenth birthday, I sat entranced at a beautiful vision on stage. Her name was Ella Retford. This was the Pavilion's Christmas panto, and she was its principal girl. She was blessed with an attractive singing voice. She could have croaked like a frog and it still would have touched my boyish ear as the music of paradise.

I think I fell in love with Ella Retford—after the fashion of a 15-year-old. Certainly for the first time in my life I was aware of female beauty, sitting up there in the Pavilion circle on my own private cloud of enchantment.

One day Mr. Robertson, who lived above our room-and-kitchen, told me to come upstairs. What he wanted to show me was a wee drum wound round with wire and mounted on a piece of wood. And to this simple contraption he had attached four brass screws. They were fitted with copper wire, and two of them had separate wires leading to a pair of head-phones. There was another little wire which connected with what was called a crystal.

"Listen to that, Sydney," he said, and helped me fix the head-phones over my ears.

And out of the air, through those little black ear-muffs, a strange voice announced: "This is 5SC, the Glasgow station of the British Broadcasting Company."

It was magic—exciting, inexplicable magic—and there followed music, which was even more exciting still.

Soon, all of us were making our crystal sets and listening in to the wireless. I remember the first night we had our own, we got Mozart in Gourlay Street, and I was so entranced I missed the fitba' for once.

I was too young, too naive, too thrilled to realise that this remarkable device we lovingly called the cat's whisker was something of a killer in disguise.

I could not recognise it then as the beginning of the decline of my beloved music-hall. How could anyone—let alone an impressionable youngster—see any connection between this new magic box and the threat of the dole queue for such sequinned goddesses as my lovely Miss Retford?

What nostalgia I have for those music-hall days. I don't think it's a regret that has no foundation. I cannot believe that distance has loaned such enchantment to the view that I am merely being old-fashioned and slightly fuddy-duddy.

These were the golden days of entertainment. They were days when an artiste had to patiently serve his apprenticeship and work away thoroughly at all the aspects of his craft.

He was out there on his own, with not one single electronic aid to disguise any flaw in his skill. He had to learn to pitch his voice to the back row of the very gods, across that great river of sound provided by a full-blooded orchestra.

Show business was a ladder, and you climbed each rung slowly and hoped for a bit of luck, and if they didn't like you, they told you so by way of that awful, frightening gesture of the slow handclap or with the mocking act of pitching pennies on to the stage.

What has happened to all those discriminating audiences who were not afraid to say boo?

Today, it would seem that anything goes. You can be young and inexperienced and dreadfully devoid of talent and still become an overnight star.

You can form what's called a group, and bellow out your tuneless nonsense, and if it's loud enough, you have a penthouse in Mayfair and a white Rolls Royce before your twenty-first birthday.

It is very wrong. It is very unjust. It must rankle with some of the few old-timers who still survive and recall the paltry pittance they sometimes received for what was comparatively such superior talent.

Sometimes I wonder what would happen if some scientist announced on the news one morning that microphones were lethal—that laboratory tests had proved they gave off rays that were definitely associated with the condition of throat cancer. And all governments throughout the world had reached agreement that mikes in future would be banned.

The entire entertainment business would fall flat on its face. Your stars would come crashing from their phoney heavens. And perhaps the resultant silence would be rather wonderful.

Between the ages of 14 and 17, I think I can claim to have seen every Christmas pantomime in Glasgow. The Princess had always the funniest ones. They were grander at the Theatre Royal. The Theatre Royal pantos were the spectacular, super, colossal shows. But give me the Princess for fun—the kind of fun that seems to me to have vanished altogether.

I saw just about every star in the business except Sir Harry Lauder.

Certainly I met him later in life. I liked the man well enough. But his fame and fortune, I must confess, were something I have never been able to comprehend.

I have never thought him funny. That false, feigned laugh of his was, to me, meaningless. He may have had a reasonable baritone voice, but with his singing alone he'd never have created the Lauder legend.

In this I may be a heretic, although the more I discuss Lauder with others, the more folk I discover who share my view. Somehow it's an opinion they've come to be ashamed of expressing. It's as if Lauder had somehow cast a spell that makes it almost an act of treason for a Scot to suggest that his genius was a myth.

Will Fyffe for my taste was a much more talented artiste. It may well be that Lauder achieved his accolade because he chanced to be the first of his kind.

It always helps to be first in the field. There will be other singing priests, I suppose. I was lucky enough to be the first. And unlucky, too—for I have always hated the title.

CHAPTER

7

I hope with these earlier reminiscences I am not making myself sound senile. It's all not so very long ago—all within less than fifty years, and yet in some ways it seems like another world.

I don't know my way around Glasgow any more. I'm a Glaswegian, and I get lost now in my very own city! Yet as a 15-year-old I knew just about its every corner.

One of the great aids towards this geographical knowledge was Glasgow's tramway system, presided over by the Great Dalrymple, and acknowledged as the best in the world.

Glasgow never talked about trams. These were cars, vehicles on wheels, so Glasgow in its logical, matter-of-fact way called them cars and pronounced them " caurs."

In this incredible half century of unpredictable change, some things have been turning so fast that they're back to beyond where they started. Dalrymple's Glasgow caurs, for instance, were a far superior public transport system than anything we have today. And so cheap!

For tuppence, as a laddie I could travel from my Springburn tenement to the bonnie, bonnie banks of Loch Lomond.

We did it often on a Sunday when the sun was out—a penny half to Dalmuir West, then change to the Dumbarton tramway system for another penny half to the bonnie banks.

For a boy who was pretty daft on boats, another penny half could make available another minor paradise—a trip to Renfrew Ferry and its seats on the Green, with a generous dripping penny wafer from the Italian's on the corner, and the whole panorama of the Clyde laid out before you with its paddle steamers and great Anchor liners and the healthy smell of the sea.

And why did they ever cancel out Dalrymple's clever colour system? Every tramway route in Glasgow town had its own distinctive colour, and never was transport made so easy.

Blue caurs, green caurs, white caurs, red caurs.

All the yellow caurs went to the posh residential sectors, and folk who spoke as if they fancied themselves were said to have a yellow-caur accent.

It made it so simple to guide the stranger.

" How do I get to Whiteinch?"

" Take a green caur and you can't go wrong."

" I'm looking for the university."

" Ah, well, mister, yer lookin' the wrang way—your best move's tae staun at that pole an' get the next white caur!"

By its colour you could see your chariot approach from afar. Now you must look for a number. And for the elderly and the short-sighted, progress has been in reverse.

I seem to remember the tramway conductors as smart, green men, with immaculately-waxed moustaches. Their tunics were always like soldiers' and the crease in their trousers would have sliced a loaf.

They wore their long-service medals proudly and called out the stops, and helped old ladies and women with prams. They seemed to like their jobs because their jobs were sure. These were the dole-queue days and security was a magic term.

So many young men went in for teaching because the teacher was certain of regular work until the day he retired.

The joiner could be out next week. The shipyard worker could be out for months. But to get the sack a teacher would just about have to kill his granny.

It was this way, too, with the tramwayman. He worked for the Corporation, and to work for the Corporation meant your future was secure.

The " caurs " have been gone for eight years and more. The last time I was in Glasgow the bus conductor wore no tie and goodness knows when last he shaved. It seems a pity men have to be scared into taking a pride in their work.

I shall always be grateful to my mother for the freedom she gave me to roam my city and drink my fill of its entertainment at such a comparatively tender age.

She was an understanding woman, with a lively sense of humour. And there was between us this pleasant, healthy attitude and trust. I think she sensed that in the early years she'd laid my foundations well. I was always in and around the church. I was active at the altar. She must have sensed that I was insulated against the city's less worthy temptations.

I was so exposed to the glitter of entertainment that pretty soon the inevitable happened—I had the urge to be actively part of it. And the chance, in a very humble form, came by way of the church.

We Catholics in St. Joseph's parish decided to form a concert party. There was nothing unusual in this. Catholic churches all over Glasgow had their pierrot troupes, along with their billiards rooms and their card tables and the weekly tea and buns.

But we in St. Joseph's decided to be original. It was long before Enoch Powell, and our distinctive touch was to blacken our faces. We were the St. Joseph's nigger minstrel troupe, and there's no suggestion that this is where Al Jolson got the idea!

Our reward was the usual tea and buns, and we played the church hall about once a month—always after most of the audience had been fortified by the evening service.

I was 14, and one of a team of boy sopranos with the not completely accurate title of the Big Six. We had a speciality number which went something like this: " O, ho, ho, my sweet Hortense, she ain't good-looking but she's got good sense!"

It used to bring the house down.

Later, I was given a solo spot, and I sang about a bull frog that sat upon a log upon a sultry summer's night. Talk about modern songs having nonsense lyrics!

But this brought the house down also. We were playing to friends. These were our own folk out there on the hard wooden benches. We couldn't go wrong.

And even when our fame began to spread and we got our tea and buns away from home, the reception was inevitably satisfyingly enthusiastic.

As well as St. Joseph's, we played the halls of St. John's and St. Alphonsus', and St. Saviour's and St. Columba's and St. Anthony's, and always the saints were on our side.

My voice broke after about a year, but I still stayed in the troupe. I fell back on my fiddle, and with brother Harold on the piano and a third man on the drums, we became the minstrel band.

Maybe we got swell-headed with all the biased applause. Anyhow, the St. Joseph's minstrels decided to turn pro!

We had in Springburn a picture house called the Well-field, its location being in Wellfield Street. It was one of my haunts on a Saturday night, because the charge for admission was in keeping with my personal financial situation. You got in for fourpence.

On to the screen between the films, a slide was flashed. It said simply: " Sunday Night—the Virginian Minstrels!"

I nudged my companion. And trying to control the excitement that threatened to restrict my throat, I said: " That's us!"

Before I describe our momentous debut, let me preface it with this—I was never so grateful that my voice had broken and thereby confined me to the orchestra pit.

Some parts of Scotland have a peculiar way of describing embarrassment. One is said to be " black affronted." Never was the phrase more apt than on this unforgettable night.

The Minstrels did the thing in style. In traditional fashion we had a chairman. He was a pleasant lad called Jimmy McBride.

Our corner-men were Neilly Reid, who was always referred to as Massa Bones because his musical talent expressed itself by way of clicking a couple of dried-out ribs from the local butcher. In the other corner was Mr. Swann, familiarly known as Duck.

Being in a corner was nothing new for dear old Duck Swann. Physically he was a remarkable specimen. His construction was rather like that of a sawn-off heavyweight. I was never very sure whether the Christian name was related entirely to his surname or was what you might call vocational. For Duck was a pug—a man who'd taken many a punch in his eventful life because he'd ducked too late.

Duck did his boxing in the rings around Glasgow. Outside of the ring, he was one of the gentlest of men. He had really a heart of gold. But the sight of one man made him see red, and that man's name was Jimmy Cosh. Many's the battle these two had fought in Springburn.

This night Jim Cosh was in the Wellfield audience!

Disaster struck as soon as the troupe went on. Massa Bones led the parade, and he stuck out his chest and swung his arms with the flourish of a drum-major.

The hand that was keeping the beat with the clicking of its bones came in contact with one of the cinema's fire extinguishers, and if we'd wanted the show to go off with a bang, this was it.

The disturbed extinguisher vented its wrath by shooting spray all over our leading performers. Whatever that foam was made of, it didn't go with our nigger make-up. Neilly Reid's face was suddenly like a zebra, and the black stuff started to trickle down his neck on to his collar and the suits we'd specially hired from McCann's in Cambridge Street.

I suppose we were immediately the first literally black and white troupe in the business, and the audience loved it. They were hilarious with laughter. And thick and fast they started pitching their ridiculing cat-calls.

I suppose even the best of shows would find it difficult to recover from such a diabolical start. We were certainly not the best of shows!

We didn't even discriminate. No one had ever done an audition. It was simply a case of, if you wanted to have a go, you were in. Mind you, one of our acts did look good on the bill. We had a world champion in the cast, no less!

His name was Jack Harvey, and it was the old, old story of having the right contacts. Jack was Duck Swann's father-in-law, and that's how we got him into our show.

His title was just a little bit vague, maybe. Glasgow has always been a great place for dancing. The craze at this time was for tap and clog.

In the tiled tunnel beneath the old St. Enoch's Station, you used to see them at it in their dozens, working out the new routines while leaning with one arm against the wall to keep their balance. The tunnel helped the sound effect.

This is where Jack did his practice for the big event of his life. " The World Clog-Dancing Championship " was what it said on the bill.

It's doubtful if there were any overseas entrants. Any from England would in fact be most unlikely. Could well have been that the farthest-travelled came from an Italian chip-shop in one of the Glasgow suburbs!

But Jack Harvey went in for what was described as the world championship, and that is what he won. And we were not that night for hiding any of our lights under bushels.

" And now, ladies and gentlemen, the World Clog-Dancing Champion—the Champion of the World himself—"

Duck made the announcement, and the abuse was immediate.

Voice from the audience: " Yer a liar!"

Duck was brave and persistent: " The Champion Clog-Dancer of the World—Jack Harvey himself!"

Again a dour, defiant—" Yer a liar "—this time backed by a rumble of discontented voices and feet.

Jack took on his little square of marble and went through his cloppity-clop routine. I thought in fact he was very skilled, but the crowd was really restless now.

Jimmy McBride tried to stem the flood of abuse by doing his " Poor Ole Joe " number. We were proud of Jimmy. Jimmy was reputed to have had his voice trained!

But the most obvious reaction to his solo was a raucous voice from the second front row: " Awa' hame! Yer ower auld tae be oot sae late!"

We had some of our faithful followers in the hall—one or two old ladies from the parish and St. Joseph's young girls who may have had a crush on certain younger members of our cast. They were suffering also. Theirs was the humiliation of seeing their local heroes cut rudely and crudely down to size.

McKenna, our tenor, sang his masterpiece from *Il Trovatore,* and somebody shouted: " Geraff! Yer rotten!"

With his blushes almost showing through his streaked black make-up, McKenna did get off. But Duck pushed him on again to do an encore. Dear Swannie was displaying the same courage in adversity that he had had to call on so often in the boxing ring. He was impressed with the adage that the show must go on.

Freddie Crumlish and his cousin Johnny did the double song-and-dance act of which they were so proud: " Little ole home, I love that little old home and do I know how to go . . ."

The rest was drowned in the stamping of feet and the shouted advice: " Awa' ye go then!"

At last it was Duck Swann's turn. We were proud of Duck in the parish halls. He was one of our stars. I suppose his voice was in fact no better than his boxing, but to us he had even Paul Robeson licked.

Usually he did a verse or two of " Rose of old Virginie, nature's placed within ye . . ." Then he went into a sort of soft-shoe shuffle routine.

That night at the Wellfield he never got that far. This was the moment his arch-rival Jim Cosh had awaited with evil, pent-up delight.

Mercilessly he lambasted poor Duck with a tongue that was as coarse as his fists. His mates took up his sadistic lead and the jeering spread all over the hall.

In sheer desperation, Duck dropped to his side his elongated arms and yelled back in a voice that went falsetto with emotion: " What the hell d'ye want for a tanner! D'ye think we're all bloody G. H. Elliots?"

It was the signal for something approaching pandemonium—all hell was let loose. Jim Cosh got up and left the hall, and his retinue obediently followed. The rest of what audience there was decided that this was as appropriate a time as any to put an end to the agony.

We were left with our dear, devoted old ladies and the black-affronted lassies who had boy-friends on the stage.

We remained in that deserted, depressing picture house for at least another hour. We were scared to go out. We had all of us the notion that our dissatisfied customers would be waiting outside, intent on some kind of physical violence.

But Wellfield Street was dark and quiet. It was raining— that soft, sooty, almost invisible rain that is peculiar to Glasgow.

So much for the beginning of the Virginian Minstrels. We went home sad and deflated. And we never performed together again. The first night of the brave Virginians was also their last!

CHAPTER

8

From as far back as I can remember I had always had this love of the Church. I used to play at Masses. I had them all off pat, and I even went the length of building an altar in the cupboard of what we called the Big Room.

The Church for me was great fun. Eventually, as an altar-server, I got involved in the real thing, and I was never happier. I liked the solemn routines, the ceremony, the mystique.

I'm not so sure that I was all that aware of Jesus Christ and what He stood for. My love was for the institution.

By the age of 18 my attitudes hadn't really changed a great deal. Certainly there had been that unfortunate period at St. Aloysius' College. There I just didn't fit. I was the boy who chose to opt out and go instead to a non-Catholic school.

But within myself I genuinely felt there was no connection between that phase and my intense affection for the Church. One was school. The other was a hobby, if you like—an activity out of which I got a great deal of pleasure.

Although I hadn't exactly hit it off with the Jesuit teachers, my love and admiration for the Jesuit priests of St. Joseph's was constant and considerable.

I didn't require a great deal of heart-searching. A priest I wanted to be, and since we'd had so much contact with the Order in St. Joseph's, it seemed natural to have a preference for the Jesuits. They were also regarded as the Church's Guards' Brigade.

" I've decided I want to be a priest," I told Brother Cragg, the kindly old sacristan at St. Joseph's.

He nodded almost as if it were something he'd come to expect.

" I'll see to it," he said. " We'll arrange it with the Father Provincial when he does his visitation in July."

But when July came, I had certain inhibitions. The interview was arranged for St. Aloysius' College, the establishment that I'd chosen to desert. And not only was I to be put through it by Father Kean, the Provincial of the English Province, there were three other priests who had to be seen, and all three had been my masters at school.

It was the first glimpse I had had of the priests' quarters at Garnethill, and I wasn't especially impressed. There seemed to be a fetish for bare wood—bare wood floors and bare wood furniture. I liked the glitter and polish of the altar. This was like the kitchen of the Grand Hotel. And everywhere, in passageways and rooms, the air was heavy with the pungent smell of stale, thick tobacco smoke.

I remember thinking they must be prodigious smokers, these Jesuits. I have since discovered that priests in general are heavy smokers.

The interview with the Father Provincial was nothing like so nerve-racking as its anticipation. Despite his status, there was a humility about the man. Certainly he had before him a large and rather frightening dossier. By its size it would seem my past little life had been investigated most thoroughly.

And still there were questions—question after question, until every corner of my personality must have been completely explored.

But the entire confrontation was relaxed and pleasant. Father Kean did his best to remove any rose-coloured spectacles I may have worn. He warned me of the difficulties that an apprentice priest would encounter. But it was never over-powering, and I seemed to make the grade.

58

Father Meyer was a joy. I'd known him at school and he was always full of understanding. And when it came to Father Gregson, we got on like a house on fire. He'd been a senior footballer, or so it was rumoured, and I'd played for the school's intermediate team.

The collision that filled me with dread—and I would say collision was an accurate word—was with my fourth interrogator, Father Stratton.

At school we'd called him Big Jake. He was the College's prefect of discipline, and he pursued his role with a Dickensian zeal.

Big Jake it was who dispensed the punishment of the corporal kind. And he didn't believe in one of the best, or even two. Big Jake's thrashings were delivered in sixes—six of the best was his minimum. But twelve was not uncommon. And often his sentence was twenty-four, or "twice twelve," as he put it.

I got his " twice twelve " on one occasion for throwing chalk: " Twelve for having the chalk, MacEwan," he said, " and twelve for throwing it."

No boy ever got the double-dozen all at once. Mine were administered in twelves on successive days. Even on this instalment basis, it still hurt.

To put it mildly, I didn't like Big Jake. I don't think anyone did. And here we were about to meet up again.

He smiled—he actually smiled. He asked for my mother and my brother. He applauded my decision to enter the Church. He was entirely the gentle shepherd. No Sister of Mercy could have been more kind. The interview with Big Jake was probably the most pleasant of all.

I told my mother I'd been accepted. " I never had any doubts," she said.

I never had any doubts myself. As it turned out, it's a pity I hadn't.

The Jesuit novitiate was at **Manresa House**, a magnificent Georgian mansion in the wealthy stockbroker, southwest fifteen suburb of Roehampton, London. It had once been the home of the Earl of Bessborough. Now it was the novitiate for the Jesuit English Province.

But I had two months still of freedom. The Jesuits' calendar remained faithful to tradition. Its novitiate didn't start until September 8, the birth-date of Our Lady, according to hallowed tradition.

That turned out to be a splendid summer, and I filled it with another sport at which I'd become not unskilled. I was rarely off the tennis courts.

I was a natural at ball games, with one exception. I still haven't mastered the sport of golf. I'm told I have a most impressive swing. In fact, my whole approach to the game is thoroughly stylish. If I played the Old Course at St. Andrews, I'm sure the spectators would be impressed.

"What a magnificent player," they might react. And when they saw me slicing and pulling and venturing into the rarely-visited jungle sectors of the course, they would probably say: "He must be having an off-day. Normally, with a style like that he must play off two at least."

But the truth is, I'm a duffer on the links. My handicap in golf, as they say, is golf. But I could well be the most spectacular wooden-spoonist in the game. In an Australian competition, I was given a prize for the most interesting golfer on the course!

On the 7th of September, I left Glasgow on the night train, and the night was grey and chilly, with wisps of autumn fog like engine steam.

There was a young man going abroad to escape the depression that bedevilled the land, and his friends had brought a piper down to the platform to play him on his way and add to his nostalgia.

The sound of the bagpipes got lost in the train noises, and Glasgow began to drift away in a series of lights that receded faster and faster as the train gained speed.

No sleeper in those days for young MacEwan. No sleepers indeed for anyone from Springburn—you sat it out on the long, long trail down the iron road to London.

I was lucky to get a corner seat, and I tried to sleep, but sleep was elusive. Outside, eventually, was only blackness. The night was down, and the only passing scene was one of remembrance and imagination.

I was thinking of the room-and-kitchen and the football and the friends, and the altar at St. Joseph's and the tea and buns.

I was utterly lonely. Try as I would, I couldn't shake off an oppressive feeling of sadness. My age was seventeen years and a half.

Euston Station was a journey of years. When I got out, with that cold, crumpled sensation that follows a night spent with your clothes on, a signboard on the Euston platform announced the next train for Glasgow. I found it hard to resist the urge to go back immediately.

I went instead to my aunt in London, and this meeting with someone familiar helped to lessen the shock of the loneliness of London.

There was a bus for Roehampton at three in the afternoon, and the stop for Manresa had a pub on one corner and opposite was a little Jesuit church.

I walked up the long drive-way, and two taxis passed and I followed their route into a quadrangle. Two young men from the taxis were going through the door, and I went in behind them and nobody spoke.

We were led by a lay brother into a large but unimpressive parlour, where young men with their little attache cases stood around. And more young men arrived in taxis, and still there was this awesome silence.

Eventually, we were thirty in all—thirty novices all in one year! Thirty young men whom no doubt a variety of impulses had directed towards this life of dedication. If the Jesuits get an intake of ten these days, it's considered a fertile year!

Some of them were wealthy boys from such Jesuit colleges as Stonyhurst, Beaumont and Mount St. Mary. Others had come up by way of Jesuit schools at Wimbledon,

Preston and Stamford Bridge. I felt out of it and even more lonely than in that corner seat in that endless night on the London train.

He looked to me about 45. He was thin and pale and bespectacled. He was shy almost to the point of bashfulness, and when he shook hands with us all, his hand was warm but limp.

Yet William Pears Smith brought to the eyes of the young men a look that went beyond respect and came close to one of wonderment. He was the Pater Magister Novitiarum—the Father Master of Novices.

We were directed towards a great, long table, and still this frightening, artificial, neurotic silence persisted. The lay brothers came in with our evening meal. They were mostly kindly, uneducated men who had chosen to serve in this kind of environment—to cook and carry and wash and scrub. Their constant act of worship was menial. They were certainly magnificent at apple-pie!

It's a long time ago and I've forgotten all the other courses in that excellent first meal at Manresa. But I shall never forget the apple pie. It was not only the most succulent of apple pies I've ever tasted before or since, it was somehow a link with the normal, physical outside world— the world I'd chosen to leave behind.

After supper—I still had scarcely spoken a word—we were led by the Father Master to the Novices' hall. Now we were in the mansion-house proper and its windows were tall and magnificent. They looked out on to Richmond Park and at the end of the lawn there was what is called a ha-ha—a broad ditch that acted as a barrier to confine to the park the royal deer.

In my silent loneliness I came near to feeling jealous of those deer in their park on the other side. I felt on the inside looking out.

Our quarters were named after Jesuit saints. I was put into St. Peter Claver's, right on the very top floor. It was a long room divided into six cubicles, and there was a magnificent fireplace at one end—a relic of the days when this self-same hall would radiate the warmth and merriment of power and affluence.

Now the fire was out.

The cubicles were curtained and each bore the name of the expected novices. There was a desk outside and opposite we each had a chest of drawers for our clothes.

Our furnishings consisted of an iron bed and a washstand with basin and jug filled with water. The water was cold. It was always to be cold. There was a small strip of carpet down the side of the bed.

I was still inspecting my spartan quarters when a bell rang and immediately we were directed back to the novices' hall. This time the Father Master assigned to each of us a Guardian Angel — a second-year novice who knew the ropes and would keep us right during our first three days.

These were the days in which we were on trial. Not until the fourth day were we officially acknowledged as novices. Four days! The Jesuit training before ordination would be no less than 15 years!

We were each of us given a Latin grammar, a book of conversational Latin and a Bible. We learned that what little talk there was at Manresa had always to be in Latin—except at recreation.

In the conversational Latin the scholars had been busy so that there was never any occasion to use even a single English word. There were appropriate words for even such modern devices as " gramophone " and " wireless " and " motor-car."

Not like the Gaelic language which has no such refinements—with results that I always find amusing.

The Gaelic speaker will be going great guns in his ancient tongue (which I regret I cannot claim to speak), and now and then in the middle of this flow of foreign sound a word like " accordion " will shoot out—or " aeroplane " or

" television." So far as such modern things are concerned, the Greeks may have a word for it, but the Gaels don't.

The Father Master informed us that first thing in the morning we must meditate, and he gave us some advice as to the pattern our meditations should follow.

That bell rang again. I discovered later that the ringer was a second-year novice called Payne. He eventually became a professor in Rome, which is a long way from clanging a milk bell.

But what power he had in that clapper of his! The bell was omnipotent. Everything stopped for that bell. The whole routine of the Jesuit day revolved around it. The bell had the power of a sergeant-major—it was the Vox Dei.

Even the Father Master stopped in the middle of a sentence, then announced that the bell was the signal for our adjournment to the chapel.

I found I could not warm to this man. He was kind and considerate. He was consistent. He never ruffled. As Father Master, his role was that of our guide, counsellor and even confessor. This was the man to whom the novice was meant to take all his troubles. The sort of man to whom you should have been able to bare your soul. But always with me there was this unseen barrier—an inexplicable reluctance to take him completely on trust.

I realise the fault was probably mine. Quite honestly, I have never been able to bare my soul to anyone. My innermost thoughts and feelings have always been my very own. Even later, when I went to Scots College in Rome, we had what were called spiritual directors and they were splendid, understanding men. They were hand-picked for their capacity for burden-sharing.

Yet none of them ever got near to my soul.

To reach the chapel, we had to pass through the Long Gallery—another magnificent link with the past in this beautiful, old house. It must have been all of fifty yards long. Its ceiling was rich in embellishment, and never have

I seen such woodwork. At intervals there were statues of various Jesuit saints.

But now it was heavy with this strange unreal atmosphere which oppressed me after the laughing, carefree, normal days of Springburn.

In the Long Gallery, talking in Latin or any language, was absolutely forbidden. If you'd something urgent to say, that couldn't wait, the ban still applied. Before a word could be uttered, you had to move into one of the ante-rooms.

We said prayers in the chapel, then silently filed upstairs to bed.

It was half-past nine. I undressed in my cubicle. The chill of autumn had already entered this house. I got in between the sheets, and they were icy cold. Yet I remember falling asleep almost immediately.

It had been a long and tiring day. And sleep was an escape from the misery I felt.

Our rising next morning was at half-past five. It arrived for me at that unearthly hour in the shape of a voice —a monotone so distant and faint that I thought I was dreaming.

" Deo Gratias! Deo Gratias!"

It came nearer and nearer, and I realised that this was the knocker-up gradually delivering his awakening chant to the three floors of novices.

" Deo Gratias!" right outside my cubicle. I creaked out of bed and prepared to wash.

By this time a fire was burning in the massive grate at the end of the hall, and I discovered that this became one of our occasional duties—to rise even earlier than half-past five and ensure that the fire was lit.

There were twenty minutes to wash, shave and dress, and despite that fire I felt chilled and half alive. We had only cold water from the jug by the bed, and you emptied your slops into a pail and the pail had in turn to be taken to a large waste-bucket on one of the landings.

The second-year novice who'd lit the fire remained in the room and ensured that we each of us kept to the schedule.

We were still in the midst of the magnum silentium—the great silence that must be observed from recreation the night before until after breakfast.

Without so much as a good morning therefore we went down the three floors to the chapel for prayers—a mere matter of five minutes, then back again up all those stairs.

The second-year man who was our "room corporal" was waiting to start us on meditation. This meditation business had to last an hour—the first quarter kneeling, the second quarter sitting, the third quarter standing and the fourth quarter kneeling again.

I wanted to lie down. I was still half asleep. How could a virile, young, red-blooded lad direct his mind to great, profound and solemn thoughts at six o'clock in the morning. I think my mind strayed to just about everything except what the Father Master had told us the night before.

When I knelt, I kept thinking of a room and kitchen in Springburn. When I stood up, my thoughts wandered off to the football and the River Clyde and its little paddle steamers.

When I sat down, I had to fight against falling asleep again. At meditating, I'm afraid I was hopeless.

There was worse to come after morning Mass. It was called the period for reflection—you had to reflect on your previous meditations.

This was a bit much.

I had nothing against meditation. In the Springburn days we used to go off for this kind of week-end—out into the country for peace and quiet, and the chance to think deeply on the things that mattered. We were all healthy, outdoor-type young men, but we treasured those occasional week-ends as something of a mental tonic. We used to go to the Jesuit Retreat House at Craighead, Bothwell, and loved the experience.

But here at Manresa it was different.

We got our hair cut in the barber's shop, presided over by a brother who had no hairdressing skill whatsoever. He didn't need it. He had only one style to deal with. He simply took your hair off!

There was a tailor's shop, and this was where we were issued with our gowns. Unlike the Franciscans, who wear brown habits wherever they are, the Jesuits have no uniform dress. Their garb, in fact, varied from country to country.

In Britain the choice of the Jesuits was black, modelled on the gown of the University of Paris, and the tailor's shop was like a jumble sale with great stacks of black gowns that looked as if they'd seen better days.

You took one that fitted roughly. It was suggested that the gown should come below the knee. That gave considerable scope for variation. Mine almost reached down to the ankles.

Pinned into my gown were what were called " examen beads." The beads were assembled on a piece of wire and the wire had a loop at one end.

I suppose you would call them conscience beads. Every time you committed a fault or thought a wicked thought or broke the rules in any way, you were meant to move one of the beads up into the circle of wire.

And at the mid-day period set aside for self-examination, you checked on your record of defaulting and entered each misdemeanour in a little black book. This was called your examen book.

It was daft. It was childish. It was completely spurious. That's how I see it looking back now.

Worse still was the issue of devices for self-punishment. One of these was a circle of barbed wire which you were counselled to wear on the thigh.

I thought it grotesquely amusing that the addendum to the instructions concerning the penance rings suggested that this kind of self-torture should be indulged in no more than twice a week.

We were also given discipline flails. They were made of what looked like window-cord knotted at the ends and attached to a sturdy rope handle.

The idea was that you applied this device to your own bare back in the privacy of your cubicle. Certain nights were set aside for this kind of ordeal, and again the limit was twice a week.

It was amazing how most of the novices accepted such incongruous, medieval practices. Certainly on the prescribed flailing nights I heard the sound of great whackings going on behind the cubicle curtains.

Many of these young men were from wealthy homes. Their boyhoods had probably been cossetted and pampered. Yet they were so caught up in the atmosphere of the novitiate that all the logic and accepted realities of the outside world were willingly discarded.

Every move they made, every act or gesture was to the glory of the Lord. They were close to the dedication of Buddhist priests who set themselves on fire.

I tried to whip myself twice. But never again. At flailing I was a failure. It hurt too much.

There was a boy called O'Flaherty in St. Peter Claver's. We discovered we had a great deal in common, and he was one with whom I could have achieved friendship. But special friends were not allowed.

" You were certainly giving it big licks last night," I said.

" Don't tell anyone, brother," he whispered. " It was my pillow I was whacking!"

I'm afraid I couldn't resort even to this kind of deceit. I couldn't pretend.

Don't think for one minute that I was cynical about the whole system of training. We were setting out to be Jesuits and Jesuit priests had it tough. Not for them the comfort and human contacts of the diocesan priest. Their lives were entire acts of self-sacrifice to the point of suffering. For this kind of future role the moulding of youth had to be strict and demanding. The discipline had to be tough.

How, you may ask, were these stern disciplines achieved? One of the methods of ensuring that you kept the Jesuit code was completely abhorrent to me. I detected in it Roman or Italian or Spanish influences. It was certainly not British.

I wouldn't like to call it spying, but we were each our brother's keeper. Each novice had an admonitor.

Every Saturday morning you had to stand outside your cubicle and your admonitor would list your minor offences of the previous week.

Sometimes they were ridiculously petty. You could be charged with breaking the silence on the previous Tuesday.

I remember one novice was accused of making too much noise when eating. One week my particular misdemeanour was that I did not observe the rule of the novitiate in the buttering of my bread. I had buttered the slice. I was reminded that I should break off a piece of the bread and butter it individually.

I'm afraid I wasn't much good as an admonitor.

What scared me was the ceremony known as The Circle. On such occasions the sixty novices assembled in the novices' hall and sat round in a circle. When the Father Master called out one of our names, the unfortunate novice had to kneel down in the middle and all of us in turn had to point out his faults.

It sounds now so much like a bizarre pantomime that I wonder that the ritual did not degenerate into a hilarious burlesque. But it never did. The Circle was always taken very seriously. Frequently I watched the novice in the middle completely reduced to tears by the shafts of reproach from his colleagues. I have seen strong, healthy eighteen-year-old youths weeping like hysterical young girls.

My name was never called. I was never nominated as the man in the middle. For that I was eternally grateful.

I suppose it could be argued that the apprentice Jesuit, by way of such ceremonies as The Circle, was being trained in humility. They could be interpreted as character-building

—as exercises in patience and the capacity for standing up unflinchingly to public criticism.

I should imagine that The Circle has now been abandoned in the novitiate.

For certain trivial breaches of discipline you could choose your own penance.

For breaking the Grand Silence you might opt to eat at the small table in the refectory. It was so low that you had to kneel throughout the entire meal.

Again, in the refectory your self-imposed penance would require you to kneel in the centre of the floor, and with your arms outstretched you chanted to the hundred Fathers and Brothers seated at the tables around the room:

" Reverend Fathers and Loving Brothers, by order of Holy Obedience, I tell my fault of having broken a plate, the property of the community, for which Holy Obedience enjoins on me the penance of kissing feet."

The defaulting novice was then obliged to scramble under the tables and kiss as many feet as he could.

Again the quashing of pride, the practice in humility. But I found that such exercises by their repetition ceased to be very effective. The novice who knelt at the small table, for instance, attracted very little attention at all. We were usually too busy eating.

The atmosphere of Manresa was tense. Without some kind of break it would have been unbearable.

As it was the frayed nerves of the novices sometimes showed. In chapel someone would titter and eventually the whole place would be rocking with laughter. It was a strained, unhealthy sort of laughter. We were all like so many schoolboys letting off steam.

So once a week we had a half-day off. The Jesuits are not enclosed monks or contemplatives. On these free afternoons we might play games or go for a walk outside the grounds.

We had no money. So we had to walk. You could walk to Wimbledon Common or Barnes Common or lovely Richmond Park. Sometimes we visited churches.

The success of the day depended on your companions, and in this you had no choice. It was the Father Master who posted up the companies, and a company consisted of three. If your two colleagues were agreeable fellows, these walks could be most pleasant. But if you landed someone with whom you simply had nothing in common, they were tantamount to another form of punishment.

Occasionally we were granted a Long Walk. This was really something to look forward to. We were off for the entire day and each of us got a shilling.

If that doesn't sound exactly like a high old time, remember that we are in the 1920s. A shilling was a shilling then. Those were days when you could rely on a shilling retaining its value for at least a decade.

In the days of my youth you could buy ten cigarettes for sixpence. And that price persisted for years and years—right up, in fact, until 1939. The constant shrinkage in the value of money is almost entirely a post-war phenomenon.

We were able therefore to travel far for our shilling. But often I still chose to walk, sometimes for miles and miles, so that my feet were blistered when I got back.

Walking was conducive to thought. And usually my thoughts took me back to Scotland. More and more I had to fight to suppress the doubts about my wisdom in ever having left it.

Some afternoons on the free day were set aside for games —handball, tennis or soccer. But at Manresa there was no rugby. It would have offended the Jesuit code. Rugby is of course played at all Jesuit schools.

Part of the Jesuit ethic was summed up in the Latin " Noli tangere." You must never touch anyone. Even if you wanted to attract someone's attention, it must only be done by pulling the wing of his gown. So rugger with its frequent physical contact was out.

Even in the playing of soccer there was a strange attitude of extreme Victorian modesty. We were never allowed to strip. We wore our oldest clothes and had to hide our necks by tying round a handkerchief. We were even obliged to wear caps. This rule could make things awkward when you jumped to head the ball.

Strangely enough, one of the weekly occasions to which I looked forward was confession. You could pick your own priest, and many of them at Manresa were what were known as curvals, an abbreviation of " curate valetudinem."*

They were old and grey and worn with age. They had done their labouring in the vineyard and now they'd come home. I suppose it should have been rather pathetic. They had in fact come home to die.

But, with those Jesuit veterans I was always aware of an almost tender bond. Their years of experience had brought them to a state of compassion and understanding. You had a great sense of comfort in their presence.

We were so far apart in years. We were at the beginning of the road and they were close to its end. Yet I got more encouragement from these great old " curvals " than anyone else. They were the real Gentle Shepherds in my days at Manresa.

For the first seventeen years of my life I don't suppose I'd ever set eyes on a three-course meal. There was nothing unusual in that. Glasgow in these days was a soup-and-pudding town with maybe a bit of meat on Sundays, and on wash-days there was boiling beef left over from the making of broth.

But now the three-course dinner was a daily occurrence. In many ways the Jesuit training may have been demanding, but you certainly weren't starved.

St. Ignatius, the founder of the Order, had no time for fasting. He asked of his followers a hard day's work and he took the commendable attitude that if a man is to give of his best, he must be well fed.

The food at Manresa was not ostentatious, but it was good and solid and plentiful. The feature of breakfast was

* Look after health.

Carleton Smith, my
international manager,
with his children,
Colombe and Christophe.

Sir Compton
Mackenzie.

Count John McCormack.

Fritz Kreisler.

the home-made bread—such mouth-watering bread, both brown and white. The breakfast table never lacked fruit, and always I've been an avid fruit fan.

We ate in the refectory, with tables for the novices down each side. The table along the top of the room was for the Rector and the Father Master and the priests. Down the centre were the tables occupied by the Juniors, who had passed from their two-year noviceship and would now do Classics and Maths and Languages for two years.

It was all rather like a posh boarding-school. Every time you entered the refectory, you walked over to the assembly of pigeon-holes, and this was where your personal linen napkin was kept, each with its identifying number.

Most of the young novices were accustomed to this sort of thing. They'd been schooled in one of the Jesuit schools where the pattern of organisation was similar.

But Sydney MacEwan from Springburn with his own linen napkin—that was one for the book, as they say!

The food came through from the kitchen in great, shining, silver tureens. Each novice had to learn to carve. And such rounds of sirloin and legs of mutton on which to practise an art that to me was completely foreign.

I can still recall my very first effort. There were carving tables at each end of the refectory, and I was given the one close to the Rector's table. At the near end of the table sat Father Ward. He was one of my favourites—an elderly, grey-haired, jolly man with a mischievous twinkle in his eye.

He watched my fumbling, hacking efforts with a huge, hot, steaming roast. And suddenly I was aware of him leaning over and whispering enthusiastically: " Put your foot on it, brother!"

I soon became pretty proficient. I discovered that in carving there is no real secret. The thing is to have a razor-sharp knife.

D

We were given a choice of refreshment—lemonade, cider or beer. Beer! I amused myself by thinking of the Springburn neighbours discussing the departure of Sydney to a monastery. And here he was being offered beer! I could just imagine their shock. Beer at the tender age of 18! And them with visions of sackcloth and ashes and nothing but God's pure water.

This was the English public school influence again.

I opted for the cider. I have never had a palate for beer. But my cider consumption became considerable. I recall the old song that was a favourite of the students at Glasgow University: "Here's to the good old cider, that makes your belly wider!"

It was very accurate. At this tender age I discovered I was developing a tum. And I'm afraid it became something of a permanency.

I have never been fat, and I've slimmed down a good deal. But down through all those many years I've never been able to get rid of my cider bulge!

There were no studies at Manresa for the novices. The two years were entirely a course in work and spiritual training. And every day you queued up outside the room of the Father Master to learn what duties you'd landed.

For indoor work you might be assigned to the library. You might have to scrub floors or polish brass. And with what enthusiasm and energy you tackled every chore. This was all to the glory of the Lord, and you gave it everything you'd got.

Even the work instructions were delivered in Latin.

Your being sent to the kitchen was described as "In Cella Poc." This meant getting busy on the great stack of dirty dishes that was the aftermath of every breakfast.

It was even more off-putting if your duty fell after dinner. That was when the mountain of crockery was usually coated with grease and the remnants of gravy—and none of your modern plastic squeezers filled with magical, grease-dissolving fluids!

74

But the order that we dreaded most was: "In a secretis!" This was your cue to be off to the lavatories!

It is difficult to accept that you are glorifying God in the act of cleaning out communal urinals. Especially when they've been coping with the essential activities of no fewer than sixty novices.

In outdoor work gardening was our most regular activity. The gardens were run by Brother Mannion, and with such a big estate to look after he needed all the novice help he could get.

Father Ward—the one who had jested at my crude initial attempts at carving—was a teacher of maths. He was in fact a brilliant mathematician. He excelled unexpectedly in another direction. He was an outstanding expert on poultry.

It was he who ran the hen farm. And his regular novice assistant was Brother Whelan, a Stonyhurst boy from a wealthy family. I liked him a lot. He remains in my memory as the boy with the five o'clock shadow.

He was dark and his growth of beard was heavy. Even at the age of $17\frac{1}{2}$ he had to shave twice daily.

I was somewhat allergic to sweeping leaves. The job was tedious and never-ending. And to Brother Whelan I said one day at recreation: " I wouldn't mind a job like yours."

The grape-vine at Manresa must have been active. Two days later I was summoned by Father Master, who said: " I understand you'd like to work with the hens."

I told him I would. " All right," he said, " we will appoint you ' assistens curator gallinorum ' " (assistant keeper of poultry).

I enjoyed this finding of a permanent niche. I was kitted out with suitable old clothes and a pair of Stonyhurst boots. They were the finest footwear I've ever worn.

It could be tiring. It could be dirty. But there was great satisfaction in shedding all the muddied clothes and stepping into a shower—the same sense of well-being that you got from the baths after a hard game of rugby for Hillhead High.

And for me there was something of a personal pride in the great baskets of eggs I carried up daily to the house.

And Father Ward was brilliant. So thoroughly did he teach us the hen-keeping art that Brother Whelan and I were eventually akin to veterinary surgeons. We could operate for instance for dyptheric roup, a common enough disease which affected the throats of hens.

Another novice was Brother Vavasour. He was a late-comer to the novitiate—aged about 25. He was upper-class —a member of one of the old English Catholic families.

There were a number of such old aristocratic families— like the de Traffords and the Vaughans—for whom it was an occasion for pride when one of their sons chose to become a Jesuit.

Vavasour was a first-class person. He had a brilliant brain. He was a pedigree article. He was extremely inventive and had the kind of initiative that makes for a natural leader.

Rather surprisingly for one from such a background as his, he was also skilled with his hands. Nowadays he would be called an expert do-it-yourselfer.

But above all he had this delightful, self-effacing personality. He had charm and perfect manners. The last time I heard of him he was Bursar at the great college of Stony-hurst.

I still found it hard to make genuine friends in the atmosphere of Manresa. You were not allowed to pick and choose your friendships.

At meal times in the refectory you had to sit at which-ever chair was vacant—even if your companion at table was the greatest of bores.

During the half-hour recreation periods when you went out into those magnificent grounds, the same rule applied. You had to walk and speak with whichever other novice happened to be nearby. You could not be selective in your companions. And your conversation was limited. There was no discussion of secular things. All talk had to be about spiritual things. And how difficult this could be with some-one who never shared the same wavelength.

The recreation period could be torture.

Once in three months there was what was called the Blandyke—after a place of that name in Holland. This was something of a blow-out, a complete day of freedom to go where you pleased and do what you pleased.

The meal that evening was an absolute banquet, com-plete with wine. And afterwards we could go out on to the front lawn and talk with anyone—no appointed companies, no strictures whatever on the nature of the conversation.

It was like breaking loose from a great mass of cobwebs. The Jesuits in their wisdom had introduced the Blandyke not as a luxury but as an essential relief-valve. It was a minor antidote to tension—a break in the monotony of the daily silences and meditations and restrictions and unsatis-factory human relationships.

The scholastic novices, i.e. those who were going to be priests, never mixed with the lay brother novices, but one could ask for leave to share recreation with them occasionally.

I took advantage of this privilege when I discovered that the lay sector included a second-year student called Hughie Smith. He used to be one of my chums in Glasgow.

But that first meeting was a flop. We used to be able to talk about the football and the neighbours and the trains. In Glasgow, Hughie had been with me on the altar, and we'd had a great deal in common.

But here our talk had to be on a spiritual plane and somehow we never got going. I tried on a number of occasions, always with the permission of the Father Master.

But in this atmosphere Hughie and I never got through to each other. It was as if we were a couple of strangers. It was all so strained and unnatural.

This worried me a great deal. It added to the doubt that kept growing up within me—that perhaps I'd made a mistake, that I'd chosen a way of life for which I was completely unsuited.

Not that I didn't try. My goodness, how I tried. I obeyed all the rules, I sang in the choir, I worked with a will at all my duties. I prayed—I prayed hard. But somehow the spiritual uplift for which I was subconsciously searching, never happened. The elation I had expected from a life of dedication eluded me altogether. Instead I became increasingly unhappy.

I had great hopes for October.

We were told to write home and tell our relatives that the Long Retreat was about to begin. All the second-year novices gave us their congratulations and good wishes. The Retreat would last for thirty days.

One evening after chapel, a small table and chair were placed in the chancel for the Father Master and he explained the significance of the thirty days.

Our indoor and outdoor work would continue. But throughout the Long Retreat we were committed to absolute silence for thirty days. And the number of our meditations was stepped up considerably.

It happened twice in the career of the Jesuit—once during his noviceship and again in the tertianship, the period when he returns as a kind of novice, after having served as an ordained priest, for what could be called a refresher course.

We learned from the second-year novices that the Long Retreat would be an unforgettable spiritual experience. I got the impression of a great cleansing process. I had high hopes that during these thirty days something would happen that would dispel all my doubts. I expected some kind of magic.

After being given the subject for each meditation, we had to return to our quarters, not to the desks in the hall, but alone inside our individual cubicles.

We had what was called the " processus peccatorum "—
the spiritual exercise in which we had to review the sins of
our whole life.

I was 18—a healthy, normal, decent 18-year-old, I would
have thought. I found I couldn't arouse any really sinful
past. My meditation was mainly spent staring into space
and drawing up from the well of memory the times when
I squeezed a lassie or told a wee white lie to get out of an
awkward corner. But sin? I was too young for a backlog
of transgression to meditate on.

Don't think that I felt self-righteous or above reproach.
My feeling was one of depression. I'd failed in my meditation again.

It was the same with the meditation on Hell. The Father
Master explained that we should even apply ourselves to
assessing the dimensions of Hell—its length, breadth and
depth.

We had to pray that if the love of God grew cold within
us, at least the fear of Hell would save us from sin.

I found this physical fire-and-brimstone Hell completely
elusive. Nowadays it would be scoffed at by most theolo-
gians.

I couldn't picture Hell. The concept of unrepentant souls
sizzling in hell-fire in eternity was something I found
incomprehensible.

Even the spiritual exercises of St. Ignatius were a dis-
appointment. I felt the actual exercises were meant purely
as guide-lines. They were the bones demanding the flesh
that an expert commentator or lecturer could provide. This
didn't happen with our Father Master.

No one is ever the same again after the Long Retreat—
that was what we were told. The man who experienced the
Long Retreat would never lose his soul—this was the sort
of build-up that this spiritual experience was given.

But I'm afraid in my case nothing happened. I had
always been a loyal member of the Church. I loved the
Church and still do. But I emerged from that gruelling

Long Retreat feeling no more profound than at its start. I expected so much and discovered so little. It was probably my fault—great minds through the years have found the riches of the spiritual exercises of St. Ignatius.

It made my predicament even more unbearable. I felt a fraud. I was living at Manresa under false pretences.

Novices who completed two years' training were obliged to take vows—simple vows that could be dispensed by Rome. They wrote them out in beautiful Latin and the following day we assembled for Morning Mass and watched them move up one by one to the altar and kneel on its topmost step.

It was a moving, unpretentious ceremony. They each read out in Latin: " Almighty, Eternal God, I . . . . , although wholly unworthy in thy sight, relying on God's clemency and goodness, vow myself to perpetual poverty, chastity and obedience in the Society of Jesus."

Thereafter they each emerged with Roman collar and biretta. Already they outwardly looked the part. But they still had a long, long way to go.

I watched and wondered—would I ever reach this stage even?

We moved up close to the time of Christmas. On Christmas Eve we went to bed early in order to rise for midnight Mass.

Vavasour whispered: " When you get up at half-past eleven, remember to pull the clothes over your bed. When you come back, it won't be so chilly."

It seemed only minutes after falling asleep, that awful voice sounded again: " Deo gratias! Deo gratias!"

I lay and thought: " I wish that fellow would fall and break his neck!"

It woke me up in more ways than one—my thinking that way, my letting this kind of thought come into my head. A terrible thing that to think on Christmas Eve—especially in the case of a potential priest!

It was on my mind as we trooped down to Mass—a strange mixture of amusement and concern. A natural enough reaction in the outside world when you're suddenly jolted from deep, warm sleep. But here the thought was positively wicked. It seemed to convince me once and for all that I didn't measure up, that Manresa and I must soon part company.

I must admit that the midnight Mass was memorable. In this holy, insulated atmosphere we came very close to the Bethlehem scene.

But back in bed my thoughts were of home. It was my first Christmas away from the Springburn room and kitchen, and I thought of the singing at midnight in St. Joseph's and the gifts and the greetings and the jolly panto-mimes in Glasgow. Ah, the warmth of it all.

We had our Christmas night concert at Manresa, but it wasn't the same. The Juniors put on a play, and one of the old priests who'd come home to die sang the song about " When you're jog, jog, jogging along the highway." I found it sad. His highway was so near its end.

I finally decided it was not the road for me.

On a bleak, sunless January day, I called on the Master of Novices. I thought it would be a difficult interview. You could not avoid this feeling of failure. I'm not one to give in easily, but I could no longer go on living a lie.

" I'm a bit doubtful about this whole thing," I said.

He was kindness itself. He showed no emotion, but his manner was gentle and understanding.

" I'm sorry," he said.

" I'm not really doubtful at all any more," I said. " I've really decided—I've made up my mind. I can't go on with this—it's not for me."

" Well, brother," he told me, " my advice is, don't do anything in a hurry. Think it over. And pray."

" I've done all that," I told him. " I think my mind's made up."

" You seem to have been happy enough," he said. " I've seen you happy. I've watched you singing and at football. Give it a little more thought—there's no need to rush into anything."

" But, Father Master, I'm being fed here and housed and I don't really think I'm entitled any more."

" My dear young man, put that thought right out of your head. You're working here for your keep — and I've watched you working hard. Think it over — that's my advice."

It was not the decisive sort of interview I'd hoped for. But I came away feeling a great sense of peace. I'd been honest at last with the Father Master. He knew what I was thinking.

I did pray. I did think deeply about my decision, but all the time I knew that there was no way back.

It was March when I told the Father Master that I was still of the same mind.

" I've prayed for you, too, brother," he said. " So let it be."

I'd been six months at Manresa.

He went on to explain the arrangements for my departure as if he'd known all along that my attitude wouldn't change.

In those days not many novices dropped out. We had one boy who lasted only three days. But the overall loss to the novitiate was small. It was later on, after the two-year training period, that the strain seemed to tell and the " casualty list " increased.

" As a matter of fact, another brother is going home also," the Father Master said. " I think I will let you both go home together."

He wrote to my mother in Glasgow, and I saw the letter later. For a misfit it was really a very favourable reference : " Don't worry—don't be disappointed—he has been a thoroughly good boy who entered into everything with great enthusiasm . . ."

There was an attitude in this kind of establishment that none of the other novices should know of a colleague's departure. It was all arranged secretly. The night before I sang as usual with the choir at Benediction, then went up along to the lumber room to pack my trunk.

The Father Master gave me five pounds for my fare and any incidental expenses, and on the 17th of March I walked out of Manresa.

And the boy who was going home with me was going all the way. It was good old Hughie Smith.

We walked together through the trees of the drive-way and we never looked back. We got on the bus for London and Hughie said to go upstairs.

And from his pocket he produced a packet of Gold Flake that he'd got from one of the old lay brothers.

We both lit up and the feeling was wonderful. Not that I've ever been a particularly addicted smoker. But this act on top of a London bus was almost something of a rite. It was a gesture of our new-found freedom. We were each being something of a devil. We were both emotionally intoxicated.

We got a great welcome home. There were no recriminations. If my mother was the slightest bit disappointed in me, it certainly didn't show. She seemed too overjoyed to have me home.

And that room and kitchen in a Glasgow tenement really felt good. My brother, who was clever with his hands, had built a real wireless set—one with a real loudspeaker. I was living with music again.

I went back to visit Manresa many a time. I loved it as a place. There was the deep, ancient well that I spoke of in the beginning. It had some of the most wonderful trees in the world—great, gnarled, dignified oaks and chestnuts, and rich, magnificent copper beeches. There was a Cedar of Lebanon that must be the largest in Britain.

I went back to please my eyes, but my heart is always elsewhere. I went back also to meet the old Jesuits. My future lay elsewhere than with the Jesuits, but the Order had and always will have my affection and respect.

Alas, Manresa as I knew it is no longer there. It serves now as a teachers' training college—surrounded by modern flats and little houses.

CHAPTER

9

There was no question of returning to Springburn as a failure. It was more of a hero's welcome they gave me. I was home, and I felt again the warmth of Glasgow around me.

I got back into the thick of church life at St. Joseph's. I got on the altar again, and Brother Cragg even let me resume with the football team—that wild and woolly lot that gave my mother so many heart-aches.

But the team had changed. The old guard had left, and anyhow it was close to the end of the season. This is one of the sad things of life. You can never really go back. The old man dreams of his youth, and he might as well cry for the moon. All those thousands of people who were starved out of Scotland and prospered in some far-away place, and always their dream is to fly into Prestwick and walk down the street that was shabby and poor and couldn't support them. It still kept a bit of their heart when they left.

And they all come back with this sad illusion, that a journey in a plane across the Atlantic will turn back the clock those forty years they've been away. And, of course, it never happens. There is no way back. Inevitably, the tenement has gone to make way for some concrete architectural horror. Or the cottage in the glen is a gaunt, grey skeleton, with the eyes of its windows picked out like the skull of a hind in the heather.

It was decided I should take a degree. I had my Highers. I was accepted for admission to Glasgow University the following October.

We were now only into the month of March, and in Scotland those were chill and hungry days. The queues of idle men were lengthening. And not for their women-folk the daily change of fashion.

There were many who were poor and wore a shawl over a striped, starched petticoat. This was their uniform of poverty week after week and month that followed month.

What they could do something about was their hair. And how they cherished their crowning glory. This was something they could constantly change for free. And what brushings and combings there must have been to coax this God-given adornment into some new shape.

I have never forgotten the magnificent hair of the shawlie wifies when Glasgow was poor.

In this kind of setting it would have been an impertinence for a student or potential student to take a job of work. In any case it was virtually an impossibility. The jobs just weren't there. I had six months ahead and nothing to do.

We moved that year to Knightswood, the second of Glasgow's great new housing schemes that were to transform the lives of thousands of folks with exciting amenities that they'd never known before—bathrooms and electric light and gardens front and back, and our garden was enormous. That kept me busy for a goodly part of the summer.

And I went again to Kilchattan Bay, one of the Clyde resorts. A small place, yet steamers made six calls at its pier every day.

I was back with the Cowcaddens gang, loyal, sincere, good-hearted lads, but a pretty uncouth, threadbare lot. Not for us the seaside boarding house with bacon and eggs and homemade pancakes. Our holiday home was a patched bell tent—ex-army stock from World War I.

Out of this humble base I walked into my first real love affair. She was only 16 and still at school. She was Hutcheson's Grammar, which marked her out as somewhat " better-class."

Certainly not one to whom it should be known that my Kilchattan address was an aged tent—shared with a rather motley crew of East-end kids.

She had soft, fair hair and a pale, oval face, and I thought she looked like a film star.

Our date was for an evening cruise, and I dressed up for the momentous occasion in blazer and flannels. I really looked the undergrad—or so I thought.

We met on the pier and behaved in the tradition of the period. It could be summed up in the phrase: " See ye inside!"

In these straitened times the boy who took his lass to the pictures always went on this basis. It saved the boy the embarrassment of having to pay for two. He probably found it hard enough to raise the money to pay for himself. And the girls understood. " See ye inside," was the courting pattern of the times.

The fare for the evening cruise was eightpence.

And with my fair-haired beauty I was making the usual arrangement on the pier—" See you on board then!"— when Jackie came along.

He was one of the scallywags from the tent. In the accent of a Gorbals scaffie, he shouted: " Hey, Sid! There's a bag o' coal fur us along the pier! Can ye gie's a haun'!"

Kilchattan Bay is a ghost place now. Its pier is closed and no steamer calls. Its tennis courts are over-grown with weeds and moss.

My romance at Kilchattan died as well. And now I can muse on what may have happened to the fair-haired wee smasher with the oval face.

After a matter of ten years, from the age of eight, I gave up my study of the violin. I was a reasonable player. The fiddle has been my companion all through my life, and I've drawn from its strings a great deal of pleasure.

But I realised that another Yehudi Menuhin was not in the making. And by now my voice had ripened smoothly into a tenor.

It was a great time for concerts in Glasgow. Every Saturday night the Corporation organised such celebrity occasions in St. Andrew's Halls. At 4d. and 6d. a time!

They were advertised in the city trams, and I used to study the names on the posters. It would be untrue to suggest that I sat and dreamed in my Glasgow caur that one day my name would be thus displayed. I never even gave it a thought.

For our fourpence we got such talent as Astra Desmond, Isobel Baillie, Harold Williams, Heddle Nash, Dennis Noble. Was there ever such a bargain!

Scotland itself had its share at this period of good singers —such soloists as Ian Macpherson, Janette Sclanders, May Ferrier, Alex. MacGregor.

And in lesser halls all over the place there were concerts going on all the time by artistes who would never make the international grade, but whose talents could nonetheless earn them a very comfortable living.

It was a wonderful time for making music.

These lesser vocalists could command a fee of three to five guineas a night. With five appearances in the average week they were doing very nicely. Especially when you bear in mind that a skilled engineer in the yards of the Clyde had a weekly wage of three pounds ten.

I was a member of the St. Peter's Harriers, and they ran an annual concert as well as their marathon races.

I'd played the fiddle for them once before, and they asked me back with my violin again. My first-half solo received polite applause—nothing more, nothing less.

At the interval I told the organisers that in the second half I'd rather go on without my fiddle. They looked as if I'd suddenly been taken queer.

" This time I'd rather sing," I explained.

Their eyebrows went up still farther.

My brother Harold was the official accompanist and he it was who came to my rescue: " He really sings quite well," he said.

88

Without Harold I'd never have made it. Even with his backing, the concession was given with obvious reluctance and considerable foreboding.

I remember I sang the Caruso song called " Trusting Eyes," and the result was incredible. They just wouldn't let me off. They were at the stage of cheering and stamping their feet. I was 18 years old.

Some of the Harriers' concert committee are still among my friends. It has been a standing joke down through the years that they were the ones who did all in their power to make Sydney MacEwan stick to his fiddle!

A few weeks later, I was booked to sing at a parish entertainment in the Woodside Hall. It was an ambitious affair. Every other act on the bill was pro.

I was very much the unknown beginner. I was still innocent enough to be self-assured. Unexpectedly, the churning of one's entire system before every show—the cross that each worthwhile artiste must bear—is something that comes with experience and fame and the fear of a performance that isn't up to standard.

In the company of professionals, however, I decided to start at least on equal terms. It was back to Cambridge Street for the hire of a penguin suit and that fashion of the day, a paper dickie.

I wish I could have kept that ridiculous shirt-front. It was my very first symbol of success, if you exclude that modest seven-and-six from the pierrot show on Kirn pier.

I was inundated with congratulations—let it be said, from most of the pros on the bill as well.

For the first time I was made aware that this voice of mine was perhaps no ordinary tenor.

My first teacher was Miss Wainwright, the niece of J. E. R. Senior, who was one of the city organists.

She lived with her uncle at 22 Royal Crescent, and I'm afraid my regular trekking up that stair to her flat played no part in my musical ascent. Miss Wainwright was a dear old soul. She played the piano nicely and provided me with efficient accompaniment. But so far as my burgeoning voice was concerned, she did not know where to begin.

I moved to the Athenaeum, the City of Glasgow's School of Music. By chance I got Mr. Reid as my tutor, and this was my greatest stroke of luck. He was something of a genius. Certainly he was the finest teacher in all my experience.

He made no pretensions at being an expert in voice production. Such wizards don't exist.

He was a practical man and a brilliant musician. This is all that any young singer needs—a really good musical coach.

Reid took the attitude that singing is as natural as running or swimming. He realised that I had the voice. It was there to be played on—as real and rare as an exquisite musical instrument.

Certainly, with exercise a tutor can stretch that kind of basically musical voice. But there is no magic about it. The finest teacher in the world can never make an indifferent singer great. No so-called expert in voice production can ever implant the heart or the soul or even the brain that is all part of the business of making great vocal music. No one other than the singer himself can do anything to imbue his voice with that precious, all-important characteristic—quality.

I am aware of vocal quality at the very first note. I can detect it immediately in the records of Caruso and Gigli and Tauber and McCormack.

There are no secrets to great singing. You can or you can't—and no techniques that man can devise will alter that situation.

I discussed this theme with McCormack and Tauber. They both agreed with my thesis.

Listen to the recording of McCormack's " Il mio tesoro " from *Don Giovanni*. His tenor is like a colorotura. For my taste this piece of singing is the pinnacle of anything ever achieved by a human voice. It is quite magnificent. It is like a human clarinet. John really only trained for one year with Sabatini in Milan—dear Vincent O'Brien would be the last to claim he could teach him anything in those early years in Dublin.

The same song by Tauber comes very close to genius also. No tutor could create such voices as those. Such singing is the gift of God and all men can do is dress it up.

That year of my long summer holiday the " talkies " came to Glasgow. At the Coliseum a black-faced coon called Al Jolson launched this exciting new medium by way of a film called " The Singing Fool."

The Coliseum had been a flourishing variety theatre. It was the beginning this early of the slow dry-rot in the historic castle of vaudeville.

I missed " The Singing Fool." My cinema-going was always on Saturday night, and my constant companion was a bricklayer called Joe Monaghan.

We had our own peculiar technique of film selection— we always went to the hall with the smallest queue. It was certainly no way of ensuring that you were in at the beginning of the super, colossal, gigantic epic.

The talkies were six months old before we saw our first —a romance called " Coquette." Its star was Mary Pickford. That was an exciting night—especially at the current admission charge of a shilling a time.

That picture-going friendship with Joe was something that never faded. It lasted in fact all our lives. To me it was a very precious relationship indeed.

Books have always been my great delight. I still read last thing of an evening, and usually into the start of another day.

To university, therefore, I looked forward impatiently. I was going to have my fill of reading. My days were to be jam-packed with study, and I could not imagine a more pleasing prospect.

School was different. School studies were prescribed—a prolonged cram with no object other than your name at the end of it all on a Higher Leaving certificate.

I was the very willing student at Glasgow because I could now read what I chose. University had no one to wield a big stick. It was the student's privilege to probe all the riches of literature, to draw on the wealth of thought and experience from all the great minds of the past.

The student was a free agent. He could choose his subjects, and his success or failure was largely of his own making.

My choice was Italian language and literature, modern European history, logic, geology and constitutional law. I decided to major in English. It could have been an awe-inspiring list. I found it only exciting.

That day of my emergence from the matriculation hall was something to be remembered. We were pounced upon from all directions by young and energetic representatives of the university's various associations.

I was urged by persistent canvassers to join the Labour Party, the Tory Party, the Liberal Party, the Young Christians' Movement, the drama group, the athletic club. There seemed to be a society for everything under the sun.

The one who sought my support for the Labour Party was an earnest young man called Hector McNeill. His Socialist fervour was to be a permanent thing. He became Member of Parliament, Minister of State, member of the Labour Cabinet and British Minister at the United Nations.

I joined the athletic club because I wanted to continue my football. And later I decided to keep in my hand at the fiddle by way of the university orchestra.

My political choice was the Scottish Nationalist Party. There was a powerful mood of nationalism throughout the land and its greatest strength was in the universities. Thus does history repeat itself.

I was active on behalf of the Nationalist group at the rectorial election. Our candidate was Sir Compton Mackenzie.

He was supported by G. K. Chesterton, that gentle pumpkin of a man whose books are still a great delight. But the sinister personality of the whole campaign was a striking figure of a man named Oswald Mosley. He represented his new Fascist Party that was to become famous or notorious as the Black Shirts.

I can think of few more handsome men. Physically he towered. His command of oratory was sometimes spellbinding. And he was rich. He was able to pour into this campaign every single item of organisation that should have led to success.

He had the most thorough party machine—a committee of no fewer than 30 students. He put at their disposal a luxurious Daimler car.

His concern for detail was immaculate. He even had Mosley ties—striped in black and McBrayne red. There were thousands of those ties. They were issued all over the university—not individually, but in boxes. Those ties of Oswald Mosley kept me going in neckwear for years!

On the morning of the rectorial we had the usual traditional " warfare " between the various student factions, when one section attempted to hold the voting hall against the others.

I was never impressed with all this nonsense. We were grown men, supposedly intelligent men, and this playing at warriors with peasemeal and flour, stale fish and rotten eggs, seemed to me pretty puerile.

And it all had absolutely no effect on the eventual result. Compton Mackenzie was duly elected and he turned out to be a first-class rector. He was, in fact, Glasgow's first working rector, who took part in all aspects of university life and was assiduous in his attendance at court and senate.

I suppose in some measure he must have therefore exerted a certain influence on students in general. In my own particular case, Glasgow's choice of rector had momentous repercussions.

I have been blessed in my life with many good friends. It would not be unkind to the others to suggest that Monty Mackenzie had been the greatest of all.

What of Blackshirt Mosley? His total poll was eighteen votes—just over half a vote for every student on his committee!

Whatever my thoughts on his politics, I was sorry for this man. He had most certainly been taken for a ride. His so-called supporters had obviously drawn on his unlimited affluence simply to have a good time.

I saw Mosley later address a rally in St. Andrew's Halls. It was, as usual, a rowdy, sometimes angry gathering. Once again I was impressed with the dignity of the man and his powerful platform manner.

Nor did he lack courage. He was staying at the Central Station Hotel, and after the meeting an ugly mob awaited his emergence from the hall.

He chose to defy them and walk to his hotel. Certainly he had a substantial bodyguard, including Ted Kid Lewis, the champion boxer. But a less fearless man would have got out a back way and reached the hotel by car.

Even in that jam-packed street Mosley stood out among men.

I remember I was twenty minutes early for the start of his rally. The platform was deserted except for a man who sat at a table writing.

He remained seated until the platform party arrived. And when he got up, he stood not much higher than the top of the table.

Most of Mosley's supporters were hefty fellows. I can only assume that the little man had been banned from the official platform parade. It wasn't Fascist policy to show off its dwarfs.

These were days when university professors were giants —super intellectual beings whom you respected and sometimes loved. Glasgow had Stockman and Glaister in medicine, Gregory in geology, McNeill, Dickson, Grillo, Medley —each an international figure in his own particular field.

I was amazed at how things must have changed, when it was announced a few years ago, that a Glasgow professor had given up his chair to become an M.P.

To my generation it didn't make sense. Men like the giants we studied under would never have dreamt of stepping down from their scholastic pinnacles to become part of the sometimes shabby business of politics.

Professor Medley's subject was European history, and this was my very first class. It took place in a lecture hall that looked like an amphitheatre encircled by seats for 500, with a gallery all around.

The place was packed and the noise was deafening. It sounded like a cup-tie in a miniature Hampden. The air was filled with flying paper aeroplanes and other less sophisticated missiles. " Why are we waiting?" was repeatedly sung to the percussion of stamping feet.

I was part of this assembly of youthful, hopeful, impatient energy by courtesy of Andrew Carnegie, the multimillionaire. I was a Carnegie bursar, and my annual award was the princely sum of nine pounds.

I chanced to sit down beside three boys who'd come up from St. Mungo's Academy.

And during the noisy prelude one of them said: " Are you going down later to get the Corporation bursary?"

I had to plead ignorance. I'd never heard of such a subsidy. But my interest was immediate. My enthusiasm for study was so irresistible that I hadn't gone deeply into the practicability of living on nine pounds a year.

That afternoon I went with the trio from St. Mungo's to the Corporation's examining panel in an office at 129 Bath Street. And it turned out to be another of those days when the angels were looking kindly upon MacEwan.

The chairman of the panel was Dr. Duncan McGillivray, my old rector at Hillhead High. Better still—he remembered me well.

His eyebrows went up with pleasant recognition as soon as I entered the room.

" Ah, Sydney," he said. " Good—very good. This is splendid—you must have worked hard. Very good."

He went into a huddle of whispers with the others on the panel. But their discussion wasn't prolonged.

Obviously on the strength of my old rector's enthusiastic recognition, I was told almost immediately: " We will put you down for thirty pounds a year."

I didn't walk out. I floated on wings of elation. My journey home had never seemed longer. I wanted too much to arrive.

My mother and I did a dance round the kitchen. We were like children at Christmas—and all for a matter of thirty pounds.

On the afternoons that we didn't have classes I studied from two to five. Every night I was at my books again—from seven o'clock to ten. There was never any drudgery. Every hour was a joy. And I tried to give myself Saturdays off—and keep my Sundays free as well.

My especial love was Italian and the literature and art of Italy. Italian for me is the most beautiful language in the world.

Our professor of Italian was Ernesto Grillo. Of all the professorial supermen, he was the most colourful. He loved his subject dearly and wanted so much to share it with others, that his every lecture was a vital, almost frenzied, experience. The sweat ran down his face and dripped off his chin. He made lecturing as physically exhausting as heavyweight boxing.

He called us all his sonnies and daughters. One of his great joys was to show us the artistic splendours of Italy by way of lantern slides.

Always, of course, when the lights went out, the hall was filled with mock squeals of distress from the girls.

And eventually when the sessions in the dark came to their end, he would hold up a hand and say: " Ah, ha, now my sonnies and daughters—be good now, be good!"

One afternoon even the volatile, loquacious Grillo was momentarily struck dumb. He was lecturing away with his usual verve, when suddenly the door burst open and in bounded just about the biggest dog I've ever seen.

This was Grillo's pet, Caesar, and he made for his master in a series of excited bounds that came near to knocking the professor on his back.

" Down, Caesar! Down, Caesar!" he shouted. But his commands were as whispers against the background of student cheers and catcalls (if that's the appropriate word).

Some engineering students had called at his house and informed the housekeeper that it was the professor's wish that they should take the dog for a walk in Kelvingrove Park. Then they brought it instead to the lecture hall, pushed open the door and made off like the wind.

He took it all in good part!

Even with that thirty pounds a year, I rationed myself to a shilling a day—three-ha'pence each way on the tram and ninepence left over for food.

I couldn't yet afford the guinea fee to join the Students' Union. I was therefore cut off from the meals provided in the Union.

My eating in the main was done at Mrs. Barclay's café. Her pie and chips cost 6d. She was generous with the chips and the pies were home-made and luscious.

Later in my studies my fortunes improved and I managed to find the Union levy. This gave me access to a bowl of Union soup for threepence. Another threepence bought a portion of substantial pudding, such as apple pie. The bread was free. I ate as much bread as I could lay my hands on, and was replete for the rest of the day.

Nevertheless, I missed Mrs. Barclay's. It was a great place to meet the girls. I am a celibate priest, but don't get the idea that at the age of eighteen I was lacking in the normal, healthy impulses of that zestful age. I liked to be with the lasses. One in particular I took out sometimes. But it was never a relationship that developed into anything serious.

Very few students of my period ever, as they say, went steady. Those who did were called mugs. It was no era for getting involved. We had no money for other than the absolute essentials. Our prospects of money were in the main, remote. Those of us intent on a career in teaching might have to wait at least two years for a post after qualifying.

We were most of us aware that our likely future was graduation to unemployment. It was no environment to encourage serious involvement in affairs of the heart.

Yet we never marched in protest. We never lay down on railway lines or squatted in public places. The thought never even entered our heads—a happier crowd I never met.

While I was at university, the German war film, " All Quiet on the Western Front " came to the Glasgow Regal. And during the Students' Charities Week the cinema management had the bright idea of making a mock-up of a German tank and kitting out ten of us students as German soldiers.

We got the uniforms, belts, helmets, boots, etc. Our weapons were collecting cans.

After driving in the Charities procession, our squad of ten " Jerries " set out to rattle our cans under the noses of South Side Glaswegians.

We weren't long in coming back! We had to beat a hasty retreat. The fact that the war was all of ten years ended made no difference.

Despite their penury, the good folk of the Gorbals were still entirely pro-British. They knew we were only dressed-up students, but even make-believe Huns roused their ire. So much so that we had to run for the shelter of our "tank" —booed all the way and pelted with stones and bottles!

It was far from quiet that day on the Glasgow front!

One aspect of my college life turned out to be an utter flop. I turned out for the soccer club's trial game and was placed at right-wing for the second eleven. I discovered I had an inside man who was not far off professional standard. We had a first half in which we could do no wrong. Our direct opposition was one of the club's established stalwarts. That memorable first half was for him almost entirely three-quarters of an hour of humiliation.

So much so, he didn't turn out for a double dose in the second half. A substitute was fielded instead.

I continued with my brilliant inside-right in the second eleven for the next five weeks. Then we realised there was never any chance of promotion.

I decided to go back to junior football and signed for Carntyne Juniors. Sometimes I got ten bob a game. Sometimes all the club funds could run to was a cup of tea and a pie. But I enjoyed my time with Carntyne.

Despite my zest for study, I managed to sing at the smoking concerts that were a regular feature of university life. My fame as a singer spread quickly through the establishment.

Mind you, these concerts were attended by only a minority. They were part of what was called the corporate life of the university—the extraneous social activities that appealed to no more than perhaps a third of the students.

To the other two-thirds my voice would be unknown— until that very first Daft Friday.

It was an appropriate title for the day of the break for the Christmas vacation—by tradition the time of mid-winter madness, the day for all of us to let off steam after the long days of playing hard and studying like mad.

Lectures were the occasion for even more ribaldry than ever. Professors could expect buckets of water to fall on their heads when they opened doors. The mood for practical jokery reached its peak.

Come mid-day, it was as if all the high spirits came together in a mass concentration on the Men's Union. Everyone wanted to be in on the Daft Friday concert. There were probably more than a thousand aspirants for the hall's five hundred seats. They would have hung from the ceiling if the rafters had not been so high. The place was like a human sardine tin.

And I was going to sing.

How the sale of toilet rolls in Glasgow must have soared the day before! The hall was a crazy firing-range for this kind of improvised missile. And the most popular target was the stage piano.

Its lid was open, and some of the students were very excellent shots. Every time one of the bombs made contact with the piano, there was a great roar of approval. And the ones that succeeded in landing inside got the biggest cheers of all.

Poor Kenny Macpherson—one of my dearest university friends—had agreed to play my accompaniment. But first of all he had to clear his piano of all the rolls of paper. And before he managed to get the lid shut, he himself was the object of a number of direct hits.

He did it with good humour—Daft Friday was living up to its name. And he started to play my introduction—the delicate, bird-impersonating lead-in to " Bird Songs at Eventide." Suddenly the hall was filled with whistles and a varied and raucous assortment of bird noises. Students called out, " Cock-a-doodle-do!" And those with space flapped their elbows in imitation of hens.

Against this madhouse background, I started to sing. And gradually the racket faded. The toilet rolls ceased their flight as if by magic. By the time I was halfway through my song, the Union hall was as quiet as a cathedral.

And such applause followed. My second song was "La donna è mobile," and this time the hush was complete.

Not until the final note did the din resume again, and it was one of concentrated approval. They cheered and stamped their feet in unison and bellowed out "Encore!"

I walked off the stage. I left it at that.

But Daft Friday had upon me a permanent effect. To silence that undisciplined mob was the act of a Canute halting the tide. I hope this doesn't sound conceited. But that day I realised that this voice of mine had some strange power over those who heard it.

When it came to the time of Charities Week I was one of the group involved in a raid on the B.B.C. It was all a stunt, of course. They had warning of our coming. But the publicity helped the campaign.

Not that the Scottish B.B.C. of that period was anything approaching a giant broadcasting fortress. It had modest premises in Blythswood Square and a mere handful of regular staff.

Our raid was such a gentlemanly affair that it developed into something of an improvised concert. We students formed ourselves into a choir and gave an agreeable rendition of "Deep River." I was persuaded to sing a solo.

A tall, handsome man came over at its end. "That was very pleasant," he said. "I wonder if you'd like to do some work for the B.B.C.?"

He was Andrew Stewart, at that time the Glasgow station's general factotum and later to become Comptroller for Scotland.

His words were music to my ears. The chance to broadcast! More important to a hard-up student—the chance to earn some pocket-money, however humble the fees might be by present-day standards.

I became a regular at Blythswood Square. I met up with Kathleen Garscadden, that charming broadcasting pioneer that the children of Scotland came to know as Auntie Cyclone!

I even helped out with sound effects for some of the early plays. The boy in this department was called Peter Thomson. He was destined for fame as well—as head of the sports department of B.B.C. Scotland.

How wonderful to be broadcasting in the early days of B.B.C. I was very much in at ground-floor level. And this before I'd even started in earnest on the training of my voice.

With my B.B.C. money I was able to join the Students' Union. This was a notable boon. You were in on what was really the social side of university, but the educational significance was also great.

I enjoyed the Union discussions with people from all walks of life. I enjoyed the exchange of ideas. I enjoyed in particular the recurring arguments about religion and religions.

There was never any suggestion of bigotry. What was remarkable was the lack of Roman Catholics. Catholic students seemed almost to boycott the Union.

There were one or two notable exceptions, such as Dr. Hugh Ryan, who remained my lifelong friend; John Bayne, who became a Sheriff; John Wheatley, now Lord Wheatley, Lord Justice Clerk; and Arthur Montague, who eventually received an important appointment with the United Nations.

But the average Catholic student seemed to choose to remain in something of a Catholic ghetto. I understand that today this attitude is changed.

One of the sources of inspiration in my university life was Professor McNeill Dixon. He taught English language and literature, and in the early 'thirties he delivered a series of Gifford lectures on " The Human Situation," a brilliant enquiry into the great mystery of life.

The lectures were assembled in book form, and what splendid reading they make. Every time I read McNeill Dixon, I can almost hear that wonderful, mellow, musical Dublin voice of his.

He used to give poetry readings, and always the lecture hall was packed. Even students from faculties that were not concerned with his main subjects—medical and engineering students, for instance—used to join the queue to get in.

McNeill Dixon ostensibly taught me English. But from him, incidentally, I also acquired an appreciation of the beauty of the spoken word. He had the gift for making music out of words. I was later to study diction as part of my voice-training process. But if I have any flair for speech at all, it came originally from contact with this literary giant.

Because I worked hard and willingly, I went through college with a carefree mind—except in the case of geology. At things scientific I am hopeless. For geology I bought all the text-books, and to start with I was stricken with something approaching terror.

I boggled at what was required to be assimilated. With my kind of non-scientific mind, it all seemed initially out of my reach—and yet I had to take one science subject.

I was not an outstanding intellectual. My brain was average. But I did have this capacity for slog. I worked like a beaver at this frightening subject of geology and eventually I made it. I understand in fact that my geology pass was far removed from border-line standard.

The finale to the study years was for me an anti-climax.

I was indifferent to the final results. I knew that I'd made it—only because I'd put into it every ounce of my energies.

I was out playing cricket at Westerlands when a fellow student came up excitedly: "You've passed," he said. "Your name's on the board."

I felt nothing. I said: "That's good," but the news aroused no more emotion than if he had made some comment on the weather.

None of my relations attended my graduation. I didn't even bother to tell them about it. My mother, of course, suggested that she would be there, but I told her it would be a waste of time.

I wished I could have felt the excitement that I had envisaged as the climax to these most satisfying years of my life. But it just never happened.

The Bute Hall was packed for what should have been a triumphant occasion. A great choir of massed voices sang the inevitable " Gaudeamus igitur juvenes dum sumus." And I almost regretted my knowledge of Latin.

" Let us therefore rejoice while we are young " was what we sang. I never felt less like rejoicing. This for me was an occasion of death—the end of the comprehending days, the days of contact with greatness, the days of fun and companionship, of well-being born out of effort. I felt it was the finale to my youth. And all my life I have never been able to throw off my nostalgia for the young and ripening years. The daft days were the wonderful days.

Duncan Morrison.

Robert Wilson.

Archbishop
Fulton Sheen.

Bronze of
Archbishop Mannix.

CHAPTER

10

My M.A. degree seemed now so insignificant. We knew
we had no hope of getting a job for years. I had my eye
on another career. Could I earn my living singing?

I still decided, however, to do my year's teacher's training at Jordanhill College. It was tough to get in. Unlike
more recent times, there were far, far more potential
teachers than jobs.

Glasgow had not added to its paltry total of two Catholic
secondary schools. Most of us graduates were reconciled to
teaching at primary level—if we were lucky!

So Jordanhill could afford to be choosey. Its acceptance
of a graduate was based on the quality of his degree. It was
also important that a good impression be created at the
personal interview.

By the time I saw Mr. Burnett, the Principal, I was quite
a regular broadcaster. One of my particular friends was
Kathleen Garscadden. By way of her Children's Hour
broadcasts she was known throughout Scotland as Auntie
Cyclone. Andrew Stewart to the children was Long Fellow.
I sang for them often.

I told Mr. Burnett about my hobby, and he obviously
was impressed. He knew my voice well. I have the feeling
that I was the only intake to Jordanhill who was selected
on the strength of Children's Hour!

For part of my college vacation I decided to visit my
aunt in London. I mentioned my journey to Andrew
Stewart and he reacted immediately: " I'll send down a

E

note to London and you'll probably get a broadcast from there."

Sure enough, I did. The fee helped to pay for my London holiday. As it turned out, the journey was free in the sense that it didn't cost me a penny. But free of incident?—ah, that's a different story!

The chaplain to Glasgow University was William Eric Brown. I feel I am at risk of running out of superlatives, but I have no description of Willie Brown other than that he was a darling man.

He had been a soldier in World War I. He suffered gassing and got the Military Cross. He was a double honours graduate of Oxford and gained his rowing blue.

His first appointment in Glasgow was lecturer in history. He was converted to Roman Catholicism and decided to study for the priesthood.

Immediately after completing his studies at Scots College, Rome, he returned to his old university—as its first Catholic chaplain.

Sadly, even the greatest of men have their little weaknesses. In Willie's case it was a passion for motor cars. It was a particularly unfortunate enthusiasm, because Willie was the type of man who would never drive efficiently. It just wasn't his kind of skill.

He decided to visit his brother at Boarshill, Oxford—the one who wrote that outstanding defence of religion and Catholicism, *Tadpoles and God*.

And for the journey he bought a bull-nosed Morris tourer—price, twenty-five pounds!

He could drive it forward. But reversing was something he could never achieve. And this was the man who asked me if I would like to drive with him to London!

We picked up the buggy from a garage at Riddrie. The proprietor—whose name was McEwan—suggested it went like a bird.

Never have I known a four-wheeled vehicle with such an insatiable thirst. It had a simple but effective way of proclaiming its need. It started to steam like a railway engine.

It turned out that I was working my passage. My role was to jump out every few miles to recharge its glass bottle from the nearest house.

Sometimes the nearest house was over two fields and up the side of a mountain. En route we bought an enamel jug in an attempt to cut down on the number of my water-carrying safaris.

Thereafter the jalopy became quite neurotic. It was obviously a Scottish Nationalist car and started to have persistent nervous breakdowns as soon as we trundled onto English soil.

I told my aunt I'd be down in two days. I went through a fortune in postcards—making daily predictions of a later time of arrival.

The two-day journey in fact took eight.

On present-day roads Willie would inevitably have had an accident. But the motor car was still something of a novelty. The roads were so quiet that somehow Willie was allowed to steer his erratic course without impediment.

The hood blew off the tourer while crossing Doncaster Bridge. Auntie got another postcard announcing a 24-hour delay while hood and car were reunited.

At last we drove into Oxfordshire and approached the town of Bicester. Its significance on the map was an R.A.F. station nearby.

The bull-nose decided to have a really acute heart attack on a very hot day in a country lane. Beneath that sun it was our turn to be assailed by harrowing thirst.

The papers were head-lining the story of a couple of raiders in open-necked shirts who'd got away in a stolen, bull-nosed Morris after robbing a bank.

Dr. Willie suggested that I should do something about our personal thirst by calling on an Oxford farmhouse.

The woman at the door was obviously suspicious. I was wearing an open-necked shirt! She hurried inside to consult her husband, and I heard the door being bolted. They came back together, and the husband was carrying what looked like an iron rod.

I pointed to the car down on the road and explained our predicament. The reaction of farmer and farm-wife continued to be non-committal and wary.

He stood on guard at the door while she again disappeared inside. Imagine my surprise when she came back again, not only with a great jug of cool, fresh milk, but a package of sandwiches also!

I never found out whether my innocence showed through or the couple at the farmhouse decided that the best way to deal with brigands was to feed the brutes.

Recharged by the food and drink, we decided to stay put. The road was so quiet that we'd settled for spending the night there, when along came a motor-bike with two R.A.F. men on board.

They turned out to be mechanics. " We'll be all right this time," said Dr. Willie. " We've got two experts on the job."

In next to no time the bull-nose had parted with a lot of its engine. The " experts " had half of the engine laid out on the roadway in a lot of separate bits and pieces that to my non-mechanical eye looked frighteningly incapable of ever being put together again.

One of the R.A.F. men said that they'd have to go to their station for a spare part: " We'll be about half an hour," he announced jauntily.

They chugged down the road on the motor-bike, and neither Willie nor I ever saw them again!

Now I really had the wind up about that collection of lifeless, oily spare parts on the roadway!

But, remarkably, another car appeared and the driver offered to take us to Bicester. There the local garageman agreed to go out and rescue the engineless Morris.

Willie Brown was blessed with a great sense of humour. He was obviously enjoying the adventure like a schoolboy. But I was worried about my aunt in London.

" Dr. Brown," I said, " I think I'll better go off by train to-morrow. My aunt will be wondering what's happening."

" True enough, true enough," he said. " I'm sorry the trip's been a bit disappointing."

I was sitting at the railway station awaiting the London train when I heard the unmistakable sound of the Morris engine.

Willie Brown came hurrying through the entrance. " It's all right, Sydney," he said, " she's going like that bird the man said. Come on!"

I traded in my ticket at the booking office and off we went to London. Old bull-nose had made it.

I was not impressed with Jordanhill. After the grown-up freedom of university, it all seemed so petty. We were like wee boys going back to school. Each teacher kept a register and you were marked absent or present. There was this feeling of being watched all the time, of being supervised.

Some of my fellow-students hated every minute of their teacher's training. I didn't find it all that irksome, despite the return to schoolroom discipline.

I discovered I hit it off with most of the lecturers. And I was soon aware that even in the oppressive atmosphere of Jordanhill the luck of MacEwan was not to desert me.

Only on one occasion did it seem that my good fairy wasn't around any more.

I now had my eye on the Royal Academy of Music. For my special teacher's training subject I therefore chose music. I was what was known as an Article 37B student, and this gave me access to two notable teachers.

One was George Scott, whose speciality was the organising and training of choirs. He always referred to us as the world's greatest male voice choir. You will gather he had a sense of humour. He wrote some lovely songs.

The other was Robert McColl, head of the department; with him I got on famously. He used to organise lots of concerts in Church of Scotland halls all over the city. And as soon as he discovered that I could sing, he asked me to join him on these outings as his soloist.

He looked upon me as his star pupil. Imagine, therefore, my amazement when the music marks were given out at the end of the year. For there it was in black and white—" Sydney MacEwan: Music—Singing—Fair!"

One other student was equally surprised when the music results appeared. He had always found the subject a bore. And of his singing powers he had no illusions. He may not have been tone-deaf, but he couldn't sing a note.

And there, against his name, was the one word, " Excellent." You couldn't go higher than that.

The clue to the solving of the strange affair of the music exam results was the other student's name. He was also a McEwan. His first name was Ernie. And obviously the marking had got mixed up.

I have met up with Ernie McEwan a number of times since and always we have a great laugh about the time that the singing of Sydney MacEwan was classed as " Fair."

The Jordanhill routine was: three weeks in college and three weeks out teaching. I was given a primary school in Scotstoun, and I found it very pleasant.

But one day the master of methods asked: " There's a vacancy at Hillhead High—any volunteers?"

My hand shot up like a streak of lightning. I hadn't been so long away. A lot of the staff would know me still. I felt I'd be meeting up again with old friends.

As luck would have it, I was allocated to Mr. Fletcher's class. He used to be our cricket coach. It wasn't so long since I'd been in his team.

And if I was looking for practical experience in teaching, I couldn't have landed with a better man. Fletcher was much more enamoured of the cricket field than the classroom.

I'd only been there a day or two when he asked me to take charge. And thereafter, at every opportunity, he got me to take over the class while he vanished into the staff-room to catch up on the cricket news or smoke a quiet cigarette.

As a student-teacher I was an obvious target for the sometimes imaginative and inventive mischief-making of those young Hillhead rascals.

When a fire-engine passed in the street outside, they all jumped up from their desks and rushed to the window—something I knew they wouldn't have dared had their normal teacher been around. They were trying me out.

A strange noise emerged from one side of the class—almost as if someone were in pain. I walked slowly in the direction of the disturbance, and next time it came from the other side of the room.

I put on my best schoolmaster's voice: " Who's making that noise?"

Back came the reply: " Please, sir, it's the pigeons!"

I knew a human pigeon when I heard one! I asked again for the culprits to stand up.

There was no response. So I went into action. I was aware that the belt was barred to students and must be administered only by a qualified teacher. But I was also impressed with the golden rule preached at Jordanhill—assert your authority right at the beginning—later is too late. Put on the tough-guy act at the start—even if by nature you are not attracted to big-stick methods.

I pulled the nearest boy on to his feet and dealt him out four of the best. He sat down protesting: " It wasn't me." I grabbed another boy close to him and gave him the same.

There were no repercussions about my using the strap. Thereafter we got on famously. I never had to bring the belt out again. And at Christmas, they gave me a present of a hundred cigarettes.

I think I would have enjoyed being a teacher.

The dread among students at Jordanhill was the random inspection by one of the masters of method. He was liable to turn up at any time during your period of practical teaching outside.

We all hoped it would be Ferguson, a firm, but pleasant and sympathetic man. The one who was feared was McLean. He was ex-army and still retained his temporary title of major. He was somewhat fiery and pompous.

My heart dropped when he walked in the classroom door to put me through my paces.

He knew I was specialising in music and talked about my singing. He mentioned my appearances on radio and suggested in his brusque and barrack-square manner that it must be rather interesting work.

" Would you like to come up sometime and see how a broadcast is made?" I asked.

He jumped at the chance. I suggested Children's Hour. These Children's Hour sessions were real family affairs, and I knew there would be no objections. I introduced him all round and he was obviously thrilled at meeting the personalities whose names were already household words.

If you wanted a school in Glasgow, you had to get a V.G. mark for teaching. Glasgow Corporation paid higher rates of salary and could therefore skim off the cream of the graduates.

I got my teaching V.G. from Major McLean, but whether it was strictly on merit I've never been sure. Let's say that my invitation to visit the B.B.C. didn't do my prospects any harm!

Not that it mattered. I was a teacher. My name was on the coveted Glasgow Corporation list. By way of evening classes I'd acquired my religious certificate without which the Archbishop could ban anyone from teaching in a Catholic school.

I had all the documents, but I couldn't teach. For the simple reason that there weren't any jobs.

I learned that the waiting period was no longer two years, but three. And no Social Security or dole. That was the prospect for all those graduates with all their impressive bits of paper and all the burning of midnight oil and sweating it out for examinations.

How strange and improbable that world seems now as you look back down through the years!

This was one reason why my mind was made up to try my luck at the Royal Academy. As I told my mother, I had nothing to lose. The alternative was unemployment with its frustration and boredom and the very real risk of the corrosion of one's self-respect.

It's an interesting conjecture that in less stringent times I might have done nothing about my singing. Had the job been there, I might have been tempted to go straight into teaching and earn some money.

I had saved up a bit from my B.B.C. work. Not that it paid all that handsomely then. But, as well as regular Children's Hours, I was getting the occasional evening broadcast. And I still went out to concerts as well.

I had enough put by for my first term's fees. I felt—like Micawber—that something would turn up, that once I was in, my good fairy would again take over and cope with the financing of the rest of my training. I had sufficient confidence in myself to believe that after that initial term, I would qualify for some kind of scholarship.

The Academy year didn't start till October, and in those waiting months of summer it was certainly brought home to me how demoralising such joblessness can be.

Oh, I got work all right—as a mobile salesman for brushes. Was there ever such a heart-breaking business as trying to sell something that nobody seems to want! I have since had a constant admiration for brush salesmen. With what powers of endurance they must be blessed. What courage and determination must be built into their characters. Were I a Captain Scott intent on probing the unknown depths of the Antarctic, I think I would have picked my exploration team from brush salesmen with more than two weeks' service.

That was the extent of my selling career—two weeks! Clean enough the job may have been. But easy! Never, never easy. No sales.

I tried to get on to the River Clyde steamers, but the companies had some sort of summer-time scheme of employing only the sons of the widows of former employees.

I thought I'd do all right at serving meals on the London train. But long lines of skilled waiters were queuing up for such employment.

I even tried for labouring work, but always it was hopeless. There were thousands of men with families and skills who found all the doors closed also. What hope for an unattached student!

CHAPTER

11

The mother of one of the Jesuit Brothers at St. Aloysius'
kept a modest boarding-house in Warwick Street, Victoria,
London. When I went down to the Academy I got fixed up
with her.

My first step was the personal interview with the
Academy's Principal. The luck of MacEwan decided that
he should turn out to be a Scot. Even better than that, a
Scot named McEwan.

Sir John McEwan was a minor composer. Strange how
Scotland has never thrown up anyone of major significance
in this line.

I was led to believe that the Academy was extremely
selective—that if it felt your basic talent was insufficient,
you were advised to go home right at the start.

Later, I was to learn that the system was far from fool-
proof.

Sir John asked me to sing, and I gave him " Bird Songs
at Eventide." I can't claim to have bowled him over completely. If he felt he was in the presence of a prodigy, it
certainly didn't show.

" A nice song that," he said. " It's by one of our old
students, Eric Coates."

My second test piece was in Italian. But no warming-up
of Sir John's enthusiasm : " Very nice," he said in a matter-
of-fact sort of way. " I think we will send you to Meux."

I was attracted to Meux. Typical of the tenor, he was
smallish, stoutish, solidly-built. A neat dresser, with a

change of button-hole every day. A pleasant, friendly, good-natured man. One-time star of Covent Garden.

It was suggested I should go down to the Duke's Hall, the adjoining building where some of the instrumental tuition took place.

As soon as I walked in, I recognised the figure standing in front of an orchestra. It was Henry Wood.

Those young players of instruments who got as far as the Royal Academy were usually intent on becoming solo performers. But it's a long, exhausting, challenging climb and there's not much room at the top.

Eventually most of the young hopefuls have to settle for playing in an orchestra. So every Friday from two to five they got this orchestral training from the great man himself.

I stood entranced. I was going to like the Academy.

Thereafter, my every Friday afternoon was spent at Duke's Hall watching Sir Henry in action. And also assimilating a very wide range of orchestral music.

The classes proper didn't start for a week. It was one of the most miserable weeks of my life. I knew no one yet. And London can be a lonely place.

That week-end I found myself in Marylebone Public Library, and what caught my eye was a section dealing with the Irish troubles of 1916 and 1921. It pressed a little switch in my memory and I was a kid again in Springburn, and the word on all the adults' lips was I.R.A. And at the close-end the talk was of the police-van that was shot up in the High Street on its way from Duke Street to Barlinnie with some Irish rebels.

For years afterwards I saw the bullet-holes on the walls. In Marylebone I read every word there was to read on those bloody days in Ireland.

It was my way of filling in the time. I became engrossed with such characters as De Valera, Frank Aitken and Tom Barrie. Little did I realise that one day I would know all three of them intimately.

On that first Monday at the Academy I was assigned to my various classes. The opera class was the most exciting. I was immediately affected by the conductor of the opera class. He was small, dark and handsome. The good-looking, little human dynamo was John Barbirolli.

You could tell the few who had money by the way they were able to dress. And they were obvious because they were the exception. Most of us were hard-up. Most of us were scraping the barrel and hoping to get by on a shoe-string budget.

Such a band of young hopefuls! All with their eye on the pot of gold at the end of the rainbow.

It was something of a dream world really. In my time in singing, there would be more than 100 students. And at the end of the day the rainbow vanished. I can think of only two for whom the dream became a reality in that eventually they achieved a certain amount of national fame.

One singer, and one only, was to make the grade internationally—the penurious young lad from Springburn.

A great number of my companions were Jewish. I took violin as my second subject, and the preponderance of Jews in the instrumental classes was even more apparent.

Later in the concert world I was to discover how dominant was the Jew. About six out of ten of the great instrumentalists were inevitably of Jewish stock. I am constantly aware of the brilliance of this race—and many are my Jewish friends.

The bohemian atmosphere of the Academy was pleasant. The musical quote about there being no people like show people may be a bit trite, but it has some truth in it. Artistes are usually a warm-hearted, generous, affectionate lot. There were no cold fish at the Academy. Cold fish will never succeed in music. Cold fish usually go for security, and there has never been any security in the entertainment world.

On that very first day I met Russell and immediately we became friends. In a way it was to be a tragic friendship.

He had been a commercial traveller in the Manchester area. On his travels he'd sung in a chain of wine lodges around this part of England. And with the best will in the world all his friends had kept telling him: " That's a great voice you've got—why don't you go professional?"

What harm they were innocently guilty of!

From his commission and his part-time entertaining Russell saved up enough to make the Academy. In my opinion, the incredible and really heartless aspect of Russell's career was that he should have been allowed to start.

He had Maurice Doysley as tutor, and I remember the first time I heard him sing. Oh, the volume was there all right—you could have heard him in Sauchiehall Street!

But I knew — and all the so-called experts at the Academy must have known—that Russell was wasting his time and money. He would obviously never make it. The tragic thing was that by now he firmly believed that he would. I, his best friend, just hadn't the heart to shock him with the truth.

He spent a small fortune on consulting throat specialists. He heard me sing and gave the credit for my performance to my tutor. So he agitated to be switched from Doysley's class to that of Meux. But as I have already said, there is no tutor in the whole wide world who can create a voice unless the voice is there by the grace of God or the work of nature, whichever you prefer.

At first I was thought to be a baritone. Compton Mackenzie suggested it was a baritone voice. He was then editor of *The Gramophone*. He knew what he was talking about.

But when Sir John McEwan decided that I was really a tenor, Meux agreed. And it was he who had the task of stretching the voice, of giving it greater range.

This turned out to be a purely physical process—a prolonged, tedious, exhausting series of exercises. The weightlifter or the heavyweight boxer can break no more sweat than a tenor in training.

I was 22. I was fully matured and therefore able to cope. But to have attempted this process at the age of 17 or 18 would have been impossible. And the most likely result at the end of the day would have been the permanent damage of the vocal chords.

From those sessions with Meux I used to emerge as limp as a piece of chewed string.

To eke out my very limited means I moved in with Russell to his lodgings in St. John's Wood, and we shared the cost of a pound a week.

We were so poor that one Thursday we just could not afford to eat. I had a penny. Russell was skint. It was a warm summer's day, and we lay in Regent's Park to conserve the human engines for which there was no fuel.

At mid-day I blew my last penny on a stick of barley sugar which we halved and sucked very slowly. It helped to see us through the hot afternoon.

On our way home we approached the little Italian restaurant where we used to buy our fish and chips. The smell of its fare was just too much.

" Come on," I said to Russell, " I give in. I could never last out till morning. We'll see if Toni will help us out."

He was a charming Italian, as most Italians are.

" Do you think we might have two fish suppers and we'll pay you on Saturday," I said. " We've had nothing all day."

He knew us as Royal Academy boys. And he beamed as if I'd offered him a gift instead of asking a favour.

" Twoa fish supper," he repeated. " Sure, yes—maybe one day you singa in Covent Garden and you give me the seats in the front row. Sure—eh—come—come—sita-down!"

The suppers steamed and smelt like heaven. He gave us coffee also.

"I have the idea," he said. "Sometimes you see, very busy—Friday, Saturday, maybe Sunday. Nine o'clock—very busy. You two boys now, maybe you come in, eh—wash a few dishes—eh—you help me—eh—I give you half-crown."

"You bet," I said.

"When do we start?" said Russell.

We were Toni's dishwashers two nights a week. That paid the rent. We cooked for ourselves. We were back on the ham and eggs again!

Meux was obviously pleased with my progress. In my very first term he cast me as "Metastasio" in the Academy production of *The Magic Flute*.

Neither Sir John nor Meux dished out compliments generously, but I knew they were pleased.

My next distinction turned out to be an embarrassment. Meux picked me to sing solo at one of the concerts in the Duke's Hall.

I had no inhibitions about my voice. What worried me was my trousers.

My entire wardrobe consisted of a university blazer and flannels. I decided that for the concert platform I couldn't go on looking like a tennis player. I must somehow acquire a dark suit.

My brainwave was to dye my flannels black!

I consulted Sheila Morant on this aspect of domestic science. She was the sister of Philip, the successful London actor.

She issued a womanly word of warning: "Don't do it!"

The concert was only a day away, and my situation was somewhat desperate. I decided to ignore her advice and immersed my sole pair of pants in a Fairy Dye, all per the instructions on the box. I spent the day in bed.

One thing I hadn't realised was that dye is a long time a-drying. The trousers were still damp on the Saturday morning. And a glance was enough to indicate that whether they dried in time or not was now immaterial.

The trousers were ruined. They looked for all the world like a cross between varicose veins and a map of the Nile delta.

I explained my predicament to the landlady and she laughed when I showed her the evidence.

I was able to turn on something of a smile myself when she said: " I think I can lend you a suit. You're just about my husband's size."

With a bit of hoisting at the waist, it fitted reasonably well. I went through that concert with the trousers hoisted so high, that I thought I might finish up cut in half.

On the Monday I mentioned the borrowed suit to Meux. He laughed as well, and I learned that he, too, had known less affluent times when trousers were a luxury.

He'd got a booking to appear at a posh hotel and for want of a pair of suitable breeks, he had to stand behind the exotic plants on the stage and sing through the foliage!

" By the way, Sydney," he said, " what exactly are your circumstances?"

I told him I was going it alone. I explained that I'd saved up just enough for the first term, but the financial future thereafter was vague.

He took it all in, but his only reaction was an indifferent nod and something that sounded like: " Mmm—I see."

A week later I was called into the office of Sir John.

I can only assume that he was made aware of my somewhat straitened circumstances. But all he said was: " Mr. MacEwan, they're wanting a tenor for St. Margaret's, Westminster, and if you go down and sing for Herbert Dawson, there's a chance—just a chance—that you might get the job."

I tried to disguise my excitement. Herbert Dawson I already knew as one of the greats among organists. And St. Margaret's—the church of the Houses of Parliament—and location of the wedding ceremonies of the fashionable and rich.

If I made it, I was to get a regular fee as a member of the choir. Better still—every wedding appearance would be classed as an extra.

Before I sang for Dawson, I thought it better to mention the religious aspect. I pointed out that I was not of the Anglican Church.

" Your religion is no concern of mine," he said, " all we have to know is, can you sing?"

One item was sufficient: " Yes, young man, you've got it," Dawson said. " I suggest you join us right away."

I was over the moon. Not only was this the answer to all my money problems. The job in itself was exciting. Dawson showed me over St. Margaret's—a lovely place.

I discovered that the liturgy of the Anglican Church is matchless. And after three weeks, Dawson took me aside and said: " I feel I should tell you, Mr. MacEwan, that in a few months' time I shall be putting you forward as a Gentleman of the Chapel Royal."

I could scarcely believe my luck. The Chapel Royal! Sydney MacEwan from Springburn as one of the select group of singers in such royal places as Windsor Castle and St. James's Palace!

Although I was taking part in these Anglican services, there was no question of a change in my own conviction. I was still a Roman Catholic. This was as much a part of me as the colour of my eyes.

And according to the Roman Catechism used in those days, one of the ways in which we Catholics exposed ourselves to the dangers of losing our faith was in taking part in the service or prayers of a " false religion."

I shall never forget that day I went to confession. I explained about my appointment with St. Margaret's and the priest's reaction was immediate: " You must give this up at once."

I walked out dazed. I just could not believe it. In a sort of mental earthquake, my happy, new, exciting world was collapsing beneath my feet.

By the time I got home to my digs, I felt that I had found the answer. The depression had been replaced by what was almost a fresh elation.

I had worked it out that if my tenor was good enough for the Anglicans of St. Margaret's—if I was good enough for the very Royal Household, why should I not offer my services to the Roman Catholic Westminster Cathedral?

I wrote off to the priest-in-charge. I had a rare feeling of inspiration as I posted that letter.

But as the days passed, the depression set in again. There was no reply. Every day I asked hopefully about the mail, but gradually the hope faded.

To this day I have never had a reply. Try as I would, I could not rid myself of a great feeling of bitterness.

All my dreams in tatters and my religious being had taken a bit of a knock as well.

CHAPTER

12

This time the luck of the MacEwans came in the shape of a letter.

As a Scottish Nationalist at Glasgow University, I was on the committee that helped to have Compton Mackenzie elected as Rector.

In the subsequent Charities Week show called " College Pudding," I was one of the singers. We met afterwards and he pulled my sleeve: " You should do something about that voice of yours," he said. " Let me know and I'll get you an introduction to Oscar Preus."

" Oscar Preus?"

" He's the recording manager with Parlophone," he said.

Well, this was Compton being as good as his word—with that letter that raised me right out of the depths—" I want you to go along to Oscar—I've told him you're coming and all about you . . ."

I was still very much the raw student. I have never been cursed with bashfulness, but for a youngster to enter for the first time that Number 1 Studio in St. John's Wood was more than a little unnerving.

Oscar came to meet me, hand outstretched, smoking his famous pipe. I could have been Caruso or Gigli or John McCormack himself. He treated me like a lord.

He was British, of German extraction. He heard me sing and immediately said: " Yes, you will make records for us."

The year was 1932. I have had a longer career than almost any other singer in the world. I recorded for the gramophone company for more than 30 years. In 1973 I'm still recording. Oscar became one of my greatest friends.

He, thanks to Compton Mackenzie, gave me the lift-up that I needed. I made three records and was assured of some kind of income again.

I threw off my loneliness and started getting around. And one place to which I was not unnaturally drawn was the Royal Scots Corporation Hall in Fetter Lane.

Every Friday they had a concert or dance, and the food was always good. And this was the place in London to meet the influential Scot—the man who'd come down from the mountains of the north and made a great go of it in some business or profession.

I joined the Gaelic Choir. I found most of the members had no knowledge of the language and no intention of learning it.

I have since had a lot of experience of this kind of musical activity—sometimes as an adjudicator—and I find it all a bit phoney.

There is something spurious about Gaelic Mods. Everybody singing in Gaelic and no one being able to speak the tongue—because they've learned their songs like parrots.

It all smacks of pot-hunting—of persistent medal-collecting, and the courting of adulation by singers who would probably never be heard of if they made their music in the language in which they converse, which is English.

Who am I, however, to pour scorn on motives? My own were probably suspect in the Corporation Hall. I met up with Duncan Morrison, whom I'd first got to know on holiday in Glasgow. We in turn made a happy, regular foursome with Eileen Murray, daughter of the former M.P. for the Western Isles, and Evie, whose father, John MacMillan, was managing director of the Shaw Savile shipping line.

I gained access to those wonderful friendships in Fetter Lane. But I must admit that I was also aware of the advantage of mixing with the mighty, of getting myself known among those with influence and power.

And this certainly happened. Duncan was something of a phenomenon from the islands of the west. He played the piano beautifully. He had no formal training, no certificates or parchments, although later he did achieve his L.R.A.M.

He started his music-making playing by ear.

Dear, musical Duncan had managed to come to London for tuition by Archie Rosenthal; an excellent pianist in his own right and a near relative of the famous Mauritz Rosenthal.

Duncan and I teamed up together. He was a first-class accompanist.

My first invitation to sing solo with the choir was for a concert at Londonderry House. Mary Stuart, O.B.E., gave me this chance. It turned out to be one of the most vital engagements of my life. But it landed me in another spot of sartorial trouble.

I hadn't the proper clothes. By now I'd acquired a kilt and tweed jacket. But such an outdoor tunic was hardly right for this kind of formal indoor occasion.

I can't remember how it came about, but a member of the Gaelic choir must have heard of my predicament.

He was a shy, quiet-spoken, gentle man. Almost apologetically he said: " I've a dress suit I've grown out of. It would probably be just about right for you. Do you mind if I do a quick measure?"

I discovered that he was a master tailor in Savile Row. He seemed to be extremely painstaking in his measuring, but I put it down simply to professional instinct.

Two weeks later he turned up with this magnificent black velvet tunic with all the frills and lace attachments.

It proved to be an immaculate fit. " It's no use to me," he said. " You're welcome to it."

Later I became convinced that this delightful, self-effacing man had never owned such a jacket as this. He'd made it specially for me. And that his charity might not be seen to be done, he'd passed it off as second-hand.

Its Londonderry airing was a great success. The Marchioness of Londonderry invited Duncan and myself back to dinner. And many similar invitations followed.

Once again my world was suddenly transformed. Sometimes we went to sing for her guests. But more often than not we were there as friends in our own right.

Not like Galli-Curci who was asked to sing at the home of a wealthy but pretentious London hostess.

" Your fee will be 500 guineas," the hostess explained. " And of course I would rather you didn't mingle with my guests."

" In that case," said the celebrated soprano, " my fee will be only two hundred and fifty!"

It was at the home of the Marchioness that I got to know Lady Cunard, one of the great patrons of Covent Garden. Any time we cared, Duncan and I had the use of her private box at the opera house.

Sir Reginald, The McLeod of McLeod, father of the whimsical, ageless Dame Flora, invited us to spend our holidays at Dunvegan Castle. We went cruising with the Guinness family on the luxury Guinness yacht.

Who would have guessed that this young man from a Glasgow room and kitchen would sup with the Duke of Argyll, the one we called Duke Neil! Or Sir Ian Malcolm. Or the Earl of Dunmore.

Not only was I rubbing shoulders with the titled and the elite. My financial position was improving as well.

Cumming Grant was a poor lad from Drumnadrochit on Loch Ness. He was almost 30 years of age when he decided that ploughing for the rest of his life was not the most exciting of prospects.

So off he went to Glasgow to study for his University Prelims. He discovered he had the right kind of brain and became one of the bright boys in medical school. He paid his way by the dish-washing method — in Rombach's famous restaurant.

As Dr. Cumming Grant he reaped a generous harvest from wealthy London patients. He was well into his eighties when I got to know him as Chief of the Gaelic Society. But still there was the fire and vigour.

Cumming Grant was a born leader, but compassionate as well. He spoke of us as his poor students and had what was almost a fetish for buying us expensive shirts.

Every morning at eleven he liked a glass of sherry in one of those picturesque little pubs that used to be part of a genteel and gracious London.

And one morning he took us both by the arm and turned in the direction of Regent Street: "It's time I bought you boys a suit," he said.

I still have Cumming Grant's gold watch. He willed that his ashes be scattered on Loch Ness, near the fields where he used to plough. I was the one who carried the casket north by train. It was I who went with the good and great Scot on his last journey home.

John McMillan, the shipping boss, was our benefactor also. With that overpowering personality of his, he more or less dragooned all the various London Scottish Societies to hire us for their concerts.

"And see you pay these young fellows a decent fee," he usually added. By that he meant no less than twenty-five guineas.

Twenty-five guineas for one night's work, and still just a student! Sometimes I wondered how long the dream could last. Twenty-five pounds in today's currency is, I suppose, at least £100.

If I were asked to name the most cultured man I know, my choice would be Sir Compton Mackenzie. But maybe I'm prejudiced. Down through the years Sir Compton has been so good to me. No father could have been more considerate to a son.

When his telegram arrived, the bowl of my life was filled with cherries. I was already giving pleasure with my voice to others, which is always a most satisfying experience. I was deeply involved in the social life of London and enjoying every minute of it. Then the telegram from Sir Compton.

I could scarcely believe that life could be so good. " John McCormack wants to hear you. Arranged you call Roehampton tomorrow at 4 p.m." That was the telegram, and it was like being summoned to Buckingham Palace!

Roehampton again—the place where I'd tried to be a priest and suffered such physical and mental discomfort.

I told Cumming Grant the exciting news and immediately he said: " You'll take the car—Leonard will drive you down." Leonard was his chauffeur and the car was an enormous, opulent Daimler.

I thought it might be a bit out of place—the struggling student craving an audience with one of the greatest of tenors and turning up like a millionaire.

So I asked Leonard to drop me well short of the great man's temporary abode. I walked the last quarter-mile or so.

Only Edward Schneider—accompanist to John for 25 years—was in the house to greet me.

John was in London getting physiotherapy treatment. He'd sprained an ankle playing tennis.

Schneider explained: " He won't be minutes," then asked me what I proposed to sing. I suggested " Far Apart." And that was me putting my foot in it right at the start of this momentous occasion.

" No, I wouldn't do that one," Schneider said, " that's one of John's."

We settled for "O del mio amato ben'," a fragile, delicate song, but a great one for " showing off."

After about fifteen minutes John arrived, if that's the right word. His entry was more like a good-natured hurricane.

" Hullo, hullo," he bellowed, " where's this young man we've been hearing about?"

He was still wearing his tennis flannels and he did the introductions—Lily, his wife, and a young, earnest-looking priest called Fulton J. Sheen.

" Come on, then," said John, " how about some tea?"

Kindly, Lily suggested that perhaps I would rather sing first. " The young man's probably nervous—you don't want to stuff him up with food."

" Nonsense," John boomed. " He'll sing all the better if his stomach's full."

The great man was right. Singing is a physical thing— certainly as physical as golf. I used to sing my best and play the better golf when I had a good meal tucked inside me.

I had a really tremendous tea and we moved into the music room and John sat down to listen.

He was round about 50, and for a tenor that's nearing the end of the road. When I'd finished my song, he turned to his accompanist and said: " Well, Teddy, did you hear that?—I used to make it ring like that!"

He went on to put me through my paces. He had me singing all sorts of songs, and all he said at the end of the recital was, " Well, young man, that was fine—just grand. You'll make it all right!"

I came away with a signed photograph and so much more. Even Compton Mackenzie at this stage was worried about my voice: " I'd rather you were a good baritone than a dud tenor," he said.

That afternoon dispelled all doubt. I was a tenor and a good one. Confirmed by the king of tenors himself.

But the real significance of that tea-party was that it started a lifelong friendship.

When John McCormack finally retired, he was a rich man. He could have picked a home for his sunset years wherever he chose—in the sun of California or the South of France or by a lake in the Italy he loved.

But John chose Dublin. He decided to come home. And shortly before he died he sent for me to come to Dublin. He wanted me to sing—just for him.

I still remember the song—the plaintive words of the Lewis poet Agnes Muir Matheson, wrapped round in plaintive music by my old friend, Duncan Morrison. It was called " Island Moon " :

" Tonight there is a restlessness in the wind,
There is a small rain that has salt in it from the sea
And the tide is turning from the seven rocks.
Perhaps the sun is shining for you in a far countrie
But the skies there are not island skies,
You will not remember the salt smell of the sea
And the little rain."

There was a little silence when I finished my song. Then John leaned forward slowly in his chair: " Your voice is all that I knew it would be," he said.

That afternoon far back at Roehampton he could claim to have predicted the future twice. I remember he turned to Fulton Sheen and said: " Sydney, me boy, if you can sing as well as this fella can preach, you'll do all right!"

Fulton Sheen became the Auxiliary Bishop of New York. He is now Archbishop of Rochester and one of America's great religious broadcasters.

John died in 1945. But my friendship with his family continued. I still correspond with his daughter Gwen. Some years ago I sang at his grand-daughter's wedding.

And among my treasured possessions is a little black book. At one time I suppose it was the most famous notebook in the world. It contained the words of his songs all neatly hand-written.

He always took it with him on stage—after the embarrassment in his early years of once forgetting the words.

It became what is nowadays called a gimmick. Chaplin had his bowler hat—McCormack his wee black notebook.

I have McCormack's prayer book also. Its pages are brown and soiled from the way he used it every day.

Not that he needed anything in the nature of a trademark. As I've said, John was one of the greatest tenors of all time. His flair for vocal acrobatics was fantastic. He had that rich velvet tone, and his diction was perfect. His pianissimo on top was quite unique—the voice throbbed like a bird song in his great years.

And his breathing! At his peak his breathing technique was phenomenal. Listen to that tremendous passage in " Il Mio Tesoro "—all in one breath.

I tried it again and again in my prime. I was always an athlete and physically strong. My chest expansion is still exceptional. I was blessed with great lung power. But I could never make that passage in one.

Neither could Gigli or Tito Schipa. Tauber came nearest but even he could only achieve it in two. John the Magnificent was the only " oncer."

If he did it today, I'd say it was faked. With modern recording techniques almost anything can be faked.

But John came too early—he was at his peak when the art of record-making was comparatively crude. And, unfortunately, most people can recall only the latter-day John —the McCormack who had passed the 50th milestone and was definitely on the way back. The McCormack of the comparatively paltry Scots and Irish songs. But the earlier John—oh, there was a man and there was a voice!

With Caruso I can draw no comparison. Compton Mackenzie has assured me that Caruso was the all-time great. I can only accept his word for it. My own access to Caruso is by way of scratchy old 78 records which do no singer justice.

Gigli had a beautiful voice—full of Latin fire and that mellow fluidity born of the Italian sunshine. After John, he was my favourite.

I still have a vivid mental picture of a faded newspaper cutting showing a lone figure arriving at Glasgow's Central Station. He's a chubby little man with a music case, and the platform is otherwise deserted.

This was Gigli arriving to sing in St. Andrew's Hall—and no one to meet him. Certainly no hordes of screaming fans, no forest of arms growing autograph books. Just a solitary man and his music.

Yet some of the bawlers and howlers and microphone slaves who earn today's mass adulation, haven't even the talent to turn the pages of his score.

The day after a Gigli concert in Glasgow, I walked into the Malmaison and was greeted as usual by Luigi, the head waiter. He looked like a Roman senator, authoritative, poker-backed, and with that vocal enthusiasm and excitement that makes all Italians so attractive.

" Well, were you at the concert, Luigi?" I asked.

" Of course, of course!" he gestured with his hands. " And the great man—he stay here, of course. What a beautiful man this Gigli. What a beautiful thing to see him eat. He come in and he have slice of melon—and then the pasta—some spaghetti, you know—what a beautiful eater —and then the meat and the potatoes and the vegetables— and the cheese—he love the cheese—and the two nectarines and the two peaches—it was beautiful to see him eat!"

Not one word about his singing! As they say, every man to his trade.

But Luigi was not all that far off the mark. So often the greats of singing were the greats in eating as well. Gigli was a toby jug of a man. Tauber was fat. McCormack had a paunch like a ship going in reverse. They all of them loved the good things of life.

My memories of Tito Schipa were rounded off with sadness. He was a brilliant artiste—a master of the art of bel canto.

I was still a student in London when Schipa was at his peak. There were always some free tickets sent to the Academy and somehow I seemed to get more than my share. It was not a bad thing to have the same name as the Principal—and Scots, in any case, are notorious for "hingin' thegither."

The applause at what I thought was the end of that concert was deafening, and we students got up to leave. We were right down at the stage, moving past the front row, when the tenor returned for a final encore.

As one of the audience, I have never been so close to any artiste. I could have stretched out a hand and touched his leg. But even at that range the sound that came from this little man was flawless—sheer perfection. Only the very few can stand up to such close inspection.

I heard him again in Australia. There he had a pretty rough time. It got around that the tenor was a Fascist and a great anti-Schipa movement spread among the freedom-loving Aussies.

It was all rather cruel and unjust. Schipa was not a political person. He was a singer—an artiste. He happened to be Italian and was probably a supporter of Mussolini. But what Italian wasn't at the time?

I got back from one of my American tours and one of the first things I noticed in Glasgow was a concert poster. Tito Schipa at St. Andrew's Halls! That's what it said —and I had to read it again to check on the date.

By now he must have been an old man. I just couldn't believe that the voice could still be ripe.

I have never forgotten that evening. It was completely disastrous. This once-great performer was past it. I came out at the interval and didn't go back. I could stomach no more of the agony of watching this parade of decay.

It was as painful as sitting in on the spectacle of a former champ being hammered around the ring.

That night I learned a most valuable lesson. I made a pact with myself that never would I run the risk of this kind of humiliation by forgetting to look in the mirror.

I stopped singing in public at the age of 51. I stepped down when the bloom was still on my voice. The act in itself was not all that difficult. But it's plagued my life ever since.

All through the silent years well-meaning people have gone out of their way to tempt me to break my rule.

"Oh, Father MacEwan, I'm sure you're as good as ever!"

I explain that this is impossible, that singing is a physical act; that to expect my voice to go on for ever is like asking Dr. Roger Bannister to run a four-minute mile or Jimmy McGrory to turn out for Celtic again.

I know full well that many of my invitations to adjudicate at Highland Mods have been made in the hope of persuading me to sing.

Sometimes the approach is rather "below the belt": "And before he leaves, I'm sure we would all like to have a song from Father MacEwan."

Often, I'm afraid, I've lost my temper. My protest is that I should be subjected to this kind of embarrassment. It has kept me frequently at home.

The persistence of people should be flattering, but sometimes it isn't: "Willie Michael O'Malley's still singing and he's over 70!"

From this kind of thing I have been a frequent refugee. I have chosen to stay away. Ironically, the singing that brought me so much pleasure has latterly curbed my social life considerably.

Because of people's lack of understanding, I've been forced into a role that is foreign to my nature, that of a minor recluse.

I know in a way I'm being intolerant and unkind. In condemning lack of understanding in others, I am showing lack of understanding myself. But I can never forget poor Schipa. By all means invite me to your party. But, please don't ask me to sing. I wear a Roman collar and can't use or may not use the language McCormack would have replied in.

The tragedy for so many of the musical giants— McCormack, Caruso, Gigli, Tauber, Martinelli, Kreisler, etc.—was that they reached their prime before the middle of the twentieth century.

The era of tape recording did not arrive until the late 1950s. It brought with it all sorts of thrilling techniques which have turned out to be a mixed blessing.

By way of such inventions as tapes and mixing devices and echo chambers, the shoddy and indifferent can be made to sound exceptional, the most pathetic little voice can be artificially enlarged to fill the Albert Hall.

The greats I speak of recorded on wax. For years they didn't even have microphones. To create his recordings, Peter Dawson, the Australian baritone, used to have to stand for hours singing into an arrangement of as many as twelve big horns.

The dramatic change in recording skill has given us so much that is nasty and spurious—and robbed us of a faithful record of magnificent vocalists whose only fault was to choose the wrong time to be born. I regret that old 78s are my best recordings.

In the 'thirties, for a singer to be asked to record at all was like receiving a knighthood. The number of recording companies was limited and they were fastidious in their choice of material.

Many fine professionals who could sing the boots off most of the so-called current stars went through life without cutting a single disc and thereby probably missed the chance of considerable fame and fortune.

This kind of situation made my own case all the more remarkable.

I was making records while still at the Academy—although recording was officially banned to students, however great their incipient talent. I can only assume that Sir John McEwan chose to turn a blind eye.

And another great stroke of luck was to land at the beginning with such a genius as Oscar Preus. I followed his advice absolutely. I was at once sufficiently naive and wise to accept that this man was probably more skilled in the art of sound reproduction than anyone else in the world.

Never once did I challenge his advice or criticism.

Jan Kiepura was a famous Polish tenor who acquired a considerable fame by way of musical films. After the success of the film called " Tell Me Tonight," he turned up at the No. 1 Studios to record its music.

Kiepura made the mistake of trying to tell Oscar his job.

He took a look at the accompanying musicians and said with some conceit: " This handful is no use to me—I must have a bigger orchestra than that!"

The gentle Oscar said simply: " Let's have a trial run and we'll see how it sounds."

Before the playback he told his engineer: " Turn up the orchestra as much as you can."

Kiepura sat back to listen to his emotional rendition of that one-time favourite, " Love, I bring you my heart."

He looked aghast. His voice was scarcely audible above the instrumental backing.

Oscar had achieved his purpose. There was no further mention of an augmented band.

Nowadays an artiste can make any number of tapes and only copies of the best one are reproduced. A modern disc may in fact be something of a deceit. It can be a selective, composite creation, incorporating only the best bits of a great many tapes, so that all flaws or inadequacies are eliminated like one of those touched-up studio glamour photographs.

In those early days we had to make two master discs in wax and they had to be as near-perfect as possible. They were the stamp for every subsequent record and they couldn't be " doctored " in any way.

Thanks to the promptings of Oscar, I quickly became expert at this hit-or-miss technique. He taught me the especially meticulous enunciation that recording deman-ded. He instructed me in the tricks of the trade, like standing on the ball of the foot, so that you could sway backwards whenever you came to a double-fortissimo high note which would otherwise have blasted the comparatively simple recording equipment.

He was a great man for taking a chance. He knew my style. He realised that with too many trial runs a singer can become jaded and some of the early sparkle can go out of his performance.

Often he would say: " Come on, Sydney, let's not waste time—let's try for a ' oncer.' "

Sometimes it didn't come off, especially when an orchestra was involved and somebody coughed into a trumpet or spluttered into his horn.

Or the balance might be elusive, for there was no clever electronic equipment to bring up one section and tone down another. You might finish up with the trombones seated on high stools away at the back of the studio.

The instrumentalists were usually hired for a three-hour session and they " downed tools " inevitably on the dot. Nobody argued when they packed up and went. Nobody argued when they ignored the " No Smoking " signs and went through an entire recording puffing at their pipes.

These men—many of them again most talented Jews—were the elite of musicians.

The same situation persists today. In London there are perhaps a hundred and fifty musicians in the recording pool. They can play anything at sight—symphonies, pop, chamber, jazz, blues. Each is brilliant in his own field. They therefore monopolise the record scene. Recording is expensive—time costs money—these brilliant players don't waste studio time. They are like the character actors in theatre. They never get the star billing, but they are constantly in demand.

The night before one of my recording sessions, I was at the home of Phil Green, the conductor, for dinner. Phil was then a Jew. We have been the best of friends for years.

It was the week before I was due to leave on one of my American concert tours. And after dinner, Phil said: " I've composed a new song—would you like to hear it?"

It turned out to be a most attractive piece: " I'd love to do that one tomorrow," I said.

" I'm afraid there's no arrangement," said Phil. " And tomorrow there won't be time."

We agreed that if we got through the scheduled programme without setback, we'd try to fit in the new song at the end.

The following day we were left with only half an hour to spare. Phil told his players: " We've no arrangement for this last one—and Sydney's off to America on Monday. Will you busk it, boys?"

There was a quick run through. Completely off the cuff we presented to the world Phil's new song, and the orchestra had no parts.

In those comparatively primitive days, Britain produced the world's best records. Its recording engineers were the finest in the world. Its musicians were magnificent. They still are.

CHAPTER

13

After my two years at the Academy, Compton Mackenzie suggested that I should do a year with Harry Plunkett-Green. After a career as a notable singer himself, Plunkett-Green had turned to teaching and achieved an even grander reputation. Among all the London tutors he was reckoned to be the tops.

His fees were 'way up at the top as well. He charged a guinea a time—when a guinea was really worth its weight in gold.

He had no secret recipe for singing. He taught me nothing in the way of voice technique that I hadn't got at the Academy. What he was able to impart was interpretation —how to study a song. His book, *Interpretation in Song*, is a recognised classic.

He was masterly at song interpretation. From him I learned how to dissect a song, sometimes as thoroughly as bar by bar.

I knew at this stage I was going to the top, and such extras were worth every penny. But never once did Plunkett-Green render a bill or even mention the question of money.

I got my year with Plunkett-Green for free, and to this day I haven't discovered the identity of my benefactor.

It was probably Monty Mackenzie himself. He is certainly the kindest man it has been my good fortune to meet.

Supposing two tramps turned up at my door and one of them chanced to say: "We're great fans of Compton Mackenzie's books."

I could phone him and explain that a couple of gentle-men of the road would like to call and talk about his work. He would receive these two hoboes with the same old-world courtesy that one would accord to a duke—and the meeting would probably last the whole morning.

It is not in Compton Mackenzie's nature to speak un-kindly of any man. He loves people. He loves the world in general. He has taken a great deal out of the world and put back so much into it.

Perhaps that is why, despite physical handicap, he has lived to such a contented old age. He is immune to such killer-instincts as hate or malice or envy.

Some day I must ask him if he it was who gave me that year with Plunkett-Green.

By this time Duncan and myself were what were known as the darlings of London society. We had access to just about every stately home that was in the social swim.

The incongruity of the whole situation appealed to our sense of humour. I was not long detached from the Glasgow room and kitchen. My recent companions were those warriors of the Woodside Rovers. And now we were living literally like lords. Almost overnight, it seemed, we'd switched from kail to caviare.

We sailed around the Western Isles in Lord Moyne's private yacht—the one that used to be a Channel steamer. Now it was a floating luxury hotel, a sea-borne oasis of gracious living.

When we wanted to go ashore, we had simply to summon the speed-boat. We had each a personal valet. I remember we landed at Dunvegan in Skye and Duncan and I sat down on a dry-stane dyke and talked about the way our good fairy had been working overtime. Eventually the pair of us were almost hysterical with laughter at the daftness of it all.

I could never fully comprehend this ritual of the cocktail party and the formal soiree. Yet for some folk this phoney way of life was an irresistible magnet. I remember one we nicknamed George—tall, very handsome, impeccable of manner and always immaculately dressed. He had no title. He had no real significance, except his looks. Yet, inevitably, he turned up at every single upper-crust party.

We discovered he was broke. He lived on his wits and was constantly in debt to his tailors.

Another who was never missing from the grand occasion was a rather insignificant little man with whom we got friendly. He was a bachelor. As a retired civil servant, his income was a princely five pounds a week—not bad in the 1930s.

Yet somehow he'd got on to the rather silly, inconsequential roundabout—and he couldn't get off.

I went home with him one evening. His bachelor flat was extremely humble—a sort of London version of our Springburn room and kitchen.

What gave it a distinctive touch was its walls. They were almost completely covered by photographs—and the subject of every picture was probably in Debrett.

Our rather pathetic little ex-civil servant hadn't made the grade himself. But at least he could claim that he moved among lords and ladies—even in his rather ignoble but-and-ben.

My most regular outings continued to be to Londonderry House. As the guest of the Marchioness, I was introduced there to Ramsay MacDonald.

I had dinner also with Philip Snowden and his Lady, with Stanley Baldwin and Shakespeare Morrison, who was Speaker of the House of Commons.

Some of the friendships of Londonderry House turned out to be real and lasting—like that with Sir Ian Malcolm of Poltalloch. Later, during my 17 years as a priest in mid-Argyll, Sir Ian's son, the present laird, was often my host at Poltalloch and Duntrune Castle.

But the mind boggles at what the lads of Woodside Road would have said to this new kind of set-up that their Syd had got himself into!

It was given an added piquancy by another activity from which Duncan and I as students extracted the occasional guinea.

We sang around London at Masonic smokers and dinners. On these modest, mercenary Masonic occasions we, who by now were honoured guests in just about every great house in town, were invariably cut down to size.

We'd be met by a Cockney committee-man, who'd show us into a dingy ante-room—usually painted in faded chocolate and cream and with a wooden form to sit on.

And always the advice was the same: " Just hang on— we'll let you know when you're on."

Our summons came after the Masonic meal—and the subsequent barrage from fags and pipes.

In this smoky, restless, indifferent atmosphere, we certainly earned our guinea. No artiste could ever perform efficiently in this kind of environment.

Without exception our Masonic audiences just couldn't care less. But the money was useful.

Most students at the Royal Academy were not earning a penny, and Duncan and I didn't mind this artistic rough and tumble—we were sure we were going to the top—all of us were convinced of this—and one day we would laugh at the poor days.

CHAPTER

14

As soon as I left the Academy, it was decided that Duncan and I should venture into the concert world. I had never been farther than London. Now I found myself making arrangements for a tour of New Zealand.

As if that weren't sufficiently exciting in itself, all sorts of wonderful things started to happen.

The Marchioness of Londonderry made available her stately home for a Sydney MacEwan—Duncan Morrison Recital. She had all her influential friends selling tickets— at a guinea a time. A guinea was still real money in 1935. So financially we did extremely well.

And when the great night of the recital arrived, it seemed that everybody who was anybody in London society had been persuaded to come.

All the programme sellers were glamorous debs—Evie MacMillan, Aleen Murray and Peggy Geddes, who later became the Grand Duchess of Hesse. And guess whom the Marchioness had been able to persuade to act as patron of the recital! None other than the Duchess of York, the most gracious of Scotswomen, who was destined first to be a Queen and later the most charming Queen Mother this country has ever had.

Into the magnificent ballroom of Londonderry House I made my entrance up the great sweep of stairway. It was a far cry from Springburn.

A few years ago I walked down Park Lane and stopped outside the scene of this unforgettable occasion. Londonderry House seemed to have come down in the world. It was an office block used by the R.A.F.

I looked inside the hallway and a smart, uniformed young man looked up from a reception desk.

" Can I do anything for you, sir?" he asked.

" This place is an old friend of mine," I said. " I was just looking around."

He asked for no credentials. " Go ahead, sir!" he said.

" If I could just have a peep at the ballroom," I said. " I can remember when it used to be filled with tiaras."

" I'm afraid we haven't got any of them left," he said. " But by all means have a look round."

I climbed the staircase and gazed at the gilded hall. Some of the pictures were still on the walls. But the gilt had faded and was worn in places. The ballroom had a business-like, efficient look—and these would have been the most incongruous adjectives in the days before the war.

I realised that Londonderry House would never again be its old, luxurious, radiant self.

I shed no tears for the decline of the aristocracy. They had a good run for their money. And measured against the present with its striving for equal shares for all, I suppose their era looks not only unfair, but that bit unreal as well.

But even as a Glasgow East End kid, I must admit that I miss the pomp. I want the best of both worlds. By all means let the working man have his fair crack of the whip. But must it inevitably mean the elimination of all that is grand and extravagant and stately?

I am scunnered by the parsimonious bleatings over the rewards of royalty. If we choose to have a monarchy, let it be on the grand scale. I don't particularly want a second or third class monarch pedalling round the markets on a pushbike as has happened in Scandinavia.

Maybe astronomical retainers for what might be called the lesser royals are no longer justified. But if we're going to have a Queen, let her be glorious. Let her be a showpiece with all the royal trimmings.

This fetish for making everything drab and plastic has affected even the Vatican. I miss the Noble Guard and the Palatine Guard and the silver trumpets when the Pope goes into St. Peter's.

I'm sure it's a feeling shared by the thousands of pilgrims who converge on Rome—and by the non-Catholic tourists also.

CHAPTER

15

On March 17 we boarded the good ship *Tamaroa*, which was to be our home for the six weeks' journey halfway round the world.

We were seen off at Southampton by Aleen Murray and Evie Macmillan, the shipping magnate's daughter—and Duncan and I were travelling free.

The *Tamaroa* was one of her father's fleet. I learned later that as we stood talking on the jetty, the purser looked over the rail and immediately ordered that our cabins be changed.

He was an astute man. On the strength of being seen with the managing director's daughter, we got the V.I.P. treatment in the shape of the ship's most luxurious quarters.

It was a switch that was achieved without any difficulty. The total passenger list numbered no more than 35.

On this, the greatest adventure of my life to date, I naturally envisaged a spot of romance. I don't think Duncan had any such thoughts. He was never a lady's man, and to this day has clung to his bachelor status.

But I had an eye for the lasses. And a prolonged cruise in luxury conditions seemed to be the traditional setting for the boy-meets-girl occurrence.

Alas, not one of the female passengers was less than 45 years old! And the majority looked as if they'd been 45 a long time ago!

For such a small company we got a most boisterous send-off. One of the passengers was an Irishman from Clonmel, where my maternal grandfather lies buried.

He was what was then called a remittance man—the black-sheep member of a wealthy family that had decided on safeguarding the family good name by dispatching the misfit as far away as possible—i.e. Australia or New. Zealand—and keeping him content by the sending of a monthly remittance.

I was soon made aware of how in this case the monthly allowance would in the main be spent.

The man from my grandpa's resting place had brought along with him for the fond farewell just about every single member of the Clonmel Hunt. They had on their scarlet hunting gear and were equipped with hunting horns and excellent hunting lungs.

John Peel himself could not have mustered a more tumultuous departure. There were loud halloas and blasts of trumpet, and so many stirrup cups were raised that the emigrant from Clonmel had to be carried on board.

He was, as they say in Glasgow, as fu' as a wulk!

This in varying degrees was more or less his state throughout the whole voyage.

There were two other interesting passengers. One was the captain of the famous Atlantic liner, the *Olympic,* indulging in something of a busman's holiday.

The other was Captain Moffatt-Pender, former Liberal candidate for the Western Isles. He never made the grade so far as Parliament was concerned, but he did have considerable success in the business of marriage.

His wife was a wealthy Australian—so that the captain could afford a home at each end of the world—in Australia and at Poolewe, Scotland.

He was also a member of the exclusive Royal Thames Yacht Club. We found him a most pleasant companion. He promised to keep an eye on us two travel-rookies.

I made friends quickly with the radio officer, and up in his cabin on the boat deck as we left Southampton Water, I heard him receive the message: " You look as if you're heading into something pretty nasty!"

148

It was a typically nautical piece of euphemism. The gale blew up that night, and it took all of eight days to blow itself out.

I love the sea. I pride myself in the quality of my sea-legs. But the occasional turbulences of the Irish Sea and that sometimes hectic crossing to the Isle of Barra were a poor apprenticeship for an experience of this kind.

On the first day of the storm I felt decidedly ill. It was on the *Tamaroa* I discovered that there are only two courses of action in coping with sea-sickness. One is a generous intake of champagne, and the other a good stiff brandy and soda.

But on this occasion even these two recommended antidotes were only in part successful. I still had to take to my cabin and lie down with that feeling that death is just around the corner.

This somewhat defeatist attitude is the only reasonable course of action. I've certainly found that the common advice about going to the galley and getting a good plate of stew inside you is so much impossible hokum.

There is nothing for it with sea-sickness but to lie down and hope for the best.

In this kind of behaviour I found I was in quite distinguished company. That first tempestuous day completely laid out even the *Olympic's* captain.

My only other sea-sickness tip is patience—be patient for old age, when the malady will leave you severely alone.

We were past the Azores when the gale slunk away in defeat and the sun came out and the dear old ladies—shaken but intact—settled down to their daily afternoon siesta from two o'clock to five.

I ignored the siesta periods altogether. I was so fascinated with ship's life that I wanted to savour every minute. And I made full use of the ship's library.

Most afternoons I went up with my book to the poop deck. Invariably it was deserted except for one grey-haired old chap, who lounged in a deck-chair reading in the sun.

I discovered he was there in the mornings and evenings also. Eventually, I asked him where he was going.

" Wherever this ship takes me," he said in a jaded, expressionless sort of voice. " I'm the chief engineer!"

Then he added: " But don't tell John Macmillan!"

His job was obviously one of those sinecures that come to some of us for good and faithful service. Each morning he would probably shout down a pipe for oil and steam pressures and various other engine-room statistics, and that would be his day's work done.

He was there at his usual place on deck that magnificent, cloudless morning when I stared towards the horizon and caught a glimpse of the first foreign territory I'd ever set eyes on.

What I was looking at was Curacoa in the Dutch West Indies. A happy choice to begin the wanderings that have since taken me many times round the globe.

Or so it seemed. For the distinction of Curacoa, if my memory serves me right, is that it has no seasons. Its temperature never varies from one year's end to the other. It can claim to have the sun in the morning and the moon at night, be it December or June.

At first it sounded like a Shangri-La. But can you imagine the absolute boredom of such a perfect climate! How quickly you'd long for the autumn mists of Argyll or the crisp rime of a Caithness March. And what would there be to talk about!

During the eight hours' sail through the Panama Canal— that fantastic, man-made linkage of the two great oceans, Atlantic and Pacific—I not only missed the afternoon siesta, but found it impossible to go to sleep at night.

There was so much to watch. The system of locks in this 40-mile waterway that raises the largest of liners no less than 85 feet above sea-level. The frightening alligators in the mud of the banks. The 20 odd miles of artificial lake in the middle, all dotted around with islands that were once the peaks of mountains. And, of course, Panama itself at the Pacific end.

There we had all of us one ambition—to visit the night club known as Madame Kelly's. It was Captain Moffatt-Pender who knew the ropes, and because the streets of Panama after dark were a lot less safe than Sauchiehall Street, he suggested we go in a party.

I dressed up in my whiter-than-white linen suit. For a comparative youngster it was all so new and exciting. I felt the helluva toff so much that I had my picture taken in that suit and kept it to show off for many years after.

This first night ashore in Panama I really wanted to cut a dash. So I asked Moffatt-Pender: " Do you think I might borrow your Royal Thames Yacht Club cap—just for this once?"

It turned out to be a perfect fit.

You approached Madame Kelly's by way of a sort of verandah, then down a winding stair to the basement premises. As I made what I thought was the grand entrance, I noticed a group of sailors at one of the tables in a corner.

The sailor at the far side of the table looked up and I heard him say: " My God, boys — here's Sir Thomas Lipton!"

Madame Kelly offered us the usual wine and women. The wine we accepted. I remember it was something called New Orleans Fizz and seemed to have a decided vinegar content.

The women we rejected, although we did sit through the floor show, and young Sydney for the very first time in his life was a witness of the fan dance.

I will not say coldly I was not impressed. I was young and virile and have never considered myself immune to the charms of the female.

But there was something seamy about this first night-club experience.

For me the highlight of that night was the walk back through the dark, humid streets and the sudden sight in great floodlit letters of the name " Tamaroa." This was our little bit of Britain. It was like coming home.

In Panama they speak Spanish, and their religion is Roman Catholic. Panama City had all the romantic atmosphere of the Spanish Main, and none of us would have been surprised to meet up with a pirate complete with golden ear-rings.

The following day Duncan and I went sightseeing and we came upon a fascinating church. At one time its altar was completely black.

The locals had it painted that colour when Morgan, the notorious pirate, was rampaging around these parts. For the altar was made entirely of gold—a most tempting piece of furniture for one such unscrupulous collector of other people's property.

The disguise must have worked. When we saw the famous altar of Panama City it was back to its breathtaking golden glory. I have still a particularly vivid memory of its spectacular beauty.

It's almost 40 years ago, but I still have two souvenirs of that first trip abroad. They are hand-carved vases in the sense that they are formed in the shape of two cupped hands.

I tell my friends: " These were made by a descendant of Fletcher Christian." And sometimes the cynics express good-natured doubts. They like my hand-like vases, but they think I was probably conned.

I got them from Pitcairn Island—our only stop on that long haul across the Pacific. This is the island discovered almost 200 years ago by Christian, the leader of the famous Mutiny on the Bounty.

It is a tiny ocean oasis—two and a half miles by one. It must have had considerable attractions, for a New Zealand dentist was among its inhabitants, he having decided to opt out of a prosperous city practice and settle for the simple island life.

Pitcairn, however, has no harbour, so we had to drop anchor inshore and wait for Pitcairn to come to us. The dentist was one of a colourful little flotilla of souvenir pedlars who rowed out to the ship.

They sang as they rowed. One of them was a most handsome young man with a film-star tan and great dark eyes.

It was with him I did the deal for the vases.

" What's your name?" I asked.

" Christian," he said.

" Don't tell me you're descended from Fletcher Christian?" I suggested.

He nodded and smiled.

So I was conned? The Christian ancestor story was nothing more than a good sales gimmick?

I prefer to think not. In fact I've always considered my Pitcairn Islander as completely genuine.

It was that kind of island. Despite its descent from rough, tough, no doubt unprincipled sea-rogues, it seemed to have become something of a little, unspoiled paradise.

The young man with the vases was as polite as a bishop. He refused a cigarette. I offered him brandy and he refused that as well.

And when he returned with the fleet of souvenir boats, the singing started again. The songs they sang were all Moody and Sankey hymns.

The descendants of perhaps the most notorious ocean highwaymen in history are deeply religious. They are all of them devout Seventh Day Adventists.

CHAPTER

16

It was night-time when we arrived at Auckland in the North Island. We dropped anchor and I looked out across the black harbour at a tall floodlit building with a radio mast.

This was the New Zealand Broadcasting Company building—the company that was sponsoring and managing my tour. I cannot deny a feeling of excitement. It was like the official signal for the start of my great adventure.

In both islands of New Zealand Duncan and I were such a success that the tour was extended to Australia—at the invitation of the Australian Broadcasting Commission.

We started at Sydney, that bustling, cosmopolitan city with its suburb of Manly, which reminded me of Dunoon, except that oysters were only a shilling a dozen.

It was in Manly that I developed a taste for oysters, something that has stayed with me all my life.

Melbourne was more relaxed—a more handsome, dignified sort of place. There I developed two lasting friendships —one with a building, the other with a man.

The building was Melbourne Town Hall. I played it so often in subsequent years that I came to look upon it as something of my own preserve. And Melbourne Town Hall appeared to like me—on one occasion it had me as its guest for nine concert appearances in a space of three weeks.

The place was always packed. And inevitably, in the seat just by the off-stage exit, there sat the same man. He was a rugged character with a jaw like a jetty and a mouth that seemed to have been pencilled in. His bald head was speckled by the Australian sun.

Although his clothes had a prosperous Australian look, there was no mistaking the Scottishness of the man underneath.

At the end of each of all nine concerts he presented me with a posy of flowers:

" Gie that tae yer auld mither!" he said. (She was in Australia with me on this 1951 tour.)

In the interval of my last performance I asked him to be brought backstage. The rugged old-timer with a love for music and flowers seemed at first to be embarrassed.

" I hope ye dinna mind," he said. " I just felt I was touchin' a bit of auld Scotland."

I gave him a silver cigarette case with my name inscribed.

" I'm afraid that's made in Australia," I said, " but the good wishes that go with it are Scottish enough."

The tough veteran lifted the box and put it to his lips. And a tear ran down his cheek.

My magnificent man of Melbourne was Archbishop Mannix. I met him on that first occasion, and every time I went back to Australia he insisted I be his guest.

He was tall and handsome, even in old age. His grey hair billowed out like the mane of a lion. He had the kind of voice that made you sit up in your chair. A majestic man. A man with that rare touch of magic in his personality.

He was born in Charleville, County Cork, on the 4th of March, 1864. On June 8th, 1890, he was ordained at Maynooth, the great Irish seminary outside Dublin. He was consecrated coadjutor Archbishop of Melbourne with the right of succession, and he succeeded to the See in 1917.

He was still in office by 1963, and I was all prepared to fly out to his 100th birthday celebration. He died five months short of the century.

Mannix retained his high office in the Australian Church all those years although he was an Irishman. Not that this was remarkable. In these days every Bishop in Australia was Irish. Australia was almost like an Irish foreign mission.

It was a situation that was accepted by everyone. Most Australian Catholics were not far removed from Ireland themselves.

When I was a boy, we had the same kind of set-up in Glasgow. Every Catholic in Glasgow had relatives in Ireland. This no longer applies, because the emigration of Irishmen to Scotland has more or less dried up completely. The current Irish with itchy feet make for London or Birmingham or Liverpool or Cardiff.

Mannix was one of the great political Archbishops. In the First World War he fiercely opposed the Australian Premier, Billy Hughes, over conscription.

In the disturbances in Ireland from 1916 to 1921 he was aggressively against the hierarchy. The official attitude of the Catholic Church was one of condemnation of the Freedom Fighters' activities. Priests were in fact instructed to deny the sacraments to all known revolutionaries.

Archbishop Mannix was a hundred per cent on the side of the rebels and made no secret of it. When the "troubles" were at their height, he set sail for Ireland, ostensibly to visit his old mother.

He was known to be such a powerful persuader with exceptional talent for oratory, that his projected trip had British diplomacy in one helluva panic.

So much so that Mannix was never allowed to reach Ireland. His liner was stopped in mid-ocean by a British man-o'-war and the Archbishop was placed under open arrest.

Eventually, he went on a lecturing tour of Scotland and England instead. But fears were so great for his rabble-rousing ability, he wasn't allowed inside Glasgow. He had to speak outside the city boundary.

On his way back to Australia, he called at Rome for his " ad limina "—the regular visit which bishops throughout the world are obliged to pay to the Pope.

The session was anything but placid. Mannix told me himself that Benedict XV blasted him for his political activities. But Mannix gave as good as he got. He was not a man to be dislodged from his principles and beliefs even in the face of the wrath of the Pope himself.

On my last Australian tour I found him at his fireside, drinking tea with a friend. The friend was his one-time arch-enemy, Billy Hughes. They were two old men with all their battles behind them.

For the journey to Perth in Western Australia I took the train. A most interesting train it turned out to be. It was equipped for one thing with shower baths. The heat of the desert lands of the Nularbor Plain was like living in a baker's oven.

There was also an entertainment room on the train with piano and equipment for various games. For the trip from Adelaide to Perth took all of four days and included stops for the unloading of provisions at points in the desert that consisted of nothing more than a couple of houses.

Australia was bedevilled by a strange attitude to rail travel, in the shape of allowing each State to have its own gauge of track.

As soon as you moved out of New South Wales, for instance, into Victoria, you had to get out and change trains—sometimes in the middle of the night. It was like changing at Polmont every time you travelled from Glasgow to Edinburgh.

I know the Australians have tremendous enthusiasm for physical exercise, but even they have since realised the daftness of such a situation and made most of their lines the same gauge.

One of the changing points on the long, hot safari to Perth was the gold town of Kalgoorlie. I took the chance of doing a concert there, and was shown round one of the mines.

They gave me a bar of gold to hold. It was no bigger than could be grasped in one hand. Its value then, when money was money, was about five thousand pounds. Today it would probably be fifty thousand. And I held it in the palm of one hand!

It was round about this time that I made up my mind to save like mad and be rich. It was probably Aunt Lettie coming out—she who used to save sovereigns under the bed in Ireland.

But I had in mind Sir Harry Lauder. He was once chided for being canny with his siller.

His reply was: " Nobody is ever going to give a benefit concert for me!"

When he died, he left three hundred and fifty thousand. He had his hey-day when income tax was sixpence. But I remember being impressed this early with the independence that money can bring.

I didn't smoke. My drinking was only occasional. I was not attracted to the expensive " wild " life. My obsession was sport, and my love was the Church.

If you wanted to be mercenary about it, this constant allegiance to the Church of mine paid off handsomely. I kept up my prayers and my Masses—even as a young man in far-away places.

The result was I could never be lonely. In all of the years of world travel, mine was never the misfortune of sitting alone in some strange, unfriendly hotel bedroom.

I discovered even on this very first tour that the Roman Catholic Church is the greatest club in the world.

Duncan, my constant companion, was of course, a Protestant. He has remained a Protestant all his life. Despite my enthusiasm for Catholicism, the matter of religion never once disturbed our friendly partnership.

My Catholics took to Duncan. He is an artistic person. He in turn was attracted by what you might call the frills of my faith—the ornate buildings, the candles, the music and incense. For Duncan the Protestant, they had an aesthetic appeal.

158

And we had a good-natured working arrangement. Whenever we were in Roman Catholic company, I would jest: " Now watch what you say—this man's a black Protestant!"

And in non-Catholic companies, Duncan would retaliate: " Be careful what you say—this fellow's a Papist!"

Perth turned out to be a charming little city—well worth putting up with all the eccentricities of the oven-like train across the relentless desert.

And again we registered such a success that the Broadcasting Company's Western Australia manager suggested an extra date. He was opening a new station up-country, and would I like to be one of the performers?

I went up with a number of local Australian artistes, and we travelled in a fleet of cars.

On the way back I didn't have Duncan with me. He was always a great talker. I used to tell him he was " aye bletherin' to somebody."

And I went off, leaving him to follow in one of the later cars.

" I'm going straight home to bed," I said. " I'll see you in the morning."

I had my usual solid, dreamless slumber—for even when the pressures were on in the later, hectic, celebrity days, insomnia was never a cross I had to bear.

I bathed, shaved, dressed, and still there was no sign of Duncan. I knocked on his bedroom door and got no reply. When I went in, I found that his bed wasn't slept in.

And just at that moment the telephone rang. Duncan was in hospital. The car he was in had overturned.

He'd badly injured an arm and hand and would be out of action for months. I saw him off on the *Orion* from Perth and continued the tour on my own.

CHAPTER

17

The broadcasting company loaned me various accompanists—notably one called John Douglas Todd. He was first-class—one of the best I had in all my career.

I was in on the opening of another new Australian station—this time away up in the outback of Northern Queensland. The two broadcasting company executives on that occasion have since become high-ranking personalities in the communications world. They had each outstanding records also in World War Two—for which both were honoured by the Queen.

But in those young and carefree early days I knew one of them as Huck. He introduced me to an outback pub—and what a morning we had there!

I remember quietly and reverently laying out the proprietor behind his own bar, and Huck and I thereafter took over the serving of the customers.

I'm proud to recall that the till was not one penny short!

That night the new station was to open with a talent contest and the auditions were held in the afternoon. My job was to introduce the various acts from a local hall, and they were heard by the broadcasting people in a studio about half a mile away. I was doing this for fun, and was in holiday mood.

I had for my assistant a local sugar-cane planter—a mischievous little fellow who discovered, as well as singing, I played the fiddle.

" Borrow one," he said. " Let's kid them."

I introduced myself. " You are now going to hear a violin selection by Ernesto Grillo," I said, recalling the name of my professor of Italian at Glasgow University.

Nobody at the other end smelt a rat. There were lots of Italians employed on the sugar-cane plantations, and Ernesto was accepted without question.

I rattled out some reels and jigs with great gusto, and awaited the reaction.

Back came Huck: " Hold that fellow, Sydney," he said, " he's definitely on tonight!"

We all of us had a beer together when the auditions were completed.

Casually I said to Huck: " You liked Ernesto Grillo then?"

He looked at me suspiciously. There was a long silence during which Ernesto tried to appear as earnest as possible.

Then Huck exploded: " It was you, ye wee bugger! All right, then—for that, I'll make you go on tonight."

In fact I got a reprieve. My public performance " down under " continued to be purely vocal!

I was as far away from home as I could possibly get, yet I never once felt lonely.

I was like the snail with its house on its back. In my case, the ever-present, comforting, shielding shell was the Church that I loved from my sapling days at the altar.

I hope this does not sound like the sentiment of a bigot when I say *my* Church—it could well be *the* Church.

After Australia, they wanted me in Canada and the U.S.A. The world was now my stage.

I had arrived; I sensed, without any undue conceit, that already I was at the top.

I had achieved the first-class bracket—first-class travel, first-class hotels, first-class companionship, first-class food and drink. Not that I bothered much with alcohol—it doesn't go with being a tenor.

My devotion to my Church was my antidote to loneliness and home-sickness.

I remember after Duncan had gone home, I arrived in my hotel, and the bedroom was large and it seemed for the moment filled with emptiness. The town was new and I knew not a soul.

But before I had time to take a shower, the telephone rang, and a visitor called. He was a gigantic man, a smiling man, a man with kindness in his eyes. And he wore a priest's collar.

" You'll be lonely now," he said, " you being new to the town. Now, why don't you just stop unpacking these things and come along and live at the presbytery?"

It was out in the country. I stayed for three days—with his dog called Sailor, and his lively, attentive, charming housekeeper and the one he called his schoolma'rm.

This was always the way it was, to whichever part of the globe I travelled. I was constantly in the company of men of the Church. And I drew from the well of their companionship.

The Archbishop of Western Australia insisted that I be his guest. His name was Prenderville—and he turned out to be a charming person.

In his native Ireland he had trained in more than one seminary. He was expelled from his first for going out over the wall without permission, to play hurly for Kerry in an all-Ireland final.

Yet he became a Bishop at the age of 36—at that time the youngest ever in the whole of the Catholic Church.

He had a trim, little holiday house, down by the sea, and one of the curates came along to ferry us in a motor-boat along that glorious stretch of coastline.

There was a peace that was soothing in that beach-hut lapped by the ocean. There was a great peace also about Archbishop Prenderville.

My boyhood ambition to be a priest was born out of awe. It was the child of a childish hero-worship. The priest was to me as a little boy in Springburn what the spaceman is to the modern child.

I could imagine no more exciting vocation. I was open-mouthed at a priest's prestige.

This attitude had changed with the years. As an international tenor I lacked nothing in the way of prestige and adulation. What was rubbing off now was the essential goodness of priests and the joy and satisfaction of their lives. Their continued presence was my continuing tranquilliser.

They were men of faith. They still are—even in these troubled, explosive, materialistic times.

There are not many priests who break the rules. That is why, when they do, it makes the front-page.

I have lived with priests all over the world and would wish for no better human contact.

CHAPTER

18

At this stage it would be effective to report a dramatic conversion—a modern re-enactment of what happened to Paul on that famous road to Damascus.

I would wish for a thunderbolt or a still small voice or a near-encounter with death.

The setting was certainly favourable for the traumatic kind of experience when I sailed from Honolulu on the good ship *Niagara,* along with members of the Canadian Empire Games team of athletes.

I was on my way from Australia to my first tour of Canada, and before we left Honolulu the warning came through that we were about to sail into a hurricane. It was only ten hours away.

There were those passengers who asked anxiously: " Why don't we stay in port till it's passed?" That seemed to make sense.

But we cast off on schedule, and the hurricane had the capacity for good time-keeping also. It struck us right at the predicted hour.

I have always had a love of boats in any shape or size. And the *Niagara* was a substantial liner. But for three whole days that hurricane treated it like a helpless dinghy.

I have never since been in a vessel that came so near to standing on its head. A less robust freighter was caught up in the same relentless storm and for 24 hours we departed from our schedule and stood by lest she give up the fight. During that period we were completely at the mercy of the frenzied wind and its equally enraged companion-sea.

In such an experience only the most bovine and insensitive of men would deny any feeling of insecurity. More than once I sensed a closeness to death. The awareness that this could be the end was very real indeed.

No doubt there have been those who have emerged as changed men from such an emotional and physical battering. When the calm came I'm afraid my only concern was of being late at Vancouver for my first Canadian coast-to-coast broadcast.

But storm or no storm, my restlessness continued. I cannot claim that this was the classical call from God. The constant beckoning was not the mystical " follow-me " of Jesus Christ.

I was in love with the Church. I was increasingly fascinated by its ritual and its ceremony. And I was more than ever impressed by those who had adopted it as their way of life.

If these men were in the service of Christ, it was a service to which I was being as instinctively drawn as the pigeon to its loft.

From Vancouver I wrote home to my mother: " I'm going to become a priest," I wrote.

I'd loved and been loved. I was in the big money. My future could not have looked more rosy.

But the pull of the priesthood was now irresistible.

At Vancouver the anxious broadcasting people were out in force to meet me at the quayside. I was whisked through Customs and rushed to the studio. I made my first broadcast in Canada ninety minutes after setting foot on Canadian soil.

There were concerts arranged in all the big cities from Vancouver to Montreal. And always it was success, success, success.

I moved down to New York. I sang in Pittsburgh, Philadelphia, Indiana. I kept broadcasting for the Columbia Company.

My lucky star continued to shine like a never-fading beacon. I had very much the best of two worlds. I was a concert soloist in the fullest sense. My repertoire was rich.

But I was also part-Scot and part-Irish. I could switch to the bitter-sweet, nostalgic folk songs that plucked at the heart-strings of dear, sentimental people who were proud to be North Americans but longed for a glimpse of a granny's Hielan' hame or the feel of the clean, moist wind blowing off Killarney.

I was a pioneer. There was just no one else in what you might call this particular export line. The remarkable thing is that up until as late as 1955 I had a monopoly of taking to the Scots and the Irish all over the globe the music of their homelands. I had by birth a foot in both camps.

I was enjoying this celebrity status before I had reached my thirtieth birthday. Everywhere I received the plaudits of the crowd, and he's a hypocrite who will deny the warm glow of wellbeing from this kind of experience. I was making a great deal of money. I could call myself rich.

In Canada and the U.S.A. I had time to think on these things. The Canadian winter is an Arctic experience. In Montreal I had to wear ear-muffs. For a time I was stranded in my hotel—locked in by snowdrifts six feet deep.

And in every quiet moment this decision of mine gnawed like a toothache. " Sydney, boy, you're a mug," one part of me whispered. " Look at how much you're giving up."

But the other part—the part that started growing inside a wee boy at the altar in Springburn—was equally persistent: " You will never be completely happy with only material things," it said.

I sailed home on the Anchor liner, *Cameronia*. And one of the first moves I made was to visit my friend Willie Brown, chaplain to my old university.

" I've decided to become a priest," I said.

I said it as off-handedly as possible. But inwardly I felt I was making the grand gesture. I awaited an appropriate reaction — like a father watching his son open up his Christmas present.

Willie didn't even look up from the papers he was tidying. " Oh, yes," he said, " we'll see the Archbishop."

He was as cool and unconcerned as if I'd said " It's started to rain."

He was not a dramatic person. He was never one to flap —as I discovered on that unforgettable safari with his aged, reluctant motor-car. But on this occasion I still have the impression that he showed no emotion because he wasn't really surprised.

Willie was wise. He was a brilliant student of human nature. I have always had the feeling that he knew all the time that one day I would make this very announcement. It was just a question of when.

Archbishop Mackintosh greeted me warmly and said I would do my studies in Rome. There were a number of seminaries throughout the world which Scotland used. It could have been Spain or France or the local college at Bearsden, Glasgow.

But Rome it was to be for me. And again I was plagued with misgiving. I was starting out on a seven-year course at an age when the brain is less receptive to study. I hadn't opened a text-book for years.

I had lost what you would call the rhythm of study. And this was perhaps the most frightening fact of all—every single lecture in Rome would be conducted in Latin—and my Latin was very rusty!

It was April, and my admission to Rome would not be until September.

It was agreed by the Archbishop that my decision should be kept a secret.

No one outside the family knew. I had still a number of concerts to do—and there were broadcasting dates from London as well.

I have always appreciated the value of publicity. It's an artiste's bread and butter. But this decision of mine was at this stage private. I had still six months of singing left. I wanted to be spared the embarrassment of being sought after by the Press.

One morning I was shocked to read on the news-stands, " Singing Star Decides to be Priest " was the headline announcement. Somehow or other the news had leaked.

Scots College Football Team, 1939.

Standing: Hackett, MacEwan, Brown, Sweeney, Morgan, McGurk (H.);
Kneeling: McKay, McGurk (T.), Banks, Cairns, Hoey.

With De Valera, Frank Aitken and Arthur Caldwell in Australia, 1948.

With Archbishop Mannix, on the occasion of a presentation to me from the Catholics of Melbourne, 1951.

With Cardinal Spellman and Countess McCormack (widow of John McCormack) after Carnegie Hall Recital, New York, 1955.

CHAPTER

19

I sang at concerts in London, Glasgow, Liverpool, Birmingham. I kept broadcasting. But I still had time that summer to renew my old love for the Clyde.

It's something we Scots may have forgotten, but this was the river that gave the world its first commercial steamship. James Watt, the inventor of the separate condenser, was a Glasgow University man.

And at Helensburgh Henry Bell adapted the new source of power for the craft that was to be a complete revolution in sea-going travel.

It was a comparatively modest beginning.

Bell's pioneer vessel was only 46 feet 6 inches long. It had a beam of only 11 feet 4, and a draught of 5 feet 9. Its steam-powered engine was fashioned by the firm of John Robertson, Dempster Street, Glasgow, and by present-day standards it would be a humble engineering achievement.

But it was the first steamboat on the Clyde.

In 1812, it was christened *The Comet*. And it was the beginning of another revolution—this time for the city-bound inhabitants of Glasgow.

At one time the Clyde had 40 passenger steamers. And suddenly the Glaswegian had access to a new, exciting world.

Although they were in fact his neighbours, such Clyde-side places as Kirn, Dunoon, Rothesay, Largs, Girvan and Ayr had been almost as remote as Timbuctoo. Now they became his playground—his convenient Riviera. The phrase that was to be Glasgow's escapist, away-from-it-all symbol, was born—" doon the watter."

I mention this because Messrs. Watt and Bell provided me with one of the great loves of my life. I grew up with the steamers of the wonderful Clyde, and for me they assumed an almost human significance.

They were my friends. Each and every one I knew by the colour scheme of its funnel—like modern boys can tell you the strips of every senior football club.

They were cheap and they were efficient. You could sail to Dunoon for two bob a time, and four-and-six, with dinner and tea, gave you the whole day's sail.

They rivalled each other for speed and beauty and the brightness of their brass-work. I remember the little *Isle of Skye,* a notable flyer in her day. Then there came on the scene the *Lord of the Isles,* and just about Bowling they sailed side by side until gradually the *Lord of the Isles* pulled ahead.

It was like an Oxford and Cambridge race on the Thames. The crew of *The Lord* waved their caps and cheered and some ribald remarks were made about the little old lady who was now past her best.

We thought Clyde steamers would go on for ever. In Scotland's West they were an institution.

We even had our own *Queen Mary,* until Cunard contracted John Brown's famous Clydebank yard to create the greatest ship of her time—a luxury liner to sail the Atlantic.

Such a floating palace had to have a royal title, and the choice of Cunard was *Queen Mary.* But Clyde Turbines Ltd. kept its little queen—by renaming her *Queen Mary II.*

That summer of 1938 I leased for three months a wee house at Dunoon, just to be in touch with the steamers. Even after the war—after sailing to ports all over the world in great luxurious liners, my infatuation with the boats of the Clyde remained as strong as ever.

When a priest, as a curate at St. Andrew's Cathedral, I always had the Tuesday off. And Tuesday was my steamer day. Never once in that time, come wind, come weather, summer and winter, in sunshine and rain, did I miss my sail on the Clyde. It was something of a weekly pilgrimage—like a regular date with someone dear.

These steamers changed our language. We talked not of grey, but Glasgow and South-Western grey. And a certain blue was always Caley blue—from the Caledonian steamship colours.

The steamers were such a revolution that the prophets got busy and predicted that all around that spectacular, jagged Atlantic seaboard of Scotland they would replace the coach completely.

It was forecast even that the land-bound roads of the West would become redundant and stonebreakers feared for their jobs.

But I was there that day the *Columba* was sentenced to death. She was probably the greatest of them all—for all of fifty years the pride of the fleet.

I saw this old friend in the wake of a tug—like a strong, virile man gone senile and blind with a young companion to show him the way.

The *Columba* was bound for the breakers' yard. And I had to force back a tear.

I returned to the Broomielaw not so long ago, and even the lamp-post had changed. It no longer carried the exciting sign—" To the Clyde steamers."

Only one of the paddle-boats now remains—the last paddler any one of us will ever again see. Her name is the *Waverley,* the same as that of her elder sister, once the flyer of the North British Railway Company's fleet and sent to the bottom at Dunkirk.

She was my favourite. And perhaps it's all a case of nostalgia—it was on to the North British Company's yards that I used to gaze from a kitchen window in Springburn.

As I sit in my study I can look still at the proud shape of the *Waverley's* jet-black hull with the red funnel tipped with black and white.

171

She is one of my oil paintings. I have more than 60, and my collection is reckoned to be the finest set of Clyde steamer memorabilia in this country.

If that sounds like a silly, sentimental, ageing man expressing in painted objects his allergy to change, I am certainly not alone in my eccentricity.

Every month in Glasgow 500 people gather together. The company is consistently all that large, despite television and its apparent widespread effect of inducing a state of voluntary domestic imprisonment.

These folk from every walk of life have one thing in common—a love of the Clyde and its steamboats. They meet to recall the halcyon days when " doon the watter " was a magic phrase that some of us thought would never die.

I am not addicted to a worship of the good, old days. They were good for the few, but frequently not so good for the many.

I nonetheless look back more often with fondness than in anger. As far as looking forward goes—I would not be so foolish.

Despite the great Clyde paddlers, the motor coach flourishes more grandly than ever. The roads of the West have not disappeared. Their network was never so complex, their motor traffic never so heavy.

And all that will soon be left on the Clyde will be those ugly vehicle ferries.

So much for the permanency of material things—even those built as solid as my lovely Clyde steamers.

CHAPTER

20

I set out for Rome with Paddy McCusker, a Glasgow boy intent on the priesthood also. Our families had been friends for years.

I was classed as " late vocation," a category that was viewed with wonderment as something of a phenomenon. Our ranks included teachers, doctors, lawyers, engineers, army officers.

Yet we were looked upon almost as freaks. Nearly all those who desired to be priests began the long trail in a junior seminary at the age of thirteen or fourteen.

Yet the original priests of Christendom were mature and experienced men. I can recall no one as young as thirteen among Christ's Chosen Twelve.

Rome even had a separate college for the oldies who got their lectures in English instead of Latin. This is where I had a mind to go, but the Archbishop decided it should be Scots College, a decision I have never had cause to regret.

Paddy and I took a taxi to the Via Quattro Fontane—the Street of the Four Fountains—and we found the place deserted. The college population was down to a solitary head boy named Hoy. He explained that the students were still up at the villa in the Alban Hills.

From the Archbishop I had two special concessions. Because of my previous studies at Glasgow, the three-year part of the course in philosophy was cut for me to two. And it was agreed that I should go home on holiday each summer.

For the others the seven-year course was a period of voluntary, unbroken exile from home. Only one complete break—after the first three years—was sanctioned.

In the searing Italian summer vacation, when the city became a giant baker's oven, even a street with four fountains was unbearably hot.

So the students annually lifted themselves, as well as their eyes, to the hills and settled in the college's country house at Marino, among the lush, thick grapevines that provided the fruit for one of the finest of Italian wines.

The head boy issued our students' raiment—purple robes, red sash and wide velour hat—and we should have felt proud in our gay, distinctive uniform as we set out for Marino.

But for me the assuming of the gown and hat was a gesture of sobering finality. This was it, MacEwan. This time there was no turning back. I'd really stepped over the frontier now and the brand was on me in purple and red.

I travelled quietly, thoughtfully, into the hills.

We got a warm welcome from the Rector, Monsignor Clapperton, and his second-in-command, Dr. Flanagan.

And Frank Duffy was there to greet us, he who became Mgr. Francis Duffy, Church representative with Independent Television. I got to know him as another Duncan, a splendid, versatile, natural musician.

I heard him play that very first night when the students had one of their concerts. My reputation had gone ahead, and of course I was asked to sing. I got the impression they were glad to have me. There was certainly comfort in their applause.

For still I was not completely committed—not within myself. I remember going out on to the villa's great, flagged patio and looking down through the warm, black ink of the night to a great assembly of beads of flickering light.

These earthbound stars were the lights of Rome. " Have you done the right thing?" I addressed myself in silence.

" Should you not be down there among the music and song and the joys of secular living?"

But now there was no turning back.

And the morrow began an eight-day retreat. I was back to the agonies of early rising and enforced meditation at six a.m.

I thought to myself: " All this nonsense again—how can anyone think clearly, let alone meditate at a time not far removed from the middle of the night, when the brain is still dulled with sleep and your very eyes won't willingly open!"

I'm afraid I frequently thought of nothing in particular and came very near to dozing off. Among my companions I swear I heard snoring.

Compared with the Jesuit establishment, this was a gay, exciting place. There was no trace of Manresa's neurotic atmosphere. This was a man's world—a healthy, happy community that had a bit of bite, a bit of muscle about its spirituality. To be fair, however, it must be remembered that Manresa was a novitiate.

The lecturers were splendid. I made friendships at this college that I will cherish till my dying day.

Friendships with men of great talent. Friendships with men of great intellect. With men of great sporting skill. Invariably with manly men.

It was the Scots College, remember, that introduced soccer to Italy. In the old days Scots College played teams like Roma which is now of world class.

It was still a college of such football talent that never once had it lost to the English College. Alas, it has this kind of record no more.

I was now in my 31st year. My enthusiasm for kicking a ball about was still as great as ever. The spirit was willing as ever to play. It was the state of things like legs and lungs that had me just a bit concerned.

But I went out feeling like a 20-year-old, and it was almost like riding a bike. The ageing fiddle had still a lot of tune. I found myself picked for the college eleven to play against the English.

If I'd turned out at Hampden for Scotland, I could not have felt more proud.

My doubts about my great decision began to evaporate fast. What worried me now was, would I make it? Would the old brain stand up to a new phase of learning?

The day I went to St. Peter's I was filled with awe and disgust. For years I had known this place from afar. This was the heart and soul of the Catholic Church. The largest holy place on earth.

From photographs I was familiar with its famous square, its great facade, its magnificent Michaelangelo dome.

The night before, I could not sleep. I lay awake like an excited schoolboy. On the morrow I would see not only St. Peter's. I was going to see the Pope.

That first real view of the basilica was like walking into a dream. No camera will ever do justice to this incredible monument to the skills to which man can rise, when his inspiration is God.

St. Peter's was an ornate Colossus—a medium for making tall men feel like flies inside a jewel-case. It can take a congregation of 60,000 people. Yet the whole was so proportioned to perfection that it was never monstrous, never grotesque, never failing in its atmosphere of holiness.

Into this most noble shrine the people came from every land. And whereas the dignity of cathedrals remains permanently intact, sometimes man can let his slip.

I was disgusted with the behaviour of this St. Peter's throng. They pushed and shoved and jostled for position. It was a saddening display of self—a gigantic brawl more reminiscent of a Glasgow cup-final.

And the most aggressive and inconsiderate, I'm sorry to say, were nuns.

Perhaps their religious fervour was to their credit. But I found them wanting in the bit about loving one's neighbour. To get to the front, they came near to knocking him down.

So that the maximum number of pilgrims could see him, the Pope was borne in on his *Sedia Gestatoria*—the processional chair, supported by eight strong men in velvet suits and breeches.

Up in the dome, the silver trumpets sounded the thrilling Papal March. Like outsize snowflakes, there was a sudden outbreak of waving white hankies. The mass cheering ebbed and flowed as if activated by an erratic wind. There was an atmosphere of ecstasy.

I felt my eyes flooding with tears. Many a time I have seen the Pope since, and always it makes me weep for joy, explain that how you will.

This was the great and glorious Pius XI, one-time Achille Ratti, outstanding athlete and mountaineer. He had stood on the peak of Parnassus as well. One of his previous appointments had been as librarian at the famous Ambrosian library in Milan.

He was small and sinewy. He brought to the Papal title a brilliant intellect married to an outdoor toughness and tenacity.

Following the annexation of the Papal States from the Church to the reunified Kingdom of Italy, Pius IX registered his protest by refusing to leave the Vatican. His successors did likewise. Pius XI it was who resolved the Roman question which had troubled Catholics ever since Garibaldi marched on Rome and the annexation of the Papal States to a unified Kingdom of Italy.

Eventually he reached agreement with Mussolini. And the losing of the Papal States turned out to be one of the best things to happen to Christendom.

It detached the Pope from the status of a mighty sovereign king, although he is sovereign of the tiny Vatican State. The Papacy was finally withdrawn from wars, battlefields and alliances.

The situation wherein the Pope was a virtual prisoner within his own Vatican created distress all over Italy among loyal Catholics who sought to be loyal Italians as well. Pius resolved the problem—by negotiating the Lateran Treaty with Mussolini's government.

The Vatican became its own little State, with all the sovereignty it needed to preserve its freedom.

Pius the Strong was also Pius the Courageous. His was the famous encyclical — " Mit Brendender Sorge " — that inveighed against Hitler.

I found it hard to associate this superman reputation with the pathetic little figure that was now being slowly carried through that yelling, elbowing mob. Here was but the husk of a man—a pale, frail, fading figure. The continuous gestures of his arms were as a cornstalk in the breeze.

It was soon to be the tenth anniversary of the Lateran Treaty's signing. I went back to St. Peter's to watch the preparations for the ceremony of celebration.

For the first time I saw the San Pietrini whose Christian calling must be the most remarkable in the world. For centuries their role has been to fly through the air to the glory of God—a sort of cross between angels and a circus trapeze act. Forty years later, I wonder if modern technology has made them redundant—I must check on this.

For the anniversary ceremony they were hanging crimson damasks hundreds of feet from the ground, high up in the basilica.

They looked like human spiders, suspended on ropes attached to the ceiling. They swung busily to and fro with seasoned skill and grace. Their ropes were so placed that no part of the great church was outwith their reach.

On this occasion their daring act of dedication was to be to no avail.

There was great excitement as to what would happen when Pius made his appearance at this tenth anniversary. He had sent out invitations to every single bishop in Italy, to be present at the ceremony. It was something that had never happened before.

He proposed to make two speeches. He was busy at their composition when he died. It was the night of February 10th, 1939.

Mussolini was reported to have said: " At last that stiff-necked man is dead!"

Back at the college there was only one topic of conversation. Why had Pius wanted all his bishops to be present? What was in his second speech, the script of which was never found?

It was known that he wished his end to be sudden. He wanted to die on his feet.

It was a heart-rending time for Italians—torn between their allegiance to their Church and a loyalty to their native land that was now hopelessly and helplessly enmeshed in Hitler's ruthless plan for world domination.

Was it the intention of Pius XI to die not only on his feet, but in full public view, with his bishops assembled in the central, sacred setting of St. Peter's?

And what historic, death-bed pronouncement had he planned? It was suggested he intended a statement of guidance to the Italians in their acute dilemma. There was also the rumour that he meant to depart with a final, damning indictment of the Fascist ideology.

We shall never know. Word got around Rome that Fascist spies had secured a copy of his second speech. But no record of any kind has ever come to light.

In these epoch-making events I sensed again a continuation of the MacEwan luck. Certainly the death of a Pope is tragic. But it is also the prelude to great excitement. It is not every priesthood candidate's good fortune to be in Rome when a new Pope is crowned.

CHAPTER

21

The college closed. Monsignor Clapperton—wise and considerate man that he was—scrapped the college time-table:

" You're lucky lads," he said. " You're in on the making of history. Get out and about and absorb as much of it as you can."

One of my particular student friends was John Morrison, Gaelic-speaking diocesan priest who still serves in the West of Scotland. He it was who achieved fame when the Army proposed to move into South Uist and instal a massive rocket-range.

John was then Uist's local priest, and he took time off from fishing his beloved trout to lead the rebel crofters in their fight against this Whitehall invasion of their native fields. He became known as Father Rocket.

I could never have predicted this role of rebel chief for John. He was a talkative, enthusiastic, delightful companion. He was near the end of his term of studies and knew his way around.

Together we went through the dark streets of Rome to snoop around at St. Peter's. The basilica was in darkness, except for the warm glow of light from innumerable flickering braziers in the Great Nave.

It was at once eerie and awe-inspiring. The doors closed and we hid behind the great pillars and watched the preparations.

This was the night of what you might call the preview. The dead Pope was being brought to St. Peter's for the eyes of the Italian nobility only.

As John and I waited, a party of young men approached across St. Peter's Square. In the semi-darkness the gowns they were wearing looked not unlike our own.

This was a privileged party of students from the college where Pius had started his priestly career. And as they filed past in threes—*in camarata*—John tugged at my sleeve and jerked his head. We tagged on behind the student procession.

That night in that giant church, lit by braziers, was something I'll never forget.

Perhaps this was going a bit too far in the carrying out of Monsignor Clapperton's instructions, but I have no regrets for our gate-crashing episode. Our hungry eyes feasted on sights that have always stayed with me.

I truly felt myself tingle with excitement. Not until the morrow was the Papal corpse to be displayed to the faithful thousands. We were that night in on the inside watching the scene being set.

We saw the body being taken down near the Confession of St. Peter, just above the spot where lie the bones of St. Peter himself.

Then we followed its journey to the Blessed Sacrament Chapel, halfway down on the right-hand side as you enter this holy place. Pius was placed on a catafalque, at an angle for all to see. This was how he would lie in the magnificence of his Papal robes for the next few days as the faithful filed past to pay homage.

Time was when a Pope's feet were placed through a grille, so that they could be kissed by the pilgrims, but the custom fell into abeyance.

Two nights later, we were back at St. Peter's, and this time with official blessing. As members of a Pontifical college, we students of the Scots College were invited to watch over the Papal body for one hour of its lying-in-state.

At each corner of the catafalque stood a noble guard—each a member of the Roman aristocracy—and we students from Scotland—40 in number—were arranged in between for our one-hour moment of glory.

I could have taken two paces forward and touched the very Papal head. It was a small head—an almost wizened head, on the body of a little man who looked even more tiny in death.

As a Catholic, I had no great feeling of sorrow in my heart. The Pope was dead. He had served his God nobly. And now it was a case of *Sede Vacante*—the chair of the Pope was vacant and awaited someone else.

But as I stood beside him on that momentous night, I thought of the enormity of this man when alive.

That letter of his against Hitler was a measure of his courage. It was the first great official document of an abhorrence of the Fuhrer, and all the Nazis stood for. As such, it astonished the world.

It was Pius also who struck fear into the heart of none other than Goering, the pompous and obese Nazi second-in-command.

When Goering paid an official visit, instead of a sovereign on his throne, he was greeted by this stern, diminutive man standing behind a desk.

It was Goering himself who later described the encounter to Commène, the Rumanian Minister: " You know me. You know I have never in my life lacked courage. But before that little figure all in white, I felt my heart jump as never before. For the first time in my life I was afraid. It's extraordinary, but that's how it was."

The French Cardinal Billot—the greatest theologian of his time—was another who suffered the demoralising power of this mighty atom of a Pope.

The wrath of Pius was directed against *Action Française*. Unwisely, the Cardinal took it upon himself to send a note of sympathy to the offending editor. And the letter was published.

Cardinal Billot was a great Jesuit, a member of an Order held by Pius in the highest esteem. But to Rome he was immediately summoned and the Papal interview was brief.

When Billot emerged from the Pope's library after only a matter of minutes, he no longer wore his Cardinal's hat. He was " reduced to the ranks." He went back to France and shut himself up in a house of the Jesuit Order.

The same fate would have befallen Cardinal Innitzer of Vienna, but for possible Nazi repercussions on the Catholic Church in Austria.

Pius was offended by the too friendly sentiments of Innitzer regarding Hitler at the time of the Austrian Anschluss. When the Cardinal—head of the Austrian Bishops —learned of the Pope's displeasure, he rushed to Rome. Pius refused even to see him.

Pius was a sovereign who was completely aware of his sovereignty. His Master of the Papal Chamber once said:

" Remembering our old friendships, I would never have believed that before Pius I would have trembled as never before in my life. He inspired a real feeling of inferiority, which did not accord with the paternal goodness of his heart."

This, then, was the little formidable giant who now lay dead on a sloping board. I remember thinking of the paternal goodness of the man—like the time he gave Scots College an audience and said to one of the students: " Scotland—that is a beautiful place. I am a mountaineer and in Scotland you have good mountains, but not so good as the Alps, eh!

" Now, tell me, is there really a Loch Ness monster?"

He had climbed his final mountain. He looked smaller than he ever had done in his life. On his feet were embroidered velvet slippers.

A couple of feet from his head stood a laddie who used to carry milk for the Co-op up the tenement stairs of Glasgow.

CHAPTER

22

The wonderful San Pietrini were busy again, switching the aerial damasks to sober shades in keeping with a Requiem.

Rome began to fill with celebrities and heads of State from every part of the world. They included a Papal Count who was also my personal friend—that most flamboyant, enthusiastic and dedicated of Catholics—John McCormack.

He invited me with him everywhere. " Guess who we're having lunch with today?" he said.

And at the table he introduced a plain, friendly, bespectacled man with an American accent. This was Joe Kennedy, America's British Ambassador, grandson of an East Boston Irish saloon-keeper. Eventually Joe was said to be worth 500 million dollars.

There were nine children in the Kennedy flock. Joe jun. was to be killed in the war that was already being borne in on the wind. In the subsequent peace he was to lose two more outstanding sons by acts of brutal assassination that shocked the world.

I was dining with the head of what must be one of the most bitter-sweet families of all time.

We were at the funeral in St. Peter's, and I can describe it no more accurately than a majestic performance. The body of Pius was lowered below, as close as could be to the bones of St. Peter.

What a strange feeling of contact with the distant past these vaults inspired with their cool, sunless tombs of departed Popes reaching back across the centuries. A complete and petrified history of Europe.

Prince Charlie is buried there—a leading figure in some of that history's most tragic pages.

While I was in Rome, there was constantly a bunch of white heather on his tomb—a gesture of remembrance by the Royal Stewart Society to the most romantic loser Scotland has ever had.

Now it was a case of the Pope is dead—long live the Pope. Pius XI was in his last unending sleep, and the world turned to the excited conjecture as to who would be his successor.

I went with John McCormack to the Vatican as the Cardinals trooped into the Sistine Chapel—that greatest of architectural gems—for the Conclave that would decide the Papal election.

They were mostly old, and it's hard for old men to be handsome. But in that grey, slow, stooping procession one figure stood out—the tall, handsome Cardinal Pacelli.

The key was turned behind them and they were prisoners for the duration of their deliberation. Time was when members of the Conclave had freedom to move around, a privilege which prolonged the proceedings to such an extent that on at least one occasion the citizens of Rome came near to riot in protest at the suspense.

The Cardinals were caged possibly that the discomfort might spur them to quicker decision. And their only link with the breathless outside world was an insignificant chimney set into a wall.

Black smoke from this modest funnel and the world was still without a Pope. White smoke for rejoicing that the Papal choice has been made.

It's all very primitive. The black smoke is nothing more romantic than fumes from the burning of the voting papers that have been inconclusive—aided by the addition of some damp straw.

This habit of announcing the most vital decision in Christendom by way of almost tribal smoke signals has not been without its twentieth-century critics.

" We have electricity," they say. " We have electronics and clever devices for flooding an entire city with light at the touch of a tiny switch. Surely the Pope deserves better than this?"

Would they have us flash on to a screen the new Pope's name? Or inscribe it in luminous writing on one of the Vatican walls?

I am all against turning the Sistine Chapel into a smoke-less zone. To an anti-smoking campaign that relates to that precious, historic, little Vatican chimney I will resolutely refuse to give my support.

This time the waiting looked like being short. According to John McCormack, it was entirely a one-horse race.

I suggested that no Papal appointment could ever be prejudged.

" It's Pacelli!" he said in that lovable, forthright way of his. " It's a certainty!"

Even as a statistical matter of sequence, the chances of Cardinal Eugenio Pacelli looked good. Leo XIII had been the aristocratic Pope. He was followed by Pius X, who came off peasant stock. Benedict XV, the successor of Pius, renewed the link with the aristocracy. And in his wake, from a working-class home, came Pius XI.

It was the turn, as it were, of the upper class again, and Pacelli was an aristocrat down to his very toes.

It showed even when we used to watch him relaxing in the Borghese Gardens—shorn of his Cardinal's finery and wearing simple black. He was still tall, impressive, regal. His face was clean-cut with heavily-shadowed jowl, as if he were always needing a shave. He looked the intellectual.

Pius had groomed him for the role. During an illness three years before his death, Pius was reported to have said : " If I were sure that the Sacred College would elect Pacelli, I would resign at once."

As Secretary of State, Pacelli had travelled the world. He was known and respected by Catholics all over the earth.

Of the 57 European Cardinals, 35 were Italian. Pacelli was also Italian. Of the 35, 26 were Roman. Pacelli was also Roman.

And among the Roman Cardinals there was an impatient mood that recognition of Rome was long overdue. There had been no Roman Pope since as far back as 1670.

It was not purely and simply a matter of prestige. Pius XI was from Milan and surrounded himself with Milanese.

It was a Papal prerogative to favour one's friends—Pius X was so loyal to the See of Venice in his choice of appointments that the jest went round the Vatican: " They've made the Barque of St. Peter into a gondola!"

Pacelli's personal record was brilliant. When he first came as a young man to the Secretariat of State, each and every one of his colleagues described him as the predestined one among them.

We were living in dangerous, difficult, explosive times, with Hitler tentatively on the rampage and the whole world threatened with unique upheaval.

The Vatican very definitely needed a diplomat. Everyone was agreed that there was no more skilled diplomat in sight than Cardinal Eugenio Pacelli.

It certainly looked as if dear Count John was backing an odds-on favourite.

To find out, we waited until 5.25 in the afternoon on the day following the entry of the Cardinals into Conclave. A plume of white smoke drifted out from the Sistine chimney. And fifteen minutes later, a St. Peter's Square that was packed with people, saw the famous balcony draped with the great fall emblazoned with the Papal arms. It had been one of the quickest Elections in history.

A massed hush as Caccia Dominioni, the Cardinal Dean, stepped forward to make the historic announcement:

" Annuntio vobis gaudium magnum, habemus Papam, eminentissimum et reverendissimum Eugenium—"

" It's Pacelli! " John McCormack shouted for joy with the gay abandon of a schoolboy at a football match.

" There's another Eugenio," I told him.

" No, no—it's Pacelli!" John persisted, and high in the air went his hat like a pigeon off with the news.

He never saw it again. Someone in Rome acquired a celebrated headpiece the day John McCormack got the Pope of his choice.

We both held hands and wanted to dance, but in that giant crowd we found ourselves singing instead.

I suppose the Te Deum in duet by myself and John McCormack should have been something of a unique musical event: nobody bothered to listen. They were too excited and busy singing themselves. We were two insignificant back-row members of the biggest choir in the world.

A mood of elation that night at the college. The Pope was back with his Church again, and this one had all the ingredients for greatness.

The college laid on a special meal, and there was wine from Monsignor Clapperton that we might all of us drink a Papal toast.

It had been a long, thrilling, hungry day. I tucked into my spaghetti.

This was a dish I'd never had before—not until I came to Rome. I must have surveyed my very first portion with a look suggesting a mixture of incredulity and mistrust.

I remember the smile of the Rector as he watched my first cautious moves towards this " stranded food." It was a smile that said: " You'll learn!"

Spaghetti I could now enjoy every day of the week—if only my figure would let me.

CHAPTER

23

I rose early that morning in March of 1939. This was the day of the new Pope's Coronation and 500,000 people would assemble for the event.

That's five times the Hampden crowd for Scotland versus England. And St. Peter's holds only 60,000—a gigantic area, indeed, but so insufficient on such a day as this.

So it was a case of admission by ticket only, and there were barriers and guards all over the place to enforce the regulation. We students got to know our way around. I had no ticket problem whatsoever.

I stood at first watching the gathering crowd in the square and chanced to look to my right. Suddenly I was back to my Saturday nights at the cinema in Glasgow.

What prompted this flashback in memory was a head of magnificent hair—and a vivacious woman to go with it.

Mary Pickford in Rome! Well, why not, I thought—and if it's her double, then no harm done. What woman of that period would not have been flattered to be taken for the famous star!

I walked over and put on my Sunday-best smile: " You *are* Mary Pickford?" I said.

" And this is my husband, Buddy Rogers," she said.

We shook hands. " Are you not going into St. Peter's?" I asked.

" We'd love to," said Mary. " But we left it too late. No tickets."

I'm afraid at this moment I showed off a bit. From my pocket I produced half a dozen tickets and fanned them out like a pack of cards: "Take your pick," I said.

We went into St. Peter's together. Mary was smaller than I had imagined, and when the Pope was brought in on the processional chair, Buddy and I hoisted her on to our shoulders so that she could catch a glimpse of the ceremony.

She would never see anything like it again. Nor would any of us. This was really almost the last of the Papal Coronations with all the trimmings.

Such colour, such dignity, such sense of occasion. The parade of the representatives of all the religious orders. The parish priests of Rome. The judges of the Rota. The Noble Guard. The Swiss Guard. The Palatine Guard. The office-bearers of the Vatican. The Papal Counts, like McCormack.

And behind the Pope that magnificent, outsize fan of ostrich feathers known as the Great Flabellae.

Pope John laughed at this item of tradition and said in effect: "No feathers for me!" Pope Paul dispensed with the Flabellae also.

Like the rest of the world, our Church is tending to break with tradition, to cut down on the pageantry. And the trend makes me sad. I'm all for a bit of show. Most of our lives need the occasional dash of the colossal and the spectacular.

And I'm sure the new generation that pretends to despise all traditional pomp and ceremony will come to regret their erasing of so much that gave some grace and beauty to living.

Already the young rebel against the new drabness and seek compensation in the riotous clothes they wear. They wrap themselves around with colour maybe because so much of life's organised colour is disappearing.

One thing of which I approve is the streamlining of most of our Church services. Even at parish level they used to be unnecessarily tedious, e.g. in Holy Week. Let's be honest, even with all its panoply this Coronation of Pius XII was tedious. It went on for hours.

Mary and Buddy knew of my concert tours, and next day at lunch we talked about travel in general and America in particular.

They invited me out to their house in Hollywood—a date I planned to keep one summer, except that very shortly the whole world was to change its course.

On the strength of that one meeting, however, a friendship flourished. That year an elaborate Christmas card arrived from Los Angeles. For years I kept on top of the piano a photograph which bore the inscription: "To Father Sydney with Fond Remembrance—Mary Pickford."

Later, when I worked in a parish in Glasgow, I started a youth club. One of its great fascinations were the photographs on the walls. We had just about every single film star—and each portrait bore the star's signature.

Our unique collection came all the way from the U.S.A. —by courtesy of Mary Pickford.

CHAPTER

24

That summer I lost all my inhibitions about studying for the Church. Scots College I loved. It was a gay, jolly, eventful place, and it had this gem of a Rector.

Certainly he saw to it that we worked hard, but there was opportunity to play hard also.

That year we students put on *Ghost Train,* and there was an ambitious production of one of the Gilbert and Sullivan operas.

Every Thursday morning I played football. In my afternoon off I was always around the Vatican, watching the parades and the comings and goings of personalities from all over the place, wandering through the Sacred Palace's art galleries and museums.

Monsignor Clapperton was a wise old bird. He knew that his Scots boys were far from home and wouldn't be back for years. The course of study was tough, and we were all of us under a certain strain. So the Rector chose to interpret the rules with benevolence and understanding.

Most of the students smoked, and one day Monsignor Clapperton told us: " You are all aware of the regulations. Smoking in your rooms is banned." Then he added, almost mischievously: " If you must smoke—please do use an ash-tray!"

In Rome there were more and more parades of the Fascisti Army and Navy. I'm afraid we British treated the Italian armed forces as something of a joke. With all their bluster and fancy uniforms, they always gave the impression of playing at soldiers.

I say that in no sneering manner. I love Italians. Were it not for my love of my native land, I would nominate Italy as my favourite spot in Europe.

But the good Lord never intended Italians to dress up in uniforms and carry guns. They are Europe's artists, and look at the legacy they've bequeathed to the world in art, music and craftsmanship.

History in its cruel way was about to cast men who were by nature creators in one of the principal roles of the 20th century's greatest and most tragic act of mass destruction.

The one I felt most sorry for was the pompous yet likeable little cardboard dictator, Benito Mussolini. Poor Il Duce! He was a man who set out to give his Italy a place in the sun and found himself hopelessly embroiled in the business of war.

With his Foreign Secretary, Lord Halifax, Neville Chamberlain came that summer to Rome, and students from what was then the old British Empire were assembled in the Vatican to bid him welcome—Scots, English, Canadians, Australians.

We were drawn up in lines like a reception party, and I shall never forget the look on his face as he entered that hall. Here he was in a hostile land—making what he must have sensed by then as a futile gesture at avoiding war.

And suddenly he was greeted by a resounding cheer. He came over to speak to some of us individually, and in his beady eyes I could see the excitement of his unexpected pleasure.

He visited the Pope, and when he came out of the Papal apartments half an hour later, the cheering was even more enthusiastic than before.

We turned out again the following day when Chamberlain and Halifax left Rome by train. We were allowed on the station platform as the British party climbed on board, and when Chamberlain opened the carriage window to say a short farewell, a remarkable sound was heard.

" God save our gracious King . . ."

Maybe I was at fault. Being a tenor, I pitched the first notes too high for most of the other students. So " The King " got off to a hesitant start.

Mussolini was standing close to the unofficial platform " choir," and who should urge it to greater musical effort than the Duce himself! He waved his arms like an orchestra conductor and repeated the Italian equivalent of " Come, on—come on!"

We were only months removed from the declaration of war.

Inwardly, most of us persuaded ourselves that of course it wouldn't happen. We subconsciously chose to ignore the logic of the situation and have faith instead in miracles.

When I went home for the summer vacation, I left behind my trunk and my fiddle. I never saw the fiddle again.

It was an imitation Stradivarius. A reasonable enough instrument, but no more valuable than thousands of others with spurious labels in attics and lobby-cupboards all over the world.

My brother had bought it years before from the Glasgow market known as " the Barrows."

When war did come, the Fascisti Red Cross moved into Scots College. And no doubt some Italian soldier thought one of his early trophies of battle was a priceless genuine Strad!

I spent that final summer of peace broadcasting for the B.B.C. and sailing the lovely Clyde. I sang from London with the conductor Stanford Robinson, brother of Eric. I did some broadcasts also with the B.B.C. Scottish Orchestra, conducted by Kemlo Stephen and produced by one of Kathleen Garscadden's " old boys," Howard Lockhart.

On the edge of the precipice, the country still laughed. What was left of the music hall made its jokes about Hitler, and soubrettes sang jolly, patriotic songs.

My mother was called back early from her school summer holidays. The emergency was by now so real that the plan for evacuating schools to the country was put into action.

Dr. Ryan was with me when I saw mother off with her boisterous, innocent brood. I affected sobbing and wiped my eyes: "My mither's awa' tae the war!" I said. And everyone laughed. We were still in the mood for jollity. There were young men impatient for the start of the conflict as a break in the monotony of their paltry, peacetime lives.

But, deep down, we who were older were haunted by the memory of 1914.

I decided to spend a week at South Uist with my friend John Morrison. The parish priest was Dr. Campbell, who later became Archbishop of Glasgow, and he asked me to sing in the local church on Sunday.

It was one date I never kept. In the peace of the Hebrides —through John's dome-shaped radio—I heard the voice of Chamberlain again—we were officially at war with Germany.

"I'm sure your congregation will have no interest now in me displaying my talents?" I said to Dr. Campbell.

He nodded in agreement. And that evening we were down at the pier instead, watching solemn young men go on board the *Lochmore*.

They were all of them, these islanders, in the Territorial Army—all Camerons or Lovat Scouts. In the dusk they were shadowy, silent figures, for already the black-out was in force, and even the steamer was a ship without light.

She sailed off into the darkness, and no one cheered. There were no bands playing this time.

In time of disaster the urge in all of us is to head for home. I was on the *Lochmore* the following night. I remember in the moonlight looking for U-boats over her stern.

CHAPTER

25

Rome, of course, was out of the question. I was told to report to the seminary at Bearsden, Glasgow. As a layman I had heard about the grim, Spartan regime of this place. I was willing to make allowances—to accept that outside gossip feeds on exaggeration and distortion.

But, oh, dear, the stories about Bearsden were all too painfully true.

It had some excellent men on the staff. Dr. Charles Traynor—the uncle of my student friend, Paddy McCusker—was Vice-Rector and took us for dogmatic theology.

From Dr. Johnny Conroy we got moral theology. Father Cahill dealt with philosophy and Dr. Sandy McQuillan ethics and scripture. Our spiritual director was Father Tom Murray.

Splendid men every one—splendid individually. But they all came under the influence of The Buff. He was Monsignor Forbes, the Rector, sometimes described as " a Pictish gentleman." He was round about 70 and looked to us like Methuselah.

I suppose you might call him a holy terror—to staff and student alike.

He presided over the establishment, exuding an atmosphere that was rather chill. As God is my Judge, I sometimes have him in an odd nightmare.

The world was in a turmoil, I agree. The bombs had started falling and whole cities were being destroyed. My own little life was undergoing a considerable somersault also.

I had been treated as a world celebrity. I had known the acclaim of the crowd, and my talents had been generously rewarded.

Having made the decision to be a priest, I willingly put all the glamour and glitter behind me. I sought no special favours. I was ready to accept whatever rigours and inconveniences my new choice of life should bring.

What I did not expect was to be treated as a schoolboy. And an approved school inmate at that!

By comparison, Scots College, Rome, was one big happy family. In the evenings, its staff were our friends. They joined in our discussions, they sang at our concerts and took part in our games.

The frigid shadow of The Buff was everywhere. When we walked in the grounds, no master raised an eyebrow of recognition—none except dear old Sandy McQuillan. What disciplinary risks he may have run for his friendly " Good evenings " I never discovered, but how grateful I was for his gestures of friendliness in this place.

If we'd stuck to the rules, I'm sure we'd have starved. Admittedly we were in the midst of war, and the rationing was strict.

But I'm sure even the soldier in some isolated outpost would not have put up with our hunger diet.

In my time at Bearsden we had fifteen cases of tuberculosis. Even in winter, the heating was negligible. I bought myself a sheepskin waistcoat, and wore it under my gown.

I had to wear gloves as well—and that was for sitting indoors! My room had bare boards and a hard wooden chair. My technique for maintaining some semblance of warmth was to sit on this chair with my feet in a cardboard box filled with straw.

Our basic diet seemed to be bread and marge. And the bread was inevitably stale. The nuns' idea of keeping it fresh was to cover the loaves with dampened cloths.

Supper was bread and marge, plus cocoa. None of us was able to drink the stuff. We used to hang about the supper-room for a couple of minutes then drift back to our quarters.

I grew troubled about the number of T.B. cases. I realised that I had a set of lungs that were tougher than average. Nevertheless, I decided to look after myself, even if it meant resorting to what some would call the black market.

Attached to the seminary was an excellent vegetable garden. We rarely saw vegetables. The nuns didn't seem to believe in fresh vegetables.

Some dark nights Paddy McCusker would join me in one of our rhubarb raids. Then we boiled up the fruit in the lumber room. We cooked cabbage in our rooms as well.

Twice a week I had an arrangement with my mother to have smuggled in two loaves of wholemeal bread. They were left underneath the gardener's shed.

Every week in the same, secret hidey-hole there was placed for me also a large beef sausage. It came from a Glasgow butcher who heard about my predicament. He probably had a special understanding of the hardship of a religious student. His son was training to be a minister— of the Church of Scotland!

We hardly ever saw eggs. There was an egg ration system for civilians, but ours was on a twice-yearly basis—Easter-time and Christmas.

So Paddy and I were forced again to embark on our nocturnal acts of crime. We found out where the seminary hens did their laying. From then on, after lights-out, we had frequent boiled-egg suppers in the inevitable lumber room.

In all my years at the Bearsden Seminary, I never once had a visitor. Thursday afternoon was the time set aside for students to receive their relatives. But it was almost like getting into Saughton Jail.

The youth who wanted to have his Mum or Dad had to climb to the room at the top and make his request to The Buff. Then he went downstairs and waited. And eventually a piece of paper would flutter all the way down the well of the stair.

This was The Buff's permission in writing. Then someone would shout: " Permission granted to Michael X to see his parents!"

How the students looked forward to their Thursday guests! For their relatives were aware of our hardships and inevitably brought with them what was called " luggie."

I never discovered its true derivation, but presumably luggie was what they lugged with them—the goodies that they could ill afford—to help keep their laddies in reasonable health.

But I told my mother not to bother; I didn't want her lugging " luggie."

The Spartan nature of Bearsden I could never understand. We had taken no vow of poverty. Our target was not a Trappist life. We were preparing for a diocesan priesthood—a life that has always been favoured with comfortable quarters and generous food and drink.

As I say, I could not blame the staff. Admittedly, at meal times they were a source of considerable envy as they sat up on their platform tucking into roast beef and gravy while we students were stuck with our Spartan diet.

I knocked one evening on the door of Paddy's uncle, Charlie Traynor. As I turned the handle, I was aware of an embarrassed scuffling inside the room. Charlie was an erudite man, a theologian and one of the finest teachers I ever had, but he must have thought my knock was The Buff. I found him standing facing the door, shamefacedly trying to hide a tiny, one-bar electric fire that he'd switched on to keep out the cold.

Once, when we complained about the cold, the advice we got was to " jump about!"

Some excellent students had been expelled from this establishment for such petty offences as smoking or being found in another student's room.

One of my contemporaries was a bright young man whose heart was not in the priesthood. The decision had not been his, but his mother's, and his every move had one thing in mind—to get himself expelled.

Ironically, he always failed. I remember Johnny Conroy doing his rounds and he stopped to speak to me at my door. Three doors along, the reluctant student was smoking like mad and the fumes came billowing out of his room. Radios were not allowed, but he had his wireless blaring.

Yet Johnny finished his talk with me and went away, and I know for a fact that Dr. John Conroy was neither stone-deaf nor devoid of sense of smell!

The student with no heart for his mother's choice of vocation finally decided on a desperate plan—to fail every single examination. In this, despite his intelligence, he was outstandingly successful.

So off he went one day to join the army. He turned as he walked down the driveway and gave the thumbs-up sign.

The Buff died shortly after I left Bearsden. And Charlie Traynor moved up as Rector. There were immediately changes for the better all round. The suppers, for instance, became more worthwhile, and the dreadful estrangement of teacher and pupil disappeared almost overnight—like the raising of an unseen curtain.

Charlie may have thought that it all came too late. On the day of his ordination, his nephew, Paddy McCusker, collapsed. And Paddy was never to serve in a parish. He spent his next two years in a sanatorium, and there he died. The cause of death was tuberculosis.

Strange as it may seem, I was very happy at Bearsden—the warmth and comradeship of my fellow students made one forget the coldness and remoteness of authority.

The Buff came from an older Spartan generation. He honestly believed this sort of regime was good for us. He was a man of prayer and he was eminently just, but, oh, how we would have appreciated a little warmth and kind-

"This Is Your Life."
B.B.C., 1963.

STANDING:

Sgt. Macpherson, Roger McDougall,
Peter Ciarella, Frances Boyne, Sgt.
O'Flynn, Harold MacEwan, Elizabeth
Boyle (*partly hidden*), Robert Wilson,
Eric Robinson.

SEATED:

Mary Stewart, Mother and myself

A " MAINLY MAGNUS " programme on the occasion of the 50th anniversary of the B.B.C. Most of those present started in the early days of 5 S.C., the Glasgow station. With me in the picture above are artistes who started their careers in Auntie Kathleen's Children's Hour, including Howard Lockhart, Gordon Jackson, Molly Weir, Moultrie R. Kelsall, Ruby Duncan, Grace ness. Nevertheless, he was " authority," and in those days we accepted authority without question.

On a day in June a year before the end of our training, we lined up in the Cathedral in front of the Bishop. He reminded us of our priestly duties and obligations. We were on the point of " taking the step "—the most momentous step in our lives.

We had one year to go of our apprenticeship, but this was the moment of committal—the conferring of the major order of Sub-Diaconate. One step forward and there was really no way back.

By this gesture we were promising ourselves to the way of life of the priesthood. It was a contract that from this point on could be broken only by special dispensation from Rome.

We took no vows of poverty, chastity or obedience—as is the case with religious orders. Nor can I recall any solemn undertaking in the matter of celibacy.

But let there be no mistake about this—every one of us was absolutely fully aware that celibacy was a part of being a priest.

What I did not foresee was that in my time this aspect of the priesthood would become a burning issue.

I am still of the opinion that the controversy over celibacy is no more than a peripheral problem of the Church.

It is not among the major problems. The really great and challenging problems, not only of the Roman Church, but of every Christian denomination in the world, are essentially doctrinal problems.

Our prime concern 2,000 years after His birth is how to bring Christ to the multitude.

But I am nonetheless aware that the traditional rule of celibacy in the priesthood is no longer as readily accepted as that day in June when I took the step.

It was something then that was never questioned— something that was as much an essential part of our vocation as getting wet is to the swimmer.

H

When we were students in Rome there used to be a lot of banter and good-natured leg-pulling concerning the " square-hatted boys " going home to get married.

The " square-hats " were those of the Eastern Church who were on the point of taking major orders. Their regulations allowed them to marry before ordination, but not after. They were intent, as it were, in achieving the best of both worlds.

There were some Americans who joined the Eastern Rites—for obvious reasons, but later this practice was stopped.

Celibacy we know is a mere law of the Church which originated in the Middle Ages. I think we all know in our hearts that it will go, but let's spare poor Pope Paul the further agony of this decision.

On 24th June, 1944, in Glasgow's St. Andrew's Cathedral, I was ordained by Archbishop Campbell—along with about twenty others. Some of them were Mill Hill missionaries. Five were my colleagues from St. Peter's, Bearsden.

The following day I sang my very first Mass. And the place was St. Aloysius', Garnethill. This was one of the places where my boyhood link with the Church was forged. This was where I sang in the choir and admired the priests and dreamed my dreams.

This was where my friends were. It was the Church of the Jesuits.

In those days there was High Mass which was sung and Low Mass which was spoken. Ninety-nine per cent of fledgling priests would obviously choose to say their initial Mass. I decided it would be good and fitting for me to sing mine.

That day at St. Aloysius' I must admit to some slight indulgence in the sin of pride.

The place was packed to the roof.

Certainly I have it from others that St. Aloysius' has never known such a day before or since. In the subsequent years I've been stopped in the street by many who've said with affection: "Father MacEwan, I was at your first Mass."

Kathleen Garscadden was there—and Howard Lockhart and the writer, Halliday Sutherland. They were with me at the banquet that followed—and I use the term accurately.

This was still a time of strict rationing, but the innkeeper decided that a Mass by Sydney MacEwan called for something very special in the way of food and drink. How he managed to achieve such a menu I never dared inquire.

One thing I treasured was a telegram of congratulation from a sick and ailing John McCormack.

Thereafter there were three weeks to relax at Dunoon— a holiday that was persistently plagued by the thought of where do I go from here?

This question of our various parish appointments had been a frequent subject of conjecture in the last weeks at college. And some of my chums used to rib me and say: "You're a cert for St. Andrew's, Sydney. You can't miss —I bet your name's down already!"

St. Andrew's Cathedral, in the centre of Glasgow and on a squalid bit of the Clyde, was the parish that nobody wanted.

The very building itself was grim and forbidding. And the Vicar General of the Archdiocese was Monsignor Daly. He was something of a bogey-man. His most common description was that of being "a tough old boy."

When the appointments were announced, I'm afraid I decided that the luck of the MacEwans had deserted me at last.

It was me for Bill Daly! I was to be the new curate at St. Andrew's.

CHAPTER

26

It was six years since I had travelled first-class. My celebrity days were all that distant. And the appointment of a humble curate to a district in Glasgow could hardly be classed as momentous news.

What did amaze me was that radio stations all over the world took notice of my ordination. Some made it the occasion for playing my records. The Australian network actually marked the event by putting on a commemorative hour of Sydney MacEwan music—coast to coast.

It was all very flattering. The loyalty of the good folk of Garnethill was understandable. But that so much of the world should remember after six years was a big and pleasant surprise.

The living quarters of St. Andrew's Cathedral were as comfortless and uninspiring inside as out. The floors were bare and the furnishings were old and faded. The place felt like something out of Dickens.

I was allocated a modest room on the top floor and for three nights I never slept a wink.

The cathedral was not only on a busy traffic route. Right opposite was an omnibus terminal that seemed to operate almost around the clock.

Great engines were revving and changing gear when I tried to get to sleep at night. There was still this infernal internal combustion racket long before the dawn.

But I was to discover that the human content of this far from desirable property was to make up a great deal for its other deficiencies.

Bill Daly was tough—of that have no mistake. He was a hard taskmaster, but eventually I discovered that he had a sense of humour.

That first week I got the impression that he was intent on stamping me into his mould. Not that this was unusual. It was still a time of downtrodden curates. The domineering, sometimes tyrannical priest was still all too prevalent.

Maybe the Monsignor detected in me the new breed of curate. I was not to be cowed. I stood my ground in argument. I refused to be overawed by his strong-arm technique.

It was probably not without significance also that he'd previously served at St. Saviour's, Govan. This was where my mother had taught for most of her teaching days. Bill Daly knew my family well.

Anyhow, the relationship that developed between us was pretty satisfactory. He was not the sort of person for whom I could work up any feeling of real affection. But he constantly had my respect—I respected him as a holy man, a dedicated man, a man who prayed hard and worked hard.

His day at the diocesan office was long. His parish was onerous—not only for its sometimes overwhelming burden of human misery, but because of its status as the Archbishop's church, a place of great ceremonies and important occasions.

Bill Daly always walked home—however hard his day may have been. Often there came from him the unexpected gesture of charity—as when he asked to see my book of visitation. He would tick off two or three names and say: " I'll do these for you on the way home."

His other side was the tendency to associate religion with gloom.

Once and once only was there wine on the table. He frowned on celebration and ignored even the traditional feast days. Our morsel of wine at St. Andrew's was restricted to Christmas Day only.

He took ill suddenly, and in hospital they diagnosed cancer, but the toughness of the man was not purely in his dealing with others. He came back and tried so pathetically hard to take over where he'd left off.

He was always the carver at table, and the sad, embarrassing evening came when his hand could no longer guide the knife and he had to ask for the assistance of his senior curate, Dr. Meechan.

He was taken to a hospital at Lanark and nursed by the nuns till he died.

As I write this, I look back on Bill Daly with kindly feelings. He was a good man. He was a man who was good for me.

We were given the keys to his desk to sort out his effects. To our surprise—and needless to say, our great delight—we found among his belongings a complete case of Chambertin!

This was a truly magnificent wine. The man who had been so sparing with the grape so far as his curates were concerned, had left this treasure to mature for years—dear old Bill probably had forgotten its existence.

It was a month before his successor arrived, and we certainly made up for so much lost time. It was Chambertin for lunch every day of the week. We even invited some of our friends to share in the luxury.

I missed out once on this daily pleasure when I was called away to Rothesay. The occasion was the funeral service of the Marquis of Bute, and Canon McQueen, the local priest, asked me to come and help with the singing. He invited also Canon Daniel, another of his friends.

We returned together, Canon Daniel and I, and on the steamer to Wemyss Bay there was one obvious topic of conversation: Who would be the new boss at St. Andrew's?

" One thing," I said, " whoever it is, there won't be any Chambertin left!"

I explained to the Canon our surprise discovery and the good use to which we were putting our unexpected gain.

He seemed to enjoy the joke. He certainly never once showed the slightest sign of disapproval.

What I didn't know was at that precise moment Canon Daniel was aware of the identity of Bill Daly's successor at the Cathedral. He'd had this advance information for one obvious reason—it was he himself who had been appointed!

Imagine my feelings three days later when the appointment was made public! And when the telephone rang and I was told: " It's a call from Canon Daniel!"

I could detect the chuckle in his voice: " Just thought I'd let you know I'm coming over to take stock of the Chambertin!" he said.

He was like a breath of fresh air at St. Andrew's. A delightful man with a great sense of fun. Suddenly our nights at St. Andrew's were comparative nights of gladness. There were films on our evenings off—some of the hilarious old Charlie Chaplin epics on my Boys' Guild projector.

It was as if somebody had pulled up all the blinds and the sun was constantly shining in. We dined as a joyous family unit, and the Canon was its presiding master who never let the twinkle go out of his eye.

I look back on this period with thoughts that are entirely happy thoughts.

The compatible team at the Cathedral included Father Dooley, who moved on later to become a naval chaplain. There was the dedicated Father Gunning for whom even the challenge of this wretched sector of Glasgow was insufficient. He now serves the poor of Peru.

We all of us had the common bond of music. Dooley was possessed of a fine singing voice, and Gunning was sufficiently skilled at piano to graduate L.R.A.M. Dr. Meechan, the senior curate, was the music-lover—the highly informed and sensitive listener.

It was Dr. Meechan who showed me round my pastures new, and oh, there was so little to make a gladsome noise about!

North Portland Street, Hume Street, Cadogan Street, Stockwell Street, Clyde Street, Balmano Brae—these were the by-ways of my district. And Rottenrow—the most aptly named of all.

This whole area was rotten—and verminous and evil-smelling and predominantly an insult to the dignity of man.

Despite my worldly experience, I was still in some ways naive. I had never known one Catholic family that did not practise its faith.

Here on this ugly bank of the Clyde there would be about forty per cent who had completely lost touch with their Church.

Nowadays, the sad fact is that forty per cent is the general average, but twenty-eight years ago I was taken aback by this state of affairs.

Yet I could never once bring myself to charge these pathetic people with neglect.

I was a long way now from Londonderry House. The sweet-smelling, good-looking world. The artificial world.

My fellow-man now was pale with hollow eyes. Sometimes he seemed permanently attached to a faded, flat cloth bonnet. If he had a shirt, it was without collar. There were thin, shabby scarves tucked into waistcoats. Often his wife sat hunched over a black and blacked-out grate.

We used to have in this derelict district our own Jesus Christ. Every Saturday morning when the priests of St. Andrew's walked to Confession, he sat on a wall at Garnethill. He was tall, erect and gaunt. It was the head that was Christlike—bearded, noble and with remarkable, sad, blue eyes.

His clothes were invariably rags.

One night I got word that one of my parishioners had been knocked down by a car. I tried the various hospitals, but at each I drew a blank.

The end of the trail was the mortuary where one of the attendants agreed to check up on the intakes that evening. I was with him as he pulled out one corpse after another in that depressing establishment's great, refrigerated chest of drawers.

I stood staring at the fourth container.

" Is that who you're looking for?" the attendant asked.

I shook my head and told him: " It's somebody else I know."

The corpse was that of my old friend Jesus. He looked even more noble in death.

You could call it, I suppose, a minor crucifixion. Our Jesus of the slumlands had died of starvation.

This was a world of orange-box sideboards and oil-drums for chairs. Of tenements linked by hollowed steps and smelly, suppurating outside toilets.

There were metal plaques on the walls of the stairs speci-fying the prescribed number of cubic feet per inhabitant. For the dwellers in these man-made caves, even God's good air was rationed!

I was daily face to face with abject poverty. To live at this level called for a strange kind of patient saintliness that had nothing to do with going to church.

How could I chide these people for neglecting their wor-ship? When the belly is so empty, it takes heroic sanctity to practise any kind of faith.

My days among such citizens of Scotland's premier city were at once revolting, inspiring, harrowing and comic.

I climbed up three stairs where hardly a complete pane of glass remained. I looked through the jagged ventilating gap, and down in the back-court rats preened themselves and played like rabbits.

It was close to mid-day when I knocked on the door, and as always the welcome was friendly: " Jist come in!"

They had no need to stand on guard. There was so little in their homes to stand guard over.

All I could see inside was an aged iron bedstead and a stale, stained cooker. There were three men in the bed, and one leaned on an elbow and said cheerily:

" Oh, it's you, Father. Sit down, Father!"

The trouble was knowing where to sit.

I leaned on the window-ledge and said: " Well, boys, you haven't been to Mass for a while, eh?"

" Ach, no, Father," said the speaker from the bed. Then as an inspired sort of after-thought: " T'tell the honest truth, Father—the Celtic's knockin' the heart oot o' us!" (Celtic is the football team that most Glasgow Catholics support.)

He brought out from under the pillow a crumpled packet of Woodbine. " Huv a coffin-nail, Father!" he said. " Dae ye less herm than the fitba'."

He could still share in his poverty-stricken state. He could still afford to laugh.

There was Paddy whose house was a single-end, but the first time I called, it stood out like a polished kettle. It actually had wallpaper and paint—and a rug on the floor. On the mantel shelf was a handsome marble clock.

" Hullo," I said, " I'm the new man on the district— from the Cathedral."

" Oh, aye, Father," said Paddy. " Very pleased tae see ye, Father. Is Father Ashe still there?"

I happened to know he was speaking of at least ten years ago.

" Naw—he's away now," I said. And we talked about the weather and the fitba' and his wife's uncle in the U.S.A.

Eventually I got round to: " You haven't been to Mass for a while?"

" Truthfully, Father, we haven't—truthfully, Father— no!" He called to his wife: " Here, Maggie, how long would it be, Maggie?"

She played up beautifully: " Now, wait a minute—three weeks, Father—aye, ah'm sure it must be three weeks!"

I said nothing about Father Ashe and how long ago that was.

Paddy, in any case, was anxious to change the subject: " Here, Father—you're a bit o' a singer, eh? Aye, we've

heard about you. Goat wan o' yer records, 'smatter o' fac'
—Maggie, put on the clergy's record, Maggie!"

Politely and patiently I had to listen to myself, not such
an ordeal as sometimes, for Paddy had equipped himself
with a very nice gramophone.

" Smashin', Father—smashin'!" he said.

" That's a nice gramophone—you've a nice wee place
here, Paddy. You'll be workin' then?"

" Me, Father? No' me, Father. Hear that, Maggie—me
workin'—that's a laugh!"

I remarked again on his trim, little home and casually
asked: " How d'you manage?"

" Crime, Father—crime all the time!"

What could I say? How do you start preaching morals
when the rats are on the wash-house roof?

One of my tenement doors was dingy and battle-scarred
with a slot for a letter-box that gaped as with a sardonic
smile.

My knock produced an immediate but unexpected reaction: out through the gap came the brief but friendly
advice: " Next door, constable!"

Again there were three in the bed next door, but this
time the one in the middle was female!

I tried to appear as if this kind of situation was an
everyday occurrence.

" I'm new," I said, " and I'm doing a sort of census—
getting to know the folk in the district. Now, maybe you
could tell me who you are."

Again there was an obvious spokesman: " My name is
James De Valera Farrell!" he said.

" And the lady?"

" That's the wife, Father!"

" And—er—this other gentleman?"

" Oh, he's no' in your parish, Father. He came oot o'
the jail this mornin'—he'd naewhere else t'go!"

Charity even in the midst of degradation—to the extent of sharing about all you had, the old iron bed and your wife!

I grew to love those people dearly. They were real. They were loyal. They were patient. They asked so little of the world, and in most cases it gave them even less.

If I have presented some of the lighter side of their miserable existence, it is not to set them up as buffoons. Rather to show their capacity for survival. They still had laughter—and not much else.

This was less than thirty years ago and nobody seemed to care. No-one other than the priest, the doctor and the district nurse, and, although we never once met, the local minister also.

The Locke Hospital was in our district, and that was the one that dealt with venereal disease. We had the Eye Hospital also—and four model lodging-houses—what a remarkable, euphemistic title that was!—and the city mortuary, and the big Royal Maternity Hospital.

The calls to the maternity wards were frequent, because even in such dread conditions, the world still went on in the shape of newly-born infants.

But there was nothing approaching the ante-natal care of today. No antibiotics or welfare foods. No regular checks of the mother's progress.

Eclampsia and child-bed fever were common. Childbirth deaths were frequent, and many a night I had to go into the operating theatre in cap and gown to give the Last Sacraments.

There is seared in my brain till the day I die the agony of one young mother.

God knows, the joyous occasion of birth was so often turned into tragedy.

What do you say to a hopeful husband when your news is that his first-born is dead? Worse still, how do you deal with a father who expects to visit a mother and child and instead you've to show him the corpse of his wife laid out on a slab?

As I say, such experience was my regular lot. And always with it the nagging " Why?"

Why pain? Why heartache? Why only for some?

The young mother I shall never forget was a lovely girl— lovely inside and out. All through the war years, her man was away and she'd held together the little home, and now they were together. She'd been faithful and loyal, and out of her marriage she was blessed with this baby boy.

The very day he was born, the policeman was at my door. There had been a works accident. Something to do with a giant press. The husband was dead. This was the news I had to take to the wife in the midst of her joy of first motherhood.

The ward was full and hers was the last bed I visited. It wasn't a case of postponing the evil hour. I had to warn the others in advance. I had no accurate notion of what would happen, but I knew it must be ugly.

She smiled. Her eyes sparkled. She was so glad to see me —here was someone with whom to share her joy.

" I'm afraid I've got bad news for you . . ."

How else could I put it? There aren't any satisfactory words for a time like this. But it was like producing a whip and lashing her radiant cheek.

You try to delay the blow and risk prolonging the agony.

She didn't seem to hear: " Your husband's been hurt— he's dead."

At least I had done the right thing in warning the other women. The whole ward was rent with that poor girl's hysterical screaming.

In that maternity hospital were many Catholic mothers who had been its guest so often that now they'd received from their doctor this ultimatum: " You must definitely have no more children. I recommend sterilisation. Another confinement could be fatal."

213

Their predicament might have involved me. I dreaded the day when one of them would ask me as her priest: " What do I do?"

The laws of our Church do not permit sterilisation. And abortion, of course, is forbidden.

But what if I prescribed complete obedience to such doctrine and the eventual outcome was fatal?

I was plagued by the fear of being faced with this kind of situation. We were told to say nothing on the subject unless we were asked.

I consider myself blessed—cowardly though it may seem —that in all my ministry at the maternity hospital, I was never once asked.

It was not unusual in those poverty days for the emotional strings to snap and another body would be pulled from the Clyde.

My very first call to the city mortuary was concerned with such a case. The body was bloated and ugly—a grotesque caricature of a human being.

That night I couldn't eat my dinner.

During your spells on call, you could scarcely leave the house. I had an arrangement by which I got a break in the fresh air by arranging to phone in every half an hour.

On these duty weeks my main port of call was a modest, little café about halfway to the maternity hospital. It was run by a delightful Italian family and they produced most excellent coffee.

They always conveniently served me in the back-shop. Little did they realise that their value to me went far beyond a refreshing drink.

They were such a gay, splendid, integrated family unit that the café became for me an oasis—a resting-point to make contact again with what I hoped was normality, when all around was so much tragedy and pain.

I had once to leave the coffee unfinished. The call was from the mortuary, where an old woman had been brought in dead—knocked down by a car.

214

It was in the afternoon. I performed the last rites, and her daughter asked would I please say Mass.

" She was in a hurry when it happened," the daughter said. " She was hurrying home to hear you on the radio."

Mary was a prostitute who hung about the riverside alleys. Sometimes in the soft, sooty Glasgow rain she would plead: " Here, Father, can Ah huv a staun in yer door."

She was always so humble, so aware of her inadequacy. She looked like a woman of 70. She may have been no more than 50. The ravages of her profession may have taken more of a toll than the actual passing of the years.

Her eyes were certainly young and alert. When she'd been on the meth or red biddy, she could spot my priestly garb a mile away.

Even when I was on the other side of the street, she would throw herself to the ground and, with outstretched arms and anguished voice, she would cry out to the dark, silhouetted rooftops: " In the name of the Father and the Son, bless me, Father, for I have sinned."

Sometimes she would disappear for weeks. But always she turned up at Easter. Mary never let an Eastertide pass without coming to me for Confession.

I'm sure the Lord would be lenient. I'm sure He would look upon the wayward Mary as one who was sinned against more than sinning.

The Cathedral was the target for scroungers—the sometimes alcoholic, sometimes ragged, always frightened few who are nowadays labelled misfits or drop-outs.

From the poor boxes of St. Vincent de Paul we had money to deal with this kind of visitor. But it didn't go far.

Those days at St. Andrew's provided no end of colourful evidence that necessity certainly mothers invention—and imagination also.

" Please, sir, Father, sir—can you help a poor man who's just about the end of the road. A tanner—anything, Father. All my family, sir, were killed in the blitz. This is me just out of hospital, sir. Beggin' yer pardon, Father . . ."

He was small and wizened, and his head and his hand were heavily bandaged. One eye had a turn, and he spoke with a stutter.

" Were you in the Infirmary?" I asked.

" That's right, Father."

" Well, you understand, it's just a formality—I can see you are genuine, but we have to check. Now what was the ward?"

Long pause and more pronounced stutter than before: " Er—er—ward—ward five, yer grace."

" Just you wait there a moment and I'll give them a ring."

I moved out into the next room. I raised the receiver, but there was no need to dial. A board creaked in the lobby floor and there was the quiet click of the front door being gingerly closed.

I went back and the bandaged man had gone.

It was fully three years later when Canon Daniel came through to see me and he sounded upset.

" I've just had to help out a terribly poor soul," he said. " His head was all bandaged and so was one of his hands, and he hasn't any family left . . ."

" Did he have a slight squint?" I asked.

" Yes, he did."

" And a wee bit of a stutter?"

" Yes, that's right—here, were you listening at the door?"

" I listened three years ago—but the story was the same. What did you give him?"

" Half-a-crown."

" Ach, well," I said, " if the red wine makes him happy. That hand will this day make a remarkable recovery, I bet."

The telephone technique must have saved our poor fund quite a little fortune. It wasn't a case of being heartless— we simply had to try and make sure that the genuine cases got what little we had.

The most persistent fable was the one about the dead mother in Liverpool: "Passed away yesterday, she did, Father. I'll need tae get down for the funeral, Father—and Father, to be quite honest, I'm skint!"

"And what's the fare?"

"Three pounds'll do it, Father."

"Very well—now just tell me the name of the priest in Liverpool. Three pounds is a lot of money, and we always have to check."

"Er—Father O'Malley!"

"All right—I'll just ring them up if you'll hold on a second . . ."

You left the room for no more than a minute and the plausible stranger had vanished.

You wanted so much to help them all—even those who lied and took you for a ride. They were always so hopelessly down—with no capacity of their own for rising again. Like little lost children.

We had one who just didn't fit somehow. He was shabby but trim—clean-shaven and lean with sad, inflamed eyes. He reminded me of an ageing film star. His accent was crisp and cultured.

"Terribly embarrassing this," he said. "Fact is, Father, I've been to the races and—well, to be quite honest, I'm broke. They cleared me out completely. Damned foolish, of course, Father, but you know how it is—and I've got to be back in Liverpool first thing—business appointment. I just wondered . . ."

I gave him two shillings. He offered no rebuke. He made no mention again of a rail fare, but backed out quickly, repeating his thank-yous as politely proper as ever.

There must have been a gap of about two years, and the day, I remember, was the Sunday nearest to November 11. In the vestry I was doffing my vestments when the stranger was announced.

It was again the prodigal punter.

"I've just been at the Armistice do," he said. "You know, the parade. Never miss it. Ex-Navy myself. Well, Father, the awful thing is some horrible creature pinched my wallet. I've got to get back to London and I thought perhaps—actually I've some clothing coupons here I could give as sort of security . . ."

"I've a better idea," I said. "Meet me at Central Station this evening at eight o'clock. I'll buy your ticket and see you safely on the train. How's that?"

He looked as if I'd slapped him on the jaw. Curtly he said: "You don't believe me, Father, do you?"

"Do you not remember?" I told him. "You were here before. I think it was Liverpool that time!"

His sallow face tinged with pink. "I must be slipping," he said. "Ah, well—no harm in trying."

As he moved towards the door, I suggested: "Why don't you come over to the house? Maybe you'd like to talk about yourself."

He was partly genuine. Certainly the Navy bit was accurate—he came off an affluent family and had achieved the rank of Lt.-Commander.

Now he was the complete alcoholic.

I gave him a pound. I knew it would immediately go on drink. But I hoped St. Vincent de Paul would understand.

I was amazed how goodness and mercy flourished in this slumland, with so much excuse for default. Just about every single youngster in that parish would nowadays be termed deprived or underprivileged.

Certainly they were tough. They were products of their environment. They might fight and they might sometimes steal. But in comparison with the affluent, free-and-easy, pagan present, the incidence of crime was paltry. Really serious, nasty, vicious juvenile delinquency was something I hardly ever encountered.

And I could claim to be in the thick of it, so to speak—by way of the Boys' Guild I ran in an attempt to bring some colour and significance into so many drab young lives.

We had our own football team and boxing club. We had a billiards hall and table tennis. And, my goodness, we had friends.

Our boxing shows on Sunday nights were sometimes almost celebrity occasions. The great world champion, Jackie Paterson, used to come along. I got tremendous help from that other champ, Johnny McMillan. He virtually adopted the club and brought along all sorts of boxers and trainers to coach and encourage my youngsters.

There was something exclusive and distinctive about those pugilistic occasions. Boxing got very close to my heart for the kind of character it seemed to attract. I was fond of the unsophisticated pug—the simple, uncomplicated man. Inevitably his rough exterior was a casing for a heart of gold.

I can smell those boxing nights yet—that peculiar masculine mixture of sweat and smoke. And there was warmth and excitement and tremendous cameraderie.

Boys came to the guild to hero-worship. There was rarely a night without some sporting personality—some Celtic star, or just as often, one of the Rangers stalwarts. We had football managers also—and my boys got their cue from real billiards champions. The great old veteran Ranger, Jimmy Gordon, was often there to lend a hand.

One morning a plain brown envelope arrived through the post. The note inside said simply: " Buy something for the lads." And with the note was a cheque for two hundred pounds.

My benefactor was Jimmy McLean, the well-known Glasgow bookie. He'd once been a St. Andrew's Cathedral boy.

That two hundred pounds gave us great prestige. We became the only guild with its own magnificent talkie cineprojector.

I had an arrangement with the distributors in London to lend us films for Sunday nights—at insignificant nominal fees.

We were in the entertainment business in a really big way. Those cinema shows on Sunday nights were inevitably packed. I had no opposition. There was no need to go for big star attractions. Our strength was in the fact that our picture house was free. For most of those youngsters it was therefore the only show. They hadn't a bean for any other.

I wish I could have said that my Sunday mornings were as flourishing as my Sunday nights. We had a Boys' Guild with a wonderful social life. But the spiritual aspect was nothing like so healthy. The audience for Mass, I'm afraid, was never a mass audience—so far as my boys were concerned.

For me the crime and murder films were always a bit tame. As unofficial chaplain to the High Court, I was regularly in touch with the real thing.

I met up recently with an old friend who is a judge: " Remember the atmosphere of a murder trial in the old days?" he said. " All the tension and high drama?"

I recalled a notable occasion—the time when one of my parishioners was tried twice for murder. It was the only such case on record.

" There's no tension now," the judge said. " All that's past. A murder trial nowadays has no more atmosphere than a case of serious assault."

There must be something wrong when we all get blasé about the business of taking human life.

I'm a fervid police fan. After working with the force so much in those Clydeside days, I accept the trite phrase about our police being wonderful as absolutely accurate.

I had my friends on the beat, like Sergeant Macpherson who used to meet me in the black-out at the junction of Clyde Street and Stockwell Street, and together we'd walk to the mortuary—or call in at a doss-house.

There was usually an invitation back to headquarters for a gossip in the early hours and the inevitable cup of tea.

The latter was a comfort that I usually had to refuse. I was due to say Mass with the coming of the dawn, and our fasting laws dictated that food and drink were not permitted any time after the midnight preceding the act of worship.

It was an era of strict obedience. However difficult the restrictions sometimes appeared to be, they never once were questioned.

My friendship with the force extended from the man on the beat to the top. The Assistant Chief Constable, George McLean, was one who was constantly a great source of help; and Charlie McNeill, Chief Superintendent, who was eventually killed in a motor crash.

When any of my lads from the guild was in trouble, I could depend on getting from such men in blue not only a very square deal, but no small amount of compassion and understanding.

I suppose it could be said I repaid them in part with song. I was a regular performer at police concerts—and at some of the more exclusive get-togethers for policemen and their families.

" I would ask you all to remain seated, as after some persuasion, Father MacEwan has consented to illustrate my most interesting talk by singing one or two songs."

I was always booked by the polis—in the nicest sense of the word—for their annual private Burns suppers. And, since they were Friday night affairs, again I presented a problem—this time regarding the haggis.

The best of haggises—as every Scot knows—is not lacking in good meat content. And our Church, as I say, was strict on such things—no Friday eating of meat was permitted.

My policemen friends overcame this hazard by introducing a special Father MacEwan haggis—a small, personal model that I could take home with me intact and enjoy at my leisure for Saturday's lunch.

For years the pleasant relationship continued—even when I was transferred from the city to Lochgilphead in Argyll.

Every January I would drive down to Glasgow and, having sung for my supper, return with the haggis, all neatly wrapped.

There was one break only in the sequence. It was a year of severe frosts, and the Argyllshire roads were as treacherous as a skating rink.

I phoned up George McLean to explain that for once I'd have to miss my date with the Bard.

The following Monday a car drew up outside my Lochgilphead cottage, and out stepped a traveller with a brown paper package.

It was my haggis from the polis. I think I enjoyed that one even more than the others.

I listen with interest to the quaint little jingles that serve as lyrics in the folk music idiom. I'm sure there is here the cue for that kind of song. Something on the lines of: "How Father MacEwan's haggis finally got its address!"

Not that I am a haggis fan. I find that a little goes a long way, and it helps if the fatted meal is doused not ungenerously with a drop of genuine malt whisky.

I should point out that the police had rules about abstinence as well. Strong drink, for instance, was quite taboo at these social occasions in the Glasgow Headquarters. Officially that is.

I started off by sitting among the honoured guests, and the top table refreshment was never more potent than lemonade.

But one year the Chief Constable leaned over and said: " Have you noticed anything, Father, about the lemonade at the other tables? You'll see it's always yellow."

Thereafter I forsook the privilege of sitting with the Chief and chose a place in the body of the hall where the lemonade bottles were mustered at attention at regular intervals along the communal tables.

Their contents, I thought, had always the fine warm glow of fermented barley!

It was the companionship of these occasions that gave me the greatest pleasure. For the average Burns supper I quite honestly wouldn't give tuppence.

I cannot rid myself of the feeling that the annual ritual is a completely phoney affair. Would it be unkind to suggest that 99 per cent of the worshippers of Rabbie haven't read a line of his worthy verse from one January to the next.

There is something ridiculous about the maudlin and starry-eyed principals who never tire annually to remind the world that Robert Burns was the greatest poet that ever lived!

I give way to no man in my admiration for Burns. I have sung Burns and read Burns. I have made the pilgrimage to the place he lived, and trodden the fields that he ploughed, but I'm sure he himself would be the first to agree that this annual insistence on his all-time greatness is not only embarrassing but inaccurate as well.

Have his sometimes frenetic devotees researched the treasure house of poetry and discovered such masters as Keats and Wordsworth, Goethe, Dante or Shakespeare himself?

I don't think it would do dear Robert harm if we Scots got his worth into proper perspective and thereafter adjusted—soberly—our January adulation.

He is a major poet—one of the greatest in the world.

Our weekends at St. Andrew's were filled with Confessions—on Friday nights and the Saturdays from four o'clock non-stop till nine.

This was a line of business that never suffered slump. Week after week the queues would form. It was challenging and exciting work, but always there was this exhausting pressure—the conflict between the will to help solve the most complex of personal problems, however long it might take, and the knowledge that out in the church were rows and rows of people with anxiety etched into their foreheads and eating into their finger-nails.

Not all of them were from our parish. Those with harrowing, intimate heart-aches came from all over Glasgow, attracted by the fact that at St. Andrew's they were unknown.

So many of my own folk found that opportunities for sinning were limited when you lived below the poverty line.

Rather was their principal Devil defined by two capital letters. These were days before the break-through of sophisticated drugs and T.B. stalked the slumlands and struck fear into the hearts of the lucky ones and death in the lungs of the others.

Tuberculosis in such a dungeon environment could be a rapid killer. Three months you might last before the blinds came down. Those fortunate enough to get away to wide-open spaces with clean, fresh air, might steal an extra year of living. Or three years even—in the rarified atmosphere of some sanatorium set in the sun.

For the great majority this kind of reprieve could only be a dream. A pleasant walk from the place I write stands a fine stone building set on the hill just below the golf course. It used to be known as Grampian Sanatorium. Now it is an old folk's home, because its trade in treating the killer-disease dwindled to almost nothing.

But on Clydeside thirty years ago my heart was broken by the number of people who would have given their right arm for admission to just such a haven.

Their rejection was not for the want of trying on my part. I had access to the City Chambers and the local health authority by way of a relative of mine called Alice Cullen. She was a woman dedicated to helping the poor and later became Member of Parliament for Gorbals, but even she had to turn me down so often. There just weren't the hospital beds to cope. Somebody pale, somebody coughing, had to be told the remedial inn was full, and I knew I'd be back in a matter of months to give the last rites.

It was the only time these parishioners of mine seemed to matter in the world. In life they were forgotten. In death they were important.

Even their very hovels were transformed. Somehow neighbours managed to produce clean white sheets with which to drape the scaly, slimy, germ-laden walls.

The coffin was laid on three chairs in the kitchen.

Temporarily, a slum attic had to be its own church. It was only the toffs who could take their dead to the Cathedral.

This was the impression that my parishioners had—they were too poor and ragged to appear in the House of God.

In the case of St. Andrew's the impression was wrong, but, with a sense of shame, I have to admit that parishes there were where Church Requiems were only for the well-to-do. I remember when my granny died, it cost £5 to take her to church. All that's past now, I'm glad to say.

A table in the funeral house was always laid out with tobacco and snuff and a neat skeleton-like row of clay pipes. This was a throw-back to the days of the wake—the custom that began as a good Christian gesture by which neighbours came in to console the bereaved—in some cases to keep them sane in their sorrow.

But the bottle was introduced as part of the act of forgetfulness and the wake degenerated so much into an orgy of boozing that it was eventually banned by the Church.

Very curious customs surrounded the dead in Ireland in former days. They all sprang from the Celtic belief (older than St. Patrick) that the dead do not die. Tobacco pipes were often left on graves instead of wreaths, and at old-fashioned wakes offerings of snuff were piled on the navel of the corpse, from which each friend took a pinch. Hence the familiar greeting of old folk exchanging snuff: " I never took a better pinch off the navel," followed by the time-honoured response: " May the souls of all yours rest in peace by the grace of God."

In the slums of my old parish in Glasgow, the pipes and snuff were still there, but no longer on the corpse—the snuff was still there, although few people snuffed even 30 years ago.

The poorer the setting, the harder I tried to give of my best on those heart-rending occasions.

Long before the vernacular was officially approved by the Church, I was reading my funeral services in English. How could I do otherwise? It would have been an insult to folk who were already deprived and ignorant. This was their important day—perhaps the only day of significance in their lives.

How could they be consoled in Latin?

The hovels of the St. Andrew's parish have all of them now gone. The greatest act of charity was to bring in the bulldozers and wipe this filthy, festering sector off the face of Scotland.

It's an area now where the sun can get in.

I found at this stage in my career that for a priest to have been something of a personality could be a very mixed blessing indeed.

My mail continued to be so heavy, it was almost impossible to cope with the flood of inquiry that had nothing to do with the Church at all.

There were letters wanting to know the numbers of specific records, about the origins of songs, about arguments concerning musical data.

I was inundated with samples of the work of aspiring composers and lyricists; and a grand new invention appeared in Glasgow that many a time I came to curse.

To record one's voice had been the exclusive privilege of the established artiste; people used to say how wonderful it must be to listen to yourself.

They were wrong, of course. The sound of one's own voice is at best a considerable surprise, at worst a deflating shock. We all of us have this built-in conceit—that the oral sounds we make, be it by way of speech or song, are a lot more attractive than in fact is the case. The play-back brings us down a peg.

Now this experience was available to all—just by walking into a music shop. If my generalisation is accurate, it certainly didn't act as a deterrent to many. As well as letters, I was inundated with the indifferent recordings of hopeful young singers and composers, and very few had heard about a stamped addressed envelope.

One man sent me a great pile of material that would have involved lots of time and expense to repack and send back. So I left it to be reclaimed.

The result was a most abusive letter accusing me of being callous and indifferent to the efforts of those less fortunate than myself:

" Dear sir," I wrote back, " if you sent me an elephant, would you expect me to parcel it up and return it at my own expense?"

There were visitors, too, by the score. It created such havoc with the Cathedral staffing arrangements that something had to be done.

I realised it was all very flattering. Many of these callers were faithful admirers who simply wanted to shake my hand. Had my position as an artiste been normal, I could have been discreetly screened from this kind of adulation, but I was a priest now, with a job to do, and the chapel-house door was ever-open to all.

So the strict regulation had to be made—no visitors unless on parish business.

This procession of fans continued even when I moved to Lochgilphead. So much so that I had to put up a notice —both at the door of my home and the entrance to my church:

" The number of social calls at the presbytery in the summer months has become so great," it said, " it is regretted that such calls can only be accepted when the visitors are personally known to Canon MacEwan."

Every week at St. Andrew's there were also people who wanted me to hear them sing. Again this demand had to be put on an organised basis.

With Father Gunning, the priest who was such an excellent pianist, I arranged to hold auditions in the parish hall on Monday afternoons.

We must have heard hundreds, and to every one I made this clear before they ever breathed a note—they must be prepared for criticism that might be almost ruthlessly frank.

This was not being unkind. I had the girls in mind particularly—the ones whose friends were convinced they had wonderful voices and " all you need is a break!"

I'd had so much experience of this before—the singer who so impressed her own little circle that her head became filled with exciting thoughts of one day being a star.

Hope can be a comforting thing, but I have seen lives ruined by the kind of hope that is falsely based. I have seen young women so obsessed with the prospect of becoming celebrities that they let the best years of their lives slip away and even destroy their chances of marriage. Their eventual disillusionment could be a cruel and bitter experience.

228

My honesty, however, was not always appreciated. I told one young man: "Your voice is quite nice—but I don't think you'll ever make your living by it—certainly not a particularly good living. Go on singing and enjoy your singing, and if you make a bob or two by it, well, that's fine; but stick to your trade and let singing be your hobby."

Oh, my goodness, such a harvest of abuse I reaped from the sowing of such words of friendly advice. I was accused of being jealous of this young man's skill. "You're afraid of the competition," he said.

And he went so far as to challenge me to a singing contest in any hall of my choosing. He even listed his choice of "informed and fair-minded judges"—three priests who were well known as authorities on plain-chant—a subject on which there would be about another 10,000 whose authority was equally impressive!

One of those sometimes frustrating Monday afternoons a girl in her teens turned up. A modest, pretty, dark-haired little lass who looked as if she could well do with a good, substantial meal. Her clothes were shabby and obviously second-hand. She looked gawky and ill-at-ease.

Almost as soon as she started to sing, I called out for her to stop. Father Gunning ceased his playing and got up from his seat.

This was the sort of voice that sent shivers up your spine and seemed to charge the little hairs on the back of your neck with some kind of electric shock.

I knew by the look on Gunning's face that his neck was bristling also!

"Hold on a minute," I said, and off I dashed to the chapel-house in search of Dr. Meechan.

"We've got a girl you simply must hear," I told him excitedly. "She's got the voice of an angel."

He puffed placidly at the inevitable pipe. "An angel, Sydney?" he said. "That sounds interesting!"

Eventually his enthusiasm was as great as my own.

I was convinced that we had on our hands a potential singer of world repute—I remember thinking: " Another Tetrazzini."

And I decided on something I've never done since—I told this girl I would be her coach.

" I can't teach you any singing," I said. " You've got that already. But if you can come along for an hour on Mondays, we'll see what we can do about giving your voice that extra bit of polish."

She was my " pupil " for a year. I put the word in inverted commas because, basically, the girl had nothing to learn. The voice was there—as pure and thrilling and natural as a nightingale's.

What I was able to do was impose upon it a technique. I tried to give her musicianship. I extended her range with the standard exercises. I widened her repertoire.

I listened to her reading, and her speech was as broad as a West of Scotland Eliza Doolittle. This speech-training was important. If you speak like a navvy, you most likely will sing like a navvy. Not—let me hastily add—that I have anything against navvies!

The exciting thing was the way she responded to all our efforts. At the end of the year I had made up my mind—this young woman who had walked in off the street was ready for the Royal Academy.

My old friend, Sir John McEwan, was no longer Principal, so it wasn't as simple as making a long-range recommendation.

She would have to go down to London and sell her own wares. A lady who was a friend of the Cathedral agreed to provide her with attractive clothes. I paid her fare and waved her off with not one twinge of misgiving.

The scholarship was hers almost for the asking. She sang herself into the Royal Academy. And thereafter her progress was exceptional.

She was awarded the accolade reserved for young artistes with the greatest potential—a Caird Scholarship.

Now she could travel and extend her experience still further. She chose Vienna.

When she came back, I happened to be in London for a series of recording sessions, and it was arranged that she should sing for me at the Royal Academy.

She got the star treatment—the Duke's Hall with a full orchestra to support her. That was one of the most memorable moments of my life. My protégé was all I had hoped for and more.

I went back to Glasgow completely convinced that an absolute world-beater was about to be launched.

But nothing happened. Not one thing.

Her letters became less regular and eventually petered out completely. Dear Oscar Preuss rang me to tell me she hadn't turned up at the recording studios where I had arranged an audition.

I learned from her parents that she'd found a boy and was married. It was a union for which they had no great enthusiasm. Probably it was because they, too, had great hopes for their lassie. Probably because the husband was of a different faith.

To this day I have no knowledge of how her life has turned out. What I do know is that the one and only star I ever discovered died virtually before it was even born.

I hope she is happy in the life of her choice. That's all that really matters.

But I cannot escape a feeling of sadness. In all my life there has been no other unknown voice that I could truly describe as magnificent.

I felt like someone who'd found buried treasure and forgotten to mark the spot.

One morning the St. Andrew's mail included a letter that bore an Australian postmark. It was from my old friend, Archbishop Mannix. The great Mannix himself was reminding me that the Melbourne Archdiocese was about to celebrate its centenary.

And this was the exciting bit—could I come out as his guest for the great occasion?

I'm afraid my excitement was pretty short-lived. I was still an extremely humble cog in the great wheel of the Church.

The long sail to Australia and back again would mean leave of absence of about six months. What hope had an insignificant curate in Glasgow of this kind of concession?

I read the letter a number of times. I sat on my own in Glasgow Green and pondered the attractions of such a journey. It was all of twelve years since my last trip " down under." And Australia had done me proud. Its pull was still persistently strong.

I decided to chance my luck.

One of the things that encouraged my boldness to ask at all was the fact that Glasgow had as Archbishop Dr. Campbell—the man I had known as plain Father Campbell in his former modest capacity as parish priest at Barra.

Upstairs in his office, I still had certain misgivings: " I've been invited out to Australia," I said as casually as I could.

His eyes twinkled.

" Oh, yes," he said, " the centenary celebrations. As a matter of fact, the bishops have been invited, but none of them will manage."

I could almost feel my confidence oozing out through the soles of my boots. If none of the bishops could get away, what hope for me?

But the Archbishop's eyes hadn't lost their twinkle.

" I've an idea," he said. " We'll send you out to represent the bishops."

I could hardly believe my ears. Me—a mere curate—to act as representative for the entire Scottish hierarchy!

Right there in the Archbishop's office I felt like doing a dance.

" There's just one thing," he went on. " We can't have you away for a whole six months."

Somehow I didn't react to this possible set-back. I felt deep down that the trip was on—that whatever the difficulties, I would be there."

Then Archbishop Campbell came up with the answer: " How about flying? Do you fancy flying?"

Would I fly? I was so keyed up about the whole affair, I could have offered to go by row-boat!

I came near to flying when I left the Archbishop's office. I was down those stairs three steps at a time.

It wasn't until later that the cold reality of going all that way by plane began to register. Travel by air was not yet an everyday affair—especially to the other end of the earth, and my one and only experience of aeroplanes had not been exactly encouraging.

I was returning from Ireland with a party of priests after singing in the Opera House at Cork.

Whatever it was I had for supper, there followed a nightmare in which the plane I was flying in went on fire and plunged into the sea.

It was all so vivid that I really felt it might be a premonition, and if ever there was a morning for paying due attention to premonitions, this was it.

December was at its very worst—rain and sleet made horizontal by a fierce, relentless gale.

" Think we'll fly?" I asked the others, trying to sound indifferent.

All I really wanted was someone to say that the flight would be off.

" Sure we'll fly!" said one of the priests.

"Och, yes, Sydney! We'll get away all right!" said another.

And when I phoned the airfield, a jolly voice replied: " Flight's definitely on, sir—don't worry!"

Don't worry! I *wanted* the flight to be cancelled!

The gale was at its height as we walked across the tarmac. You just about took off without the help of a plane.

I

The nightmare was followed by a nightmare flight. It was terrifying. There were so many air-pockets, it was like repeatedly falling off a wall. Everyone was sick.

I decided that if we ever made it, I'd never go near a plane again.

And here I was making all the preparations for flying halfway round the world!

CHAPTER

27

I was booked to leave from Southampton—by flying-boat. Somehow I found the flying-boat bit a comfort. I have always had a love of the sea. It was quite illogical, I know, but there was something less frightening about the possibility of crashing on water than on land. Illogical because I understand that hitting the sea from a height is like making contact with reinforced concrete.

The old Sunderland took it leisurely. Over to Marseilles and an all-night stop. I took the chance to go with some of the other passengers to a friendly little estaminet in Aix en Provence. In the bar we found a pleasant chap playing the piano.

One of the passengers let out that I could sing, and of course there was the request for a song.

" Do you know ' Bird Songs at Eventide '?" I asked the café pianist.

To my surprise he rattled out that lovely, little, fragile introduction. He'd spent most of the war years in England.

When we reached Cairo there was something of a musical welcome again. The man who was there to meet me at the airport was Gerald Shaw—one of the last survivors of that body of displaced persons, the cinema organists.

Gerald took me to dinner and we talked of old times. He was at one time something of a celebrity in a number of London cinemas, but the times we recalled in Cairo were his days at the Regal, Glasgow.

I stayed that night in Shepherd's Hotel. I was back on the first-class luxury circuit — one of those privileged periods in my strange, mixed life that made me all the more bitter about the awful conditions of my dear, helpless folk in Rottenrow.

Our scheduled route from Cairo should have missed the Pyramids, but by this time I had struck up a friendship with the pilots and they were persuaded to make the slight detour.

Not only that. In a Sunderland you can actually go upstairs. " Not a word to anyone," one of the pilots said. " But once we're up, go upstairs and I'll leave the cabin door open."

So I got my first sight of the Arabian Desert from the vantage point of the " driver's seat." And across that great wonderland of sand came a Scots voice on the aircraft's wireless: " Rangers, 1—Morton, 1." It was the result of the Scottish cup final of 1948.

I took the chance of the stop-down at Rangoon to visit the shrine that is to Buddhists what St. Peter's is to Roman Catholics—the great golden-domed Shwe Dagon pagoda. I walked along this great, long, dark corridor with rows and rows of counters, offering for sale little umbrellas, joss-sticks and other various Buddhist offerings.

At its end was the magnificent shrine filled with the silhouettes of solemn, bowed worshippers. They were burning candles. I could have been in one of our own cathedrals. How close in many ways are the devout, however different their beliefs and doctrines may be.

At Surabaya in Java I went off with one of my fellow-travellers on what now seems the daftest of ploys. We visited the local cinema. There was a shock awaiting us when we emerged again into the street. A curfew was in force. The place was deserted. We shouldn't have been out at all.

Instead of being locked up, we were allowed to return to the hotel and the place was virtually in darkness. It was back to candles again.

This was rather effective, I thought—dinner by candle-light. Then I discovered that the romantic touch was not a matter of choice. Someone had blown up the central power station! I was grateful they hadn't picked on the cinema. The Communists were in revolt.

The posh Raffles Hotel in Singapore was filled with British types—bank clerks, minor civil servants and the like. I amused myself by watching the way they ordered the natives around, the way they played the big white boss and revelled in their artificially-inflated status. They'd had a long run. Good luck to them. Their time was running out. It wouldn't be long before the under-dogs of the world rebelled and had them back in their own back-yard, bringing in their own sticks and coal and washing their own soiled nappies.

When the Australian Broadcasting Commission heard that I was coming out for the centenary celebrations, they wrote and asked me to do three concerts—two in Sydney and one in Melbourne.

It was going to be very much a nostalgic occasion, meeting up again with Huck and his various companions—one now Sir Charles Moses and head of the A.B.C. Those springtime days were twelve years away, and I wanted to relive them as far as I could. I got off the plane at Darwin. My plan was to take the train to Melbourne on that long, slow, reminiscent journey across Queensland and New South Wales.

I wanted to see again the places where it was good to be young and we laid out the publican in his very own bar and I played my fiddle and pretended to be an Italian discovery.

There was also a more practical reason for contriving to delay my arrival. The Sunderland was due to arrive at Sydney on Anzac Day—a public holiday with everything shut—and the broadcasting boys suggested that the timing would be bad from the point of view of publicity.

The train stopped again at Bowen, and I wondered if I were seeing things. They had out a reception party on the platform. The local priest took me off to his house and announced I was due at the convent school.

All the school-children were on parade, and they sang me a song of welcome and presented me with a magnificent illuminated address.

It was all very touching after so many years. Some of those youngsters weren't even born the last time I passed that way.

The publicity boys had been busy in Melbourne. The platform was crammed and there were pressmen and photographers all over the place.

I was rushed off to Raheen, the Archbishop's palace, gifted to Mannix by an admiring Australian millionaire. It had been redecorated specially for the occasion and looked lush and inviting with its furnishings predominantly in cardinal red.

I was introduced to the famous U.S. Cardinal Spellman, and that exciting moment was the birth of a long and, for me, profitable friendship.

Fulton Sheen was there — now a Monsignor — and I recalled that unforgettable meeting at the home of John McCormack, when dear, kind John predicted notable futures for both of us.

Later that same day, De Valera turned up with Frank Aitken, the Irish Minister for External Affairs. It was my first encounter with the great Irish leader and again a warm and lasting friendship was to develop.

My exciting news from Archbishop Mannix was that I was down to sing Mass in the presence of Cardinal Spellman; at the final Mass at the close of the festivities, mine was to be the honour of acting as Deacon to Spellman.

I paid an advance visit to Sydney to meet again my old accompanist, John Douglas Todd.

But my first move was to visit St. Mary's Cathedral. I wanted to go to Confession, and I wanted to meet up again with the Cathedral's administrator—a lovely, gentle prince among men, as Irish as the hills of Donegal and one of my friends from the days of yore.

I found out his particular Confessional and went in to say my piece. In all innocence he listened patiently, then gave me absolution: " Go in peace."

" Hello, Paddy—it's me—Sydney!" I said in not much more than a whisper.

He was full of concern at the most normal of times—an infectiously enthusiastic, bustling, excitable personality. Even through the Confessional wall, I could almost sense a minor emotional explosion.

" Sydney—Sydney, me boy!" he said. " Come on now—right round to the Cathedral house. Off you go and we'll be seeing you!"

Cardinal Gilroy was there and invited me to be his guest. Then off I went to find again that splendid musician, John Todd.

The twelve years were shrinking into a matter of days. With John it was a case of dropping immediately into the old prescribed pattern—thorough rehearsals so that everything would be near perfection on the night. And again I took my other inevitable precaution—to visit the hall where I would sing.

I enforced this discipline on myself before every concert. Sydney Town Hall was all right—its acoustics were excellent. Melbourne's auditorium also filled the bill.

At Brisbane the hall looked extremely handsome. It cost over a million a long time ago when the value of a pound was less like a snowball in the sunshine, but the acoustics of this planner's dream were most unsatisfactory.

That's the funny thing about halls. You can build them with all the expert know-how concerning sound-waves, etc., and in the resultant arena the greatest basso profundo will sound like a mouse.

Like theology, the science of acoustics is just about as exact as the science of betting on horses.

Once upon a time Cork City Hall had this kind of trouble, but when I appeared on its stage, the most delicate pianissimo winged its way to the most distant corner.

There are three huge metal drums in Cork City Hall and they've nothing to do with the band. They're halved down the middle and are cleverly painted to blend with the general décor. They are Cork's secret weapon against dead sound—the little magic touch that makes all the difference between a hall that's good to sing in and one that isn't.

That brilliant conductor of choral music, Sir Hugh Roberton, always rehearsed his Orpheus Choir in a wee church hall in Glasgow. Not only that—often he refused to go to a clever, scientifically-constructed studio to make his actual records. Many of his recordings had to be done in the uninspiring atmosphere of those very ordinary, unpretentious church hall premises. For this " sound " reason— by some strange chance and without one word of expert advice, they were blessed with perfect acoustics.

What a magnificent job the Aussies made of the celebrations! They're absolute masters at this sort of thing. It was a case of Mass in the mass with enormous congregations of 50,000 to 60,000 in football stadia and other sporting arenas. I recall a most impressive Mass in the ground of Melbourne Cricket Club.

At one of the dinners the guests included Mannix the Mighty and Archbishop Panico. The latter was not exactly the Australians' pin-up boy. He was the Apostolic Delegate and he was Italian. He spoke with a pronounced Italian accent. He had been known to proclaim that one of his ambitions was to de-Irish the Church in Australia.

It was probably a commendable enough sentiment. Ideally, every bishop in Scotland should be Scots. Every bishop in Ireland should be Irish.

But bear in mind that it was the Irish who really built the Church in Australia. They were the pioneers; typical of their race, they were the ones who did the spadework.

240

Up in the sugar-cane country of Queensland, there were enclaves of Italian Catholics. The South had some small communities of German Catholics.

Certainly on my first visit to Australia twelve years previously I got the impression that the Church was virtually an Irish foreign mission.

During his after-dinner speech, Panico inevitably introduced his pet theme. In his quaint, clipped English, he said: " I look forward to the day when every bishop in Australia will be Australian . . ."

For one trained in diplomacy at the Noble College in Rome, that was not particularly clever—especially in front of Mannix.

When it came to his turn to reply, the great man rose like an elongated lion and out came the words in that port-wine voice that had a dignified music all its own:

" I was most interested to hear," he said, " what the Apostolic Delegate had to say—that he looked forward to the day when every bishop in Australia would be Australian. I would like to say to the Apostolic Delegate that I look forward to the day when the Apostolic Delegate will be Australian."

A beautiful barb. A penetrating barb. A barb that got home. The applause was thunderous and prolonged. It needed courage to say a thing like that. Panico after all was the representative of the Pope himself. His power and influence was considerable. Mannix not only looked like a lion, he behaved like one as well.

For me it developed into an embarrassing situation. Mannix, as I have said, had the topmost place in my roll of honour, but I liked Panico as well. I discovered that the feeling was mutual.

He was a skilled musician and one of his delights was to accompany my singing at the Delegation. He came to one of my concerts and gave it that extra bit of pomp by being greeted with a fanfare of trumpets.

As I write, there sits opposite a handsome clock—my farewell gift from Panico.

I will not say that the two archbishops were arch-enemies also. But it was difficult for me to have two friends who could not be described exactly as bosom companions.

I found myself in a similar situation with Cardinal Spellman and Bishop Fulton Sheen. I had great regard for both, and in each case this was reciprocated. But if Spellman didn't like Sheen, Sheen was no more enamoured of Spellman.

I was somewhat in the position of the famous servant of two masters. I think I coped. As far as I am aware, my friendships with all four remained intact. I think I could claim to have behaved more diplomatically than the graduate in diplomacy of Rome's Noble College!

One of the things I especially enjoyed were the evenings round the fireside in the Palace of Mannix. These were notable occasions. Each and every one in that wide half circle was an important Church dignitary. I should have felt out of it. I was Father Sydney MacEwan, a priest situated on the very bottom rung of the ecclesiastical ladder.

Yet I was treated as an equal. I don't suppose I contributed a great deal to the erudite conversation, but I certainly was listened to.

I should point out, however, that so far as the Press of Australia was concerned, I was the most publicised man in that room!

One of the lasting friendships which grew out of this tour was with the former Australian Cabinet Minister, Arthur Caldwell. He first got in touch with me because of his interest in Celtic music and folk song.

We got on famously together, and only last year there was a pleasant reunion in Largs. I travelled to meet him from Glasgow at Her Majesty's expense in a Government car. Arthur was always one who knew how to treat his friends.

It was he who suggested a trip to the Eureka Stockade near Ballarat with De Valera. With typical consideration he got into the seat beside the driver and left me in the back with Dev.

That was a fascinating journey. My mind went back to my student days in London when I spent hours in the library swotting up on the Irish Rebellion. Something of a hero-worship had developed for De Valera then. Now I was with him, side by side in the back seat of a car, and the reality of the situation only served to enhance the mental image that I'd carried around for years.

He was a fascinating personality. He chuckled as he told me the dramatic tale of his escape from Lincoln Jail. He had been in prison before, of course, and was condemned to death. He escaped the noose by the accident of birth. Dev was American-born and an American citizen. The story he told me of the Lincoln escape was hilarious.

He talked of those who fought with him for Ireland's freedom—the artists, the poets, the littérateurs, the musicians, the aristocrats, men of vision and intellect.

I knew most of it already—from my student days in London. It was intriguing to hear it first-hand from the lips of the leader himself.

How sadly debased in Ireland today has the fight for freedom become. Somehow the idealism has got all mixed up with gangsterism. I find that any comment is feeble on a situation that seems to be without hope.

It was back to Sydney Town Hall—and the door-keeper hadn't changed. He'd presided there for Gigli and McCormack and myself those dozen years back.

We shook hands heartily and he wished me luck. I needed a lot of that kind of greeting. I was nervous as a kitten. The butterflies in my tummy had assumed the size of bats.

This was a come-back and a unique one at that. My first concert in Australia wearing a Roman collar.

The Press boys with their kindness didn't help the situation. The advance ballyhoo grew to such proportions that I was near to a state of panic at the standard they'd set me to reach. I had so much to live up to. I was the personal equivalent of the film that gets so much super-colossal trailer treatment that it can scarcely avoid being below expectation.

I wasn't the brash and confident youngster any more. Usually the tension was a pre-concert hazard. This time it shadowed me when I went on stage—and throughout my entire performance.

I wanted to run away. In my own opinion I was right off colour. The nerves had almost taken over. I hadn't given of my best and I went home to await, in a mood akin to fear and trembling, the forthright critics of the morning after.

At the Cathedral where I was staying, some of the priests shook my hand and patted me on the back. Their verdict was—a wonderful show. I told myself that they were only being kind. I knew that I'd sung badly.

That night I didn't sleep a wink. I tried left side, right side, then lying on my back. I kept seeing visions of newspapers—each of Sydney's half-dozen dailies.

I pulled the cover over my head. I saw newspapers under the bedclothes.

They had bold, black, centre-page headlines. This was not imagination's titivation of reality. The Australian Press really went to town on its critical coverage of cultural occasions.

I must have been a pretty bleary, dejected specimen when I turned up for breakfast. I gave a flat " Good morning!" greeting and one of the priests looked up and said: " By jove, the critics liked you last night all right!"

All the papers were spread on a table. Trying to be as casual as possible, I read their every line on the concert.

One heading said boldly: " A Lesson in Song Art— Sydney MacEwan Banishes Time and Space."

Every paragraph was a eulogy. I searched in vain for a word of dissent.

I had two more concerts in Sydney. I sang with a confidence that I wished I could have brought to that come-back occasion—the most remarkable, successful flop (in my own opinion) that I've had in all my career.

Sir Charles Moses, the Broadcasting Corporation's chief, called: "Look, Sydney," he said, "you've seen the audiences. We just can't cope. There are thousands still who want to hear you. Can we extend the tour?"

I said I thought it could be arranged.

"Instead of three concerts, I'd like fifteen," he said.

As well as Sydney and Melbourne, I took in Adelaide, Perth, Canberra, Albury and Brisbane. It was a case of a sell-out every time.

At Brisbane one of the critics came backstage and asked for more detail of one of my songs. I took immediately to Ernest Briggs. Criticism was only one of his talents. He was one of Australia's outstanding poets. Ernest was also a spiritualist.

One evening he told me: "John McCormack came through the other night."

I was taken aback. All I could say was: "John? Oh, no!"

"He did indeed."

I told Ernest: "Far be it from me to deny the spirit world. This is what my life is all about. Of course, I believe in a next world or I wouldn't be a priest. But you've rather taken my breath away."

"All right," said Ernest, "I will get all who were there to sign a letter stating on oath what happened."

Sure enough, I got the full written account. But still I was sceptical. Only because dear John was involved was my doubt mixed with persistent curiosity.

Next time we met, I asked Ernest: "Can you call up anybody you like?"

" Afraid not," he said. " We might never make contact again."

I had only a short time left in Australia. " I'd like you to do me a favour," I said. " If John does turn up before I leave, will you ask him something? Ask what Lily McCormack, his wife, gave me to give to his sister in Dumfries."

It was a question that no one in Australia could possibly answer. To this day I doubt if half a dozen people in all the world could have that information.

The day before I left Australia, I got another letter from Ernest. This is what it said:

" John McCormack's widow gave you a gold pencil to deliver to his sister in Dumfries!"

That was absolutely accurate. I must admit to being somewhat shaken. There I let the matter rest. I choose to make no further comment.

Before I left, I gave a dinner to some of my Australian friends—a pretty lavish affair, with a hundred guests, including Church dignitaries and various representatives of the Broadcasting Corporation.

Australia is a long, long way from the little London Italian café where I begged as an impecunious student for fish and chips on tick!

That memorable night, Sir Charles pleaded: " Come back again next year, Sydney!"

" Not next year," I said. " Perhaps in two years' time."

John McCormack had a golden rule—never sing in the same town two years in succession. Keep them asking for more. It's a maxim I've never forgotten.

In show business you can die from over-exposure. Nowadays television has increased the risk a hundredfold.

CHAPTER

28

I began to give thought to my future as a priest. As what was known condescendingly as " late vocation," I was one of a minority.

About 90 per cent of the priests in Scotland have set out on their choice of career at the age of 12 or 13. They might achieve their own parish by the age of 50, for the waiting period in Glasgow was on average 25 years. But if I had to wait as long as that, I'd be coming up for 60!

I decided to try for a change of direction.

In my young days as a student of singing, one of my regular friends was a young curate at St. Mary's, Pollokshaws. His name was Kenneth Grant. Many's the jolly musical evening we had together at the home of Mr. Besant, a man who was able to gild his life with lilies as well as lieder. He was director in charge of Glasgow's parks.

Kenny Grant had made his way in the Church. He was now the Bishop of Argyll and the Isles.

I decided to take the train to Oban.

He gave me the hearty welcome I expected: " Well, Sydney, this is a surprise! What brings you to this part of the world?"

" Lochgilphead," I said.

" A delightful place."

" That's what I think, My Lord. Yet I believe it's still vacant."

" That's right. Has been for some time, unfortunately. We're short of men all over Argyll, I'm afraid."

I paused.

" If I were to get away from the Cathedral in Glasgow,"
I said, " would you give me Lochgilphead?"

He beamed. It was as if I had offered him a prize· " Of
course, Sydney—that would be splendid!"

My next move was to sort things out at the Glasgow end,
and that might not be quite so simple.

For most of my fellow-priests that climb up the stair to
the Archbishop's office was as nerve-racking as the ascent
of the north-facing cliffs of the Eiger.

I had no such inhibitions. I had known Archbishop
Campbell of old. His own roots were in Argyll and he had
graduated by way of the Argyll and the Isles bishopric
himself.

" What can I do for you, Sydney?" he said.

" Release me from the Cathedral, Your Grace. If you let
me go, I happen to know I could get a parish tomorrow."

" What parish?" he asked.

" Lochgilphead."

He looked up and that old twinkle was in his eyes again.
" Lochgilphead," he mused. " Lovely Lochgilphead—you
could do good work there, Sydney."

He sat back as if to work it out. " We're now into May—
I couldn't let you go until September—how would that
do?"

" Wonderful!" was all I could say.

" Mind you," he added, " I'm not letting you go at all
really. You will only be on loan."

My next seventeen years were to be in Lochgilphead. I
will call them my simple, satisfying years·

Lochgilphead is a bay window on to lovely Loch Fyne.
A little town with little shops and a little square at the end
of its street. There is a war memorial looking constantly
out to sea through the eyes of its Celtic cross. And a little
fountain to share its vigil.

The loch that is famed for herring had aesthetic appeal
as well. It was a bit of the sea that I've always loved, with

248

all its moods and restlessness and the mystery of its horizon. It is also MacEwan country.

As well as Loch Fyne, I had Loch Awe, Loch Gilp and Crinan with its canal—all virtually on my doorstep. From my sooty, sour-smelling slums, I was suddenly in contact with fragrance. For Argyll is one great, landscaped garden.

Its air was clean, and even its rain was pleasant. And it had sufficient silence to make the seagulls loud.

Argyll is the Highlands, where all our hearts are supposed to be. And maybe the song was not so far wrong. But there are Highlands and Highlands.

I could not be more Highland than where at this moment I write. Kingussie is at the core of the proud Cairngorms, and my neighbour is Aviemore, which youth has turned into a winter playground. I am 47 miles from the Highland capital of Inverness. The sunsets can be spectacular and the hills are handsome, especially when they don their white winter caps.

But, oh, the hellish noise!

I have one of the most handsome stone-built houses in the length and breadth of Scotland. It is very stout and solid. But I am on the road to the north that is called the A9, and the traffic that roars past day and night makes even this domestic citadel tremble.

Last year, on the second day of August, ten thousand vehicles passed through Kingussie, and huge lorries day and night rattled my windows.

Every time I venture out of my door I take my life in my hands. In my moments of foolhardiness I may choose to add my own car to this frightening flood of power.

In the holiday months of July or August, I may have to wait as long as ten minutes before I can venture out of my gate.

Were not the two most abominable inventions of the twentieth century the internal combustion engine and the concrete block?

I am not impressed either with the new breed of laird that is evolving in the Highlands of Inverness-shire. The beer barons and the property tycoons and the cigar-smoking smart guys from the south. If their heart is in the Highlands it is only for two months of the year. They are the latest model of the absentee landlord.

If we must have an aristocracy, I prefer the blue-bloods every time—like the ones in Argyll. They are predominantly the cadet branches of the ancient Campbells.

This is the land of their fathers—something to tend and be sentimental over. Not just a casual howff for a summer's slaughter of its birds and beasts.

There is a constant love affair going on between the blue-bloods of Argyll and the earth from which they sprang. That is why they are such great gardeners—dressing up their native countryside with great Himalayan splotches of colour—rhododendron and azalea, and ensuring its annual raiment of evergreens.

It was one of the blue-bloods, Lady Margaret Macrae, who built the lovely little St. Margaret's Church of Lochgilphead. She was the daughter of the third Marquis of Bute, that great benefactor of good causes in general, and the Church in particular. However, the St. Margaret's I saw had come down in the world. It was, as they say, the worse for wear. West Highland wind and rain had battered it.

It leaked in the roof and the lime had been wrenched from its joints. Its interior was without a single bench— there were only cushions to kneel upon. The floor was like a storm at sea, and for an altar it had a kitchen table. There were no Stations of the Cross in its solid walls. Its candles and vestments were sadly depleted.

St. Margaret's was a challenge.

It had long been the Cinderella of the diocese—latterly kept alive and no more by a gallant Canon Butler who was retired to Rothesay, but who journeyed to the outpost every weekend to say Mass and keep the little Lochgilphead flame alive.

I was determined to restore the Cinderella. I had the floor ripped out and replaced with terrazzo marble, a marble altar built. I repointed the walls and made the roof secure. In its every window, St. Margaret's eventually got stained glass.

I called in Carmichael's, the great construction company that had its birth in Lochgilphead. And they brought in their earth-moving equipment and cleared the jungle that threatened to swallow the little church. And the place of God was given a godly setting of flat, smart lawns and shrubs and flowers.

I got to work on my house as well—a modest little bungalow on the edge of the town. Seventy-two roses were planted in its garden. I installed my two cats and my mother's old furniture. I liked familiar things around me— even if the gramophone needed some books to prop it up.

What wonderful folk I had landed among. I hesitate to call Lochgilphead a paradise, lest too many people decide to sample its charms and thereby destroy them.

It was a paradise based on a most remarkable feature— a mental hospital. Lochgilphead was the centre of treatment for cases of mental sickness in the West Regional Hospital Board territory.

Its every house had some one involved. Nursing was the town's main breadwinner and the townsfolk reacted by making this place an absolute haven for those in need of understanding and care.

When the patients emerged from the hospital grounds, they were not suddenly in some strange, unfamiliar, hostile territory. They were still among friends—the same friends as they knew on the hospital staff.

There was a wave and a welcome at every door. They were out in the great big world, but still they felt secure.

In many cases the remedial effect of this kind of environment was great. The hospital was in my parish. Over the years, I had hundreds of letters from former patients, recalling with heartfelt gratitude the healing power of Lochgilphead folk, off duty as well as on.

For a minority, however, the welcome on Lochgilphead's mat produced another reaction. Some patients were so insulated in this mental harbour of a town that they feared to venture beyond.

The lowest ratio of success was with the alcoholics.

Their hospitalisation is still in this country on a voluntary basis. They can sign themselves out when they choose.

Many stayed for only two or three weeks and they went off no better than when they came in.

When I began my link with the Lochgilphead hospital, I had this common attitude of doubt, if not disapproval, of psychiatry. It was a new science and an inexact one at that.

I no longer think that way. One of our monasteries in Mount Melleray in Ireland used to attempt the curing of alcoholics. The intention was good, but really they hadn't a clue.

They tried to taper down a patient's drinking in the belief that eventually the craving would go altogether. This was playing at treatment. There is no such thing as an alcoholic who will settle for a little, getting less every day.

It might work for the heavy drinker. But this is a man who, no matter how much he likes his dram, is always in control.

The alcoholic has no control whatsoever. He is sick. It was brought home to me very forcibly that this is an illness like diabetes or cancer or tuberculosis—except that its ramifications can be a great deal more disastrous. The alcoholic can bring down not only himself, but those near and dear to him also.

He needs the professional. He needs the psychiatrist. And, oh, how he needs our sympathy.

Thank God it is less a subject for jest than it was not so long ago.

Recently I was in Dublin and had lunch in the Four Courts Hotel. I had just sat down when in streamed a number of lawyers and barristers and court officials.

One of the barristers sat down at my table and we got on the talk.

" Would you like a drink, Father?" he asked.

" I hope you will join me," I said.

" Oh, no thank you," he answered. " I'm an alcoholic."

At first it came as a shock. Then I thought—this is splendid, this is how it should be. Here was a man who had this dread disease but was able to cope as simply and rationally as someone with diabetes.

I trust this digression will not strike you as out of place in such a volume as this. I would crave your support and prayers for all who are trying to cope with this disease.

For be sure it is on the increase. It strikes now at the very young. I have seen at close quarters the awful problems it brings. Not only have the psychiatrists and psychologists and specialised nursing staff my every support, I would wish to see far greater interest shown by the Church. Church students of every denomination should have a measure of understanding of the scourge included in their training.

As a nation we should be spending far more on research.

I needed a motor-car. As well as the hospital, I had two hydro-electric camps in my parish—one 24 miles away at Inveraray for the dam at Glen Shira, the other another 15 miles on at Butterbridge as part of the great Loch Sloy project.

Cars were scarce in 1949, and people were willing to pay double the actual market price. I managed to get a ten-year-old Morris Eight in reasonable trim.

It wasn't long, however, before I decided to equip her with new engine and tyres. Thus reinforced, she kept me on the road for all of three years. She was one of the last of a sturdy breed.

I sold her eventually for two hundred pounds. By then she was thirteen years old.

They were predominantly Irish, these tunnellers of Argyll. Most of them came from Donegal. They had a habit of getting drunk on Fridays, and the unco guid said " Such rough fellows! It's trouble for Inveraray."

How wrong they were! Of course they got merry once a week, but the local police will back me up when I say that those who made any real trouble were very much a black-sheep minority. They were in camp 12 years, and never one serious crime.

Their weekly blow-out was their only pleasure. They were far from home and their work was hard—in mud and rain and wind and sleet, and living for long hours the life of a mole.

I got to know them as first-class men. They made big money, but they sent it home. Their bonds with their families were as strong as the muscles of their mighty arms.

I think now of those who were proud to sweat in order to pay their sons and daughters through college or university. And the ones who invested in little crofts and farms and went back to Donegal every spring to plant out their plots with tatties and corn.

They were off again when the harvest-time came to bring in their crops and meet up with their loved ones.

I was proud of my Friday-night drunks. They were men of the kind of mettle that is nowadays all too rare. They were workers before the word got debased.

And they feared their Lord and were faithful to their Church.

In the mud of their camp-site they built me a place of worship—with rough-hewn benches to seat 200 and an altar that was appropriately crude.

When the Communists in North Vietnam made the Christians run for their lives in the 1950s, there was wide-spread suffering and hardship. All the Churches throughout the land were asked to come to their aid.

To the rough, tough Paddys in my little wooden church, I announced without warning a special collection. I have never forgotten the way they responded. Just by putting round the plate, we raised no less than £144—a goodly sum in 1950.

With the two camps to serve on a Sunday, I had to stay in Inveraray on the Saturday night. Mine host was Jimmy Carmichael, one of the contractor family, and I will always be grateful for his kindness.

He never seemed to send any bills. I used to have to badger him for an account. And the one he would render say, after three months, would be for a quite ridiculous sum. I would reckon that from Jimmy I got three times the amount of hospitality that he ever made me pay for.

I loved those Saturday nights with Gentleman Jim. All that spoiled them was the thought of the early rise next morning. I had to be up at six to make my preparations and hear Confessions.

Mass at Shira used to be at seven. Then on to Butterbridge for another Mass there. And all on an empty stomach. From Saturday night till three on Sunday afternoon I went without food and drink.

Those were the days of the fasting laws. Anyone saying Mass or partaking of Holy Communion had to fast from the previous midnight.

Eventually Pius XII reduced to three hours the fasting period. It was a worthy mitigation.

I was forever grateful to Bishop Grant. For me in my peculiar far-flung parish he got special dispensation from Rome—I was able to break my fast before Mass.

All that is happily in the past. The period of fasting is now one hour.

I am aware that there are older Catholics who say: "I still fast." All right—if that is as their conscience dictates, but they shouldn't be more Catholic than the Pope. They shouldn't be more Catholic than the Church.

They should remember that the Last Supper was in the evening. The disciples were not fasting from midnight. The wording of the Consecration of the Chalice is worthy of quotation here: "When supper was ended, He took the cup."

This modern one-hour ruling is splendid. It has increased tenfold the number of the faithful who can partake of Holy Communion. It has made it possible for priests to say three Masses a day without risk of stomach ulcers.

Gradually I was able to change the timing of my Masses to more convenient hours. I had Mass at Lochgilphead at 10 a.m., travelled to Shira for Mass at 6 in the evening with an 8 o'clock Mass at Butterbridge.

The new arrangement meant I was never home before 10 o'clock. It was a long, exhausting day—but always extremely worthwhile. It was mainly the faithfulness of my friends, the mountain-borers, that made it so.

When I told Dr. Mathieson that I'd bought a yacht, he said: "You'll have to see Swallow." Then he added: "His real name's Alec McCallum."

Not unnaturally, I asked: "Why Swallow?"

"You'll see," he said.

Alec was a man with red, strong hands that had pulled many a boat across Loch Fyne in search of the silvery herring.

His face had a lovely, ruddy glow. Alec liked his dram. I got the impression that he'd probably bestowed the title on himself, for I never saw him the worse of drink.

His pal was Bob Bruce, and they had this in common—both were ex-fishers. But there the similarity ended. Bob was a sober, serious man—an elder of the Presbyterian Kirk.

They jointly agreed to adopt my yacht. They set down moorings in the anchorage at Ardrishaig, and never has a craft been more tenderly cared for. The yacht was their baby. They scraped and they painted and watched over it like guardian angels.

There was never thereafter a gale or storm that gave me qualms. I knew that Swallow and his loyal chum would be down at the harbour adjusting its ropes and securing its shackles.

I suppose in a way I was emulating the Master Himself. I had two staunch disciples, and both of them fishers.

It wasn't long, however, I must confess, before we entered into an unholy partnership. We started poaching.

The plot was hatched because we were unanimous upon one thing—one for the pot was the right of every Scot.

We invaded no river or laird's preserve. Our beat was Loch Fyne, and our prey was salmon trout.

Many's the summer's night, with Swallow and Bob, I sailed out from Ardrishaig into the dusk and across to the Kilfinnan side of the loch, and out went our nets.

And round about two the following morning the whole of Lochgilphead might have been wakened by the screaming of my two pet cats.

They knew the drill. There was no need to open the door of the house. As soon as I parked the car, their impatient howling began. Their master was home, as it were, from the sea, and some of his booty would be coming their way.

I sometimes grew jaded with my diet of salmon trout in Argyll. I never lacked for salmon either. Not that I ever poached the salmon. There wasn't any need. My friend, Malcolm of Poltalloch, Clan Malcolm's chief, saw to that by regularly sending down sufficient supplies for myself and my fellow-hunters.

I suppose our nocturnal escapades sound like a highly dangerous practice. Imagine the headlines had we ever been caught! A Catholic priest netting salmon trout in Loch Fyne! And aided and abetted by an elder of the Kirk!

Somehow I never worried. Somehow I knew we would never be caught—not with a wily, old veteran like Swallow.

He knew that Clyde estuary like the back of his hand— its every mood, its every creek, its every bay, its every rock.

There was only one other who rivalled his expertise. And that was Bob Bruce.

My poaching nights were spent with an easy conscience. I had always an equally easy mind. I enjoyed the sense of security of working with two real experts—and the " polis " were my friends.

Those two cats of mine were magnificent creatures. One of them puffed a lot and was therefore called Puffer. He was an enormous blue-grey Persian and he lived to the age of 14.

To the other I gave the name of Jimmy Edwards, a comedian of whom I am particularly fond. And comic and cat had this in common—a most gorgeous set of whiskers.

I liked to think that my cats were of genuine royal blood. The Shah of Persia once paid a visit to Malcolm of Poltalloch, and he brought as a gift two handsome cats. There are cats all over mid-Argyll—at cosy Scots firesides and on the cottage walls. All of them have the Persian look.

George Malcolm, the laird of Poltalloch, was one of those who made this Lochgilphead era so memorable. Not only did he keep me supplied with salmon—he was generous with his invitations to dine at Duntrune Castle. It was there I was able to indulge my taste for oysters. Always they were succulently fresh—for Poltalloch had its own, private oyster bed.

CHAPTER

29

I was still commuting regularly to London to sing for the B.B.C. and meet up again with dear Oscar for recording sessions.

I looked upon these journeys as interludes—as little deprivations inserted into my life to make me appreciate all the more the peace and quiet and beauty of Argyll.

The truth is—emotionally, I was not cut out to be an international tenor. I enjoyed the singing. I had this gift, and there was undoubtedly great satisfaction in its exercise.

It was pleasant to visit far-away places, but basically I am a home bird. For me the greatest joy of travel is the coming home at its end.

But the pace of the concert tour, its schedules and time-tables, the late nights and the plaudits, the artificiality of what I call the racket—these I found a necessary evil.

In one of my Melbourne concerts my programme included " Deirdre's Farewell to Scotland." Halfway through I almost broke down. There were tears wanting urgently out of my eyes. I feared my voice would trail into silence because of the lump in my throat.

Suddenly, as I sang, I was stricken with home-sickness. I had a persistent mental image of the steamer *Loch Fyne* with its two red funnels gliding through the matchless beauty of the Kyles of Bute on the route home to Argyll.

When at last I got back to Glasgow, I could have gone straight home to Lochgilphead by road. I chose instead to travel to Gourock, so that I could sail the last lap through the gorgeous Kyles on the boat with two red funnels.

The Australian Broadcasting Commission ensured that I didn't forget my promise. It was arranged I should return to Australia in 1951.

I got my usual generous contract—fifty per cent of gross receipts, plus all travel and expenses. It represented a tidy sum if you got packed halls wherever you went. This had always been the pattern in the past. I had no reason to think it would change.

This time I decided to give the money away. I told Bishop Grant: " I want to do this tour for your Cathedral."

At one time the Catholic church in Oban was not much more than a small tin shed. It needed tremendous courage for this kind of non-urban diocese to replace its undignified, inappropriate base with the finest Catholic church in the country and one of the most handsome churches of any kind built since the Reformation.

That's what Argyll decided to do—initially inspired by Bishop Martin, who passed on his enthusiasm to Bishop Campbell. This act of faith was not yet complete.

That's why Kenneth Grant's eyes lit up with approval when I told him what I had in mind.

My other decision was not to travel alone. My mother had earned this kind of first-class treat and I booked for two on the liner *Oronsay* for what was to be her maiden voyage.

Mother got one of the few air-conditioned cabins. I felt that at the age of 72 to sail through the Red Sea without this sort of amenity was asking a bit too much.

We were seen off on the five-week voyage by my brother and his family—and Annie Cleary, a splendid, loyal, life-long friend, who has since proved herself invaluable as my ever-attentive housekeeper and cheery companion.

At Naples, I took my mother ashore to fulfil a long-standing promise. We were off by taxi to the Campo Santo to visit Caruso's tomb.

It was never my privilege to hear him in the flesh, but I have the assurance of Monty Mackenzie that Caruso was the greatest—the king of them all.

It's a sentiment that was obviously shared by the profession, for the shrine we saw at Campo Santo had its marble inscribed with the names of singers from all over the world who'd left behind this evidence of their pilgrimage.

I was back at the Caruso memorial two years ago and no signatures had been added. No homage was paid to the king any more. It was an age of new affections—of constantly-changing adulation for strange successors to the throne, with names like Beatles and Rolling Stones.

Australia was as I had left it—the pressmen were loyal and the cameras clicked. I met up again with Sir Charles Moses and good old Huck Findlay—and, of course, my faithful accompanist, John Douglas Todd, and Arthur Caldwell, Leader of the Labour Party.

It was to turn out to be the most successful tour that the A.B.C. had ever handled for any artiste. Sometimes I doubt if this kind of response was entirely due to my vocal merit. I was after all a hybrid person—half Scots, half Irish. I had a foot in both camps. And the Scottish and Irish content of the Australian population was considerable. Possibly had I been only half as good, I would still have got the crowds. I could have traded on nostalgia for the old country.

Everywhere, with one exception, the press notices were kind and enthusiastic.

Geelong is a town outside Melbourne. It is not a particularly large community. You may not in fact have been aware of its existence, although it did achieve a more recent fame when Prince Charles did a year at a boarding school there.

In all my life I have received one unfavourable criticism in the press. And that was in Geelong.

I always read what the critics had to say. I sometimes found their comments helpful. No matter how long I was in the business, I was never allergic to informed, constructive reaction.

One of the critics in Melbourne called Sinclair wrote thoroughly helpful notes. A music critic in Cork pointed out that he did not agree with my interpretation of " I Know My Love."

I got out my record of that particular number and played it again and again. The man was right—of that I am sure. So I made the change he had suggested.

But sometimes the conceit of the Australian critics was appalling—especially in Melbourne and Sydney. Not that I ever suffered. But Yehudi Menuhin was one of the visiting performers who was given pretty rough treatment. I felt it was a bit of effrontery that such a musical genius should be sniped at by immature, incompletely-informed university students posing as seasoned experts. One critic was a medical student.

And Australia was exhausting—so much so that in Perth I finished up in hospital with nervous exhaustion, complicated by pneumonia.

America was easy by comparison. I did each concert, and that was it. I was left completely free to go off to my hotel—or train or plane for the next assignment.

But Australia was so demanding. After every show I was expected to be charming to various local personalities and committees.

Part of the publicity build-up was to fit in frequent visits to hospitals and old folk's homes.

However commendable this kind of gesture may be, it was really asking a bit too much.

These appearances of mine were solo. Apart from dear John Todd, I was out there on stage on my own for all of two hours and twenty-four songs.

The physical strain was considerable. Emotionally I was completely drained. After taking this kind of battering, it was well nigh impossible to radiate and be the life and soul of the party. All I wanted was to slip away quietly to bed and go to sleep with a dram.

I hope this does not sound ungrateful. For me, Australia has been a wonderful audience. I think in part it was fear of letting my audience down, of not giving them full value for money, that made me inwardly rebel at the extra demands that were put upon me.

The resultant cheque I was able to present to Bishop Grant represented thousands of pounds.

One of the compensations of that hectic Australian safari was to meet up again with Archbishop Mannix. He insisted, of course, that I be his guest. Despite his aggressive, outspoken nature, to me he was always kindness and understanding.

After my every concert he would say: " All right, Sydney—off to bed and I don't want to see you tomorrow until ten o'clock."

And in the morning this grand old man—in my experience one of the greatest of churchmen—would serve my Mass.

One morning I slept in. Despite our close relationship, I always accorded Mannix the respect befitting his office. And you don't keep an Archbishop waiting.

To save time, I pulled on a dressing-gown and dashed downstairs. It was one of the more flamboyant items in my wardrobe. Joseph's coat of many colours had nothing on this!

There was no word of reprimand. When I apologised for my lateness, Mannix looked round, then looked again:

" My God!" he said· " For one moment I thought we were going to have Mass in the Oriental rite!"

Before my final performance in Melbourne, we asked for requests. I said to Archbishop Mannix: " Is there anything you would like me to sing?"

" ' Oft in the Stilly Night,' " he said.

I could see him from the stage—right in the middle of the gallery, just behind the clock.

I reached the lovely bit of what is a lovely song:

> "When I remember all the friends, so linked together,
> I've seen around me fall like leaves in wintry weather . . ."

He was 87. I knew how he was feeling. I sensed his reason for the choice of song. At that age a lot of leaves have fallen.

When we said our farewells at the Palace, the old man wept. I am not ashamed to say that my eyes were wet also. We both of us realised that this was not just another goodbye. It was very likely the final handshake—the last contact on earth between two human beings who came near to being as close as father and son.

His parting gift was to hand me his red Archbishop's biretta—to this day one of my treasures, with the McCormack prayer book and Tauber's cane.

It was typical of Mannix that he almost beat the prophets. There were many, many winters left for him yet. He lived right up to his hundredth year, and when the celebrations were being planned for his glorious centenary, he asked me to come out.

But that farewell at which two mature men cried was to be the finale after all. Mannix died just a few months short of the hundred.

Things had changed since my last time out. Archbishop Gilroy of Sydney had been made a Cardinal.

The appointment caused something of a national sensation. Arthur Caldwell, former Cabinet Minister and Leader of the Australian Labour Party, asked questions in the House of Representatives.

Gilroy was a man of great holiness, an excellent administrator, a good Archbishop, but he paled by comparison with Mannix. Every Australian Catholic realised that if any red hats were being given out, the most eligible head was that of Mannix.

He had been a rebel, of course. He had been a political bishop, and in this day and age the political bishop is no longer in favour.

The *Duchess of Rothesay*, one of my beautiful Clyde steamers.

Beloved Lochgilphead.

Photo by courtesy of the *People's Journal*, Dundee.

Photo by courtesy of the *Scotsman* Publications Ltd.

Sir Compton Mackenzie's 82nd birthday party. Among those present: Lord Cameron, Lord Wheatley, Eric Linklater and Moray McLaren.

Rome played safe with Gilroy. It avoided controversy. This is currently the pattern of the hierarchy—to appoint good men, but grey men rather than those who stand out fearlessly in black and white.

Perhaps Rome is right, but does the Church thereby get the right type of leadership?

One outstanding leader I have in mind was Argyll's own Bishop Grant. He was possessed of this rare, indefinable, magnetic quality. He was a soldier in the trenches in World War I. He volunteered for service as a chaplain in 1939, was captured at St. Valery and spent five years in a prison camp.

No doubt many in that camp blessed the fact of his companionship. The blue-bloods of Argyll who were captured with him all affirmed his undoubted leadership.

What was the effect of his appointment to Argyll and the Isles? He exuded inspiration wherever he went. The whole diocese took on a new lease of life. To please Bishop Grant was the constant delight of the clergy. There were those who would have laid down their lives for this man.

This is what leadership means—and what leadership can achieve. Alas, he died too soon—at the age of 59.

I came in contact with the same kind of personality at a very different level. Because of my love of boats, I was invited by J. Herbert Thom to crew with him in the Clyde Week races. I was thrilled to bits. To a yachtsman this sort of invitation was tantamount to a knighthood.

Among helmsmen, in my opinion, Thom was the greatest. He told me himself that he had little interest in boats unless they were racing. And his interest in racing was only to win. He had, if you like, the killer instinct. In *Circe* he won the Seawanhaka Cup in America and defended it against Sweden on the Clyde successfully.

He presided over his crew like a modern Captain Bligh. Yet as soon as he stepped ashore, he was the gentlest and most modest of men.

With such natural sailing genius as Thom, why is it we never manage to win the America Cup?

A few years ago he helped in the preparations. In fact, he whacked the new challenger for the Cup in the old challenger.

He was not only the greatest of helmsmen—he was also the most neglected. He has never once been invited to take part in the most famed of all sailing events—the America Cup. His fault would seem to be that he misses out on one thing only—he is not a member of the Royal Yacht Squadron!

CHAPTER

30

The day before I sailed for New York, I walked in Kilmory, looking down on Loch Gilp, and I decided it was my favourite view.

I thought to myself: " Tomorrow I'll be leaving all this. I hope nothing happens. This place is too good to leave in a hurry."

I remember reprimanding myself up there among the quiet, clear hills. " You're an idiot, Sydney, boy! Why don't you decide once and for all that you're not cut out for this globe-trotting nonsense and settle down in this corner of Scotland that is safe and peaceful and sane?"

I sailed out the next day for Glasgow. I always went by the steamer—the *Loch Fyne* or *St. Columba.* They knew me as a steamer addict, and I always got my place on the bridge.

I walked alone down Sauchiehall Street, alone along Hope Street, alone into Glasgow's great Central Station. No fuss. No crowded farewells. I even forbade my own brother to see me off.

Southampton brought sight of one compensation to all this touring about the world—the tall, proud funnels of the *Queen Elizabeth.*

The concert round sometimes got on my nerves. But the bits in between I loved—the combination of sailing and living on a great liner.

I always travelled the Atlantic first-class on the *Queens* —it was built into my every contract. Ridiculously expensive, of course. My suite in the mid-1950s cost round about fifty pounds a day. But Cunard did give you your money's-worth—you travelled fast and the service was fit for a king —and I wasn't paying the bill!

I had watched the *Elizabeth* as she grew on the Clyde. I saw her during the war—all grey and miserable, gliding through the grey and miserable waters with fifteen thousand American troops on board.

Now she was back to all her radiant, polished, peacetime finery — the second-greatest floating luxury hotel in the world.

I say second-greatest because she never quite matched the *Mary*. There was a solid, quality, stately-home feel about the *Mary*. She came in at the end of the great days of craftsmanship. You seemed to sense that somehow this gigantic article was entirely hand-made—right down to the very knobs on the doors. The *Mary* was the Queen of them all.

I'll give you an example of her kind of service. Always Cunard served smoked Scotch salmon for lunch. At dinner the menu said Irish salmon.

To one of the head waiters, I teased: " Surely this salmon business is just a bit of pretence. I mean—it's obviously the same salmon—you just change the name at midday, then in the evening again?"

It was the wrong thing to say on the *Mary*. He was hurt —politely hurt, but hurt. And after dinner he beckoned me into the kitchens. " There you are, sir," he said. " Scotch salmon, and here, Irish salmon."

There was a difference, even in appearance. And the texture of the flesh was not the same. Cunard on the *Queens* never missed a trick—not at fifty pounds a day.

All my American concerts were organised by Carleton Smith, President of the National Arts Foundation of New York. Carleton is a one-man Debrett, a human *Who's Who*. He simply knows everybody who amounts to anybody.

The last time we met he came to see me at Kingussie and announced casually that he was just back from a visit to the Dalai Lama. He had his two children with him, and they were able to tell me all about it.

They were baptised by Cardinal Spellman of New York, and confirmed by Cardinal Koenig in Vienna.

All very normal for the offspring of a man whose oyster is the world. He knows Kruschev and Paul Getty. Name any celebrity and Carleton has been his guest. The other day he dropped me a note to say he was off to Oslo to see an honour conferred on his friend Willy Brandt.

I met him once in London, and he was in a hurry. He was on his way to Buckingham Palace to have a look at the paintings.

He uses aeroplanes like taxis, and his bus-stops are the various countries of the globe.

To maintain this sort of super contact-man status, you have to be something of a human dynamo. Carleton is a human dynamo.

He met me at New York, introduced my road manager, Elwood Emerick, and it seemed just about every press photographer in that mighty city had been tipped off to record the event.

We were rushed in among the skyscrapers with a mayor's reception committee in suitably gigantic automobile, plus a police escort wailing like banshees.

Carleton had fixed me up in the Biltmore Hotel, and from my bedroom window I could look down on the harbour. I spotted the *Queen Elizabeth's* funnels and was stricken again by the same kind of feeling that I'd had up there on the hills of Kilmory—an overwhelming urge to click shut my case and sail back home forthwith.

There was a knock on my door, and some of my homesickness went out with its opening. Here was the comforting, kent face of Lily, Countess McCormack, over like a shot to say hello and remind me of the burgeoning years. Since John's death she'd lived in New York's Park Avenue, making each summer a pilgrimage to Ireland.

I joined her later at her flat for a meal, and we listened through the evening to her husband's voice. The records still made her weep. And her weeping was infectious. I thought—how significant, how inevitable, that my first night back in New York should finish up with tears.

One of the things that struck me this time about the U.S. was the remarkable status of its clergy. The denomination didn't seem to matter.

Clergymen travelled half-fare on the railroads. When you approached a lift, that collar was a passport, and everyone stood back to make way.

In Chicago and New York the power and influence of the Catholic Church was particularly remarkable. The Catholic priest in either metropolis was assured of cream on his porridge all right!

The priest who knew the ropes could just about park his car wherever he liked—so long's he left his book behind. The book was the breviary—which we use for the saying of our daily office. So long's it was obvious—like on the front seat or up at the wind-screen, the priest could forget about parking tickets.

One day my taxi-driver was going like mad and I saw him look scared in his mirror. He'd picked up a couple of speed cops, and they came roaring in for the kill. But as they drew alongside, one of them saw me in the back— Roman collar and all. They gave a salute and turned about.

" Thanks, Father!" the taximan said. " Lucky me having you for a fare! Guess I should start going to church a bit more!"

A lot of Americans did. Every Sunday it was reckoned 54 per cent of the U.S. population would be at church. In Britain it was something like 17 per cent at that time.

Carleton had me along to audition a number of accompanists. The first in line was Ralph Liebe, a young man of German extraction. I shoved all sorts of music in front of him—stuff that he obviously didn't know and hadn't even seen before. He was in the same class as Gerald

Moore. He had that extra subtle sensitivity to register almost immediately his soloist's mood and approach to a song.

" This will do me," I said. " We needn't keep the others waiting."

He turned out to be not only a formidable musical companion. He knew his way around in the matter of travel as well. In 1954, I sang 36 concerts throughout the U.S.— from the Atlantic to the Pacific, from Wisconsin in the north to the southern centres of Texas and Louisiana in the south. I repeated this in 1955 and 1956.

That meant a great deal of travel by rail, and in the land where so much is on a grandiose scale, American railroads had an elaborate ticket system which I never fully comprehended.

To travel any distance at all you didn't buy the usual voucher. You invested in a positive library of tickets. It must have been about a yard long, and throughout the journey an official would appear and appropriate a certain portion or punch a hole in another.

I always left the handling of this frightening document to Ralph, my accompanist. He was American after all— he'd been brought up on this kind of thing.

But when we were going through his home state of Pennsylvania, he asked if he might break off to see his wife, and rejoin me in New York.

From Cleveland, Ohio, I was accordingly on my own with my alarming yard of tickets.

I was dozing off in my sleeper about eleven o'clock when a little car attendant called. He took this great substitute for a Christmas decoration and said: " Here, mister, you ain't got the right ticket. You gotta get off if you can't pay!"

I had only a cheque book and odd change.

In something of a daze, I told him: " Don't be silly— I can't get off. I've got to be in New York—and anyhow I'm in my pyjamas."

" Sorry, mister," the attendant persisted. " You gotta get off at the next stop. Better get dressed."

" Look, be reasonable," I said. " If there's something wrong with the tickets, we'll square up at the other end!"

" No ticket—no train! I got my orders!"

" Phone ahead and tell the cops!" I said sarcastically.

I thought he had decided after all to listen to common sense. I went to sleep. At New York I was dressed in my priestly garb and all set to disembark.

I saw the little man at the end of the carriage and detected, I thought, a look not far from consternation. He seemed intent on my Roman collar. Instead of my usual reception committee, there was a cop on the platform to meet me.

The little man had phoned ahead.

The policeman of course was Irish. He, too, was fascinated by my clerical neckwear: in a kindly mixture of brogue and Bronx, he asked: " Whassa trouble, Father?"

I explained about the ticket.

By this time the little railway official was looking decidedly ill.

" You bloody stupid sonofabitch!" the big cop said. " Can't ye see his reverence is bonny fyde!"

Before an argument developed about a priest in pyjamas looking like anyone else, Carleton Smith arrived with his entourage and sorted things out at the office.

The press coverage of my arrival was fantastic. It looked like my American sponsors certainly knew their business.

I headed for Detroit. A packed hall, of course, and evidence of nostalgia all over the place.

A fervid ex-Scot kept shouting out: " You're taking us home—you're taking us home!"

I remember thinking uncharitably: " If you feel all that bad about it, why the hell did you leave Scotland in the first place?"

My sleep that night was far from sound. I was up with the dawn and down to the reception desk for a check-up on the press reaction.

Every single notice was excellent.

Minus breakfast, I dashed out excitedly to see Carleton, who was staying in the Athletic Club—one of those peculiar American institutions that didn't seem to have anything to do with sporting prowess except that you probably ran up a very large account.

He was still in bed and half asleep. " Have you seen the crits?" I said.

" Nope!"

" They're great—terrific, in fact!"

" Sure, sure!" an almost indifferent voice from the bed. " What you expect?"

I had a strange sort of feeling that it was all arranged— that even instant success was something that these slick American whiz-kid organisers could somehow pre-arrange.

One of Carleton's multifarious contacts was a large, stout, affable Jew with the name of Nate Grose. Nate wrote a column for the *Chicago American.*

Chicago was the greatest rail centre in the world, and every time I passed through, Nate would give me a ring and duly record the meeting.

He was read as something of a Walter Winchell. But Nate wrote with a most benign pen. He was no keyhole gossip-man. Nate's writings never harmed a fly. He got his following by way of a fascinating vocabulary and a distinctive flair for being witty and wise.

One day he asked me : " Sydney, it's time you came to see my ranch."

He sent round a taxi and off we went. My surprise was that we should proceed no farther than one of the expensive down-town hotels. Nate's " ranch " was one of its suites!

It was rigged out like a mid-West bunk-house—with every single item in a cow-hand's inventory. Guns, pistols, holsters, chaps, ten-gallon hats and sombreros—even a mock-up of a swing-door saloon. He was a cowboyphile, if that's the right word, a devotee of the great outdoors, who compensated for his enforced big-city environment by living in this remarkable den.

Nate was a minor Carleton Smith—his contacts were legion in every walk of life.

He phoned me up once that he had some pals he thought I might like to meet. I found the " bunk-house " occupied by about a dozen colourful characters all sat around the table. Nate did the introductions, which were pretty vague, and later I asked one of my quaint companions: " And what line of business are you in?"

" Gambling, Father," he said. " I'm a gambler."

What he really meant was gangster. I was in a nest of hoodlums—Las Vegas boys, riggers of fruit machines, guys who worked the protection racket and pushed certain records on juke-box circuits.

I was assured they were all of them backing my Chicago concert. " Don't you worry about the papers, Father," one of them said. " You'll be all right!"

I had tea with the head of the Church in Chicago, Cardinal Stritch. He almost made me choke on my cake by asking: " Somebody said the gangsters were going to back this concert of yours? I'm sure that can't be right?"

" Gangsters?" I managed to say. " Of course not. I wonder how that got around?"

But to this day I was never sure.

One of the big shots that Carleton decided I should meet was Colonel McCormick. He was of Scots extraction. He owned the *Chicago Tribune* and a whole string of news-papers right across the country. I kept off the subject of Britain. I'd been warned that McCormick was fiercely anti-British—something I couldn't understand in a land where anyone with a Scottish granny is fervently proud of the fact.

By now the colonel was old. He reminisced about his roots in Scotland and mentioned the name of his mother.

The name was Irish. I remember thinking: " There's the answer. With an Irish mother I know where he gets his hate of the English."

Despite any feelings he may have had about the old country, he was certainly good to me. He told his papers all over the place that Sydney MacEwan was to get the full treatment. He proved to be a powerful ally.

I wondered what my old Catholic friends would have thought in their single-ends in Rottenrow and Stockwell Street if they'd seen the life I was leading now.

That time, for instance, with the Alden-Carpenters in their magnificent home at Lake Shore Drive on Lake Michigan.

The late husband of Mrs. Alden-Carpenter had been a noted poet and musician, and her social circle was a golden ring. In my honour she threw a dinner party, and it turned out to be like a dollar-millionaire's convention.

Everybody who was anybody in this dynamic Chicago was there that night. The Du Ponts were on my left, and over there to the right, the Cunios and the Marshal Fields.

I looked around at the galaxy of diamonds and emeralds sparkling from ears and necks and wrists and fingers. Maybe there were some on toes as well—I wouldn't know.

" Are these real?" I asked Mrs. A.-C. in a mood of mischief.

She looked aghast.

Carleton told me, Eunice, one of the Kennedy girls, was throwing a cocktail party on my behalf.

" *The* Kennedys?" I asked.

" Sure thing," he said.

This one was Mrs. Sergeant Shriver, daughter of Joe, whom I'd met away back in the student days at Rome. In 1972 her husband ran as the Democratic Vice-Presidential candidate.

There was an Italian touch to that party as well. I got into a corner with the Italian Consul and his wife, and I was telling them of my love for Italy when a young man came in and was introduced.

He was one of those persons who stood out in a crowd—handsome, tanned, immaculately dressed, with that extra something that we ineffectively describe as magnetic.

He apologised for being late. He said his plane had been stacked above Chicago—and I must have looked puzzled.

" That's when you're kept circling around up there till you get the O.K. to land," he explained.

He made conversation easy. He was interested and interesting. We talked about Ireland and the persecutions. I explained that the Scots had suffered a similar fate in the shape of the Highland Clearances.

" It's pretty awful what some guys will do to other guys," he said.

About six years later, I waited up all night to hear the fate of this same young man. I hurried into my mother's bedroom and told her: " They've elected Jack Kennedy. Jack's the new President."

I sent him a telegram of congratulation.

And when he was assassinated, I couldn't help thinking of what he said at his sister's cocktail party.

As I say, I tried to keep a curb on charity shows—not out of any lack of compassion, but just to get the priorities right. People were paying good money to hear me sing, and I felt they should hear me at my best and not tired out from what you might call extra-mural activities.

But when the command came from a Cardinal, I had to break the rules.

Anyhow, Cardinal Stritch was having his annual concert for charity and he wanted me to sing. The timing couldn't have been more inconvenient. I was due next day in Omaha, Nebraska, and I had to catch a train that night.

I did my spot and was rushed from the banqueting hall with a special escort from the police department. It was also arranged that the train wouldn't leave until I was safely on board.

For a bemused Scottish clergyman who sometimes wished he was back on Loch Gilp, that great American express was in fact held up for no less than fifteen minutes.

That was quite a night. Never before or since have I sung for patrons who'd paid three hundred dollars to get in. That's what the Cardinal charged for his charity dinner—per person!

The following year I toured U.S. again. In New York the newspapers were more enthusiastic than ever. I walked into Times Square and all the news-stands had their usual displays of publications from all over the world.

One New York tabloid had settled that morning for a front page composed entirely of two large pictures. One of our Queen Mother—the other of Sydney MacEwan!

The Queen Mother was on a visit to the U.S. I suppose she would see it. I was intrigued thereafter that she might have said: " I know that face." She it was who consented to be my patron when the Marchioness of Londonderry loaned Londonderry House for my recital with Duncan in 1935.

March 17 is the day they paint the traffic lines green in New York—in honour of St. Patrick!

This is the occasion when every New Yorker with an Irish granny shines his boots and puts on his best suit and goes out and proclaims the fact.

The climax to the giant parade is the march up Fifth Avenue past St. Patrick's Cathedral, where the Archbishop of New York takes the salute.

Cardinal Spellman said: " I want you to be there, Sydney. Keep close to me all the time—it won't do you any harm—you'll see."

With the Cardinal therefore I watched this endless procession of Celtic pride. With drums beating and bands playing, it came down the Avenue like a gathering flood through a man-made canyon. It took about three hours to pass.

The Men of Cork marched behind the Men of Kerry, and the Men of Kerry behind the Men of Sligo, and the Men of Sligo behind the Men of Armagh, and so on through the whole of the atlas of Ireland.

Each group displayed its gay, individual identity banner. The Irish in the United States don't stick at being hewers of wood and drawers of water. There were judges and senators and lawyers among this mass demonstration of loyalty to St. Patrick—and doctors and surgeons and business tycoons. The U.S. is the great racial melting-pot, and a lot of the devotees of the shamrock were now ostensibly Jewish.

As the flood of Erin flowed past, the bishops in the entourage of Cardinal Spellman were like racehorses at the starting-post. They jostled for the best position at the Cathedral—if possible alongside the Cardinal himself.

"Don't move," said Spellman every so often; I stuck close to his side right throughout the entire parade.

I realised what he was after when the newspapers came out next day. The photographs of Spellman were everywhere. I learned later that the pictures went all over the world as well.

And, of course, wherever the Cardinal appeared in print, I was by his side. I've never since had a full-blown Cardinal as my public relations man. But that day Spellman did a magnificent publicity job for me.

Afterwards he took me to lunch. He was a man who was not without critics. His treatment of me was always wonderful and he it was who arranged for me to appear on the Ed Sullivan show.

A cherubic, little man whom his close associates referred to as Spelly—yet a man to be feared for the power he wielded.

So far as Pius XII was concerned, Spelly was very much on the inner circle. From New York, it was said, he phoned Rome once a week.

One time in Italy I had personal experience of the extent of his influence.

In the Via Veneto the Cardinal was living at the Excelsior Hotel. One of his Monsignors telephoned and asked me to come over immediately.

Spelly was waiting for me at the door, and I thought I detected a twinkle in his eye—a look that suggested that this was no ordinary, afternoon-tea sort of visit.

" We're going out tomorrow, Sydney," he said. " We're going to see the Pope! You're coming with me for a private audience!"

I didn't answer right away. You don't react so fast to this kind of situation. A private audience! The sort of honour reserved for royalty and heads of State, and the very occasional celebrity! At first I couldn't believe it.

That night I remember thinking—I wonder if it's trouble. A ridiculous thought, of course. But I pondered at my unique position. No other priest had my kind of freedom— not only to sing in public, but to travel the world as an international tenor.

Eventually, I dismissed the thought as nonsense—the Pope had more to do than bother his head about me!

Next day a Vatican cadillac drew up outside the Excelsior, and we were off to St. Peter's.

I don't think I've ever had a more exciting journey. Remember, this was still basically the Springburn laddie who worshipped the Church and built his own altar and was never more happy than in the company of men of the Church.

And now—to meet the Pope!

It wasn't a day for taking in detail. I remember at St. Peter's, Spelly and I went up in a very smooth lift and then, it seemed, there followed an endless procession of various luxurious halls and apartments.

A Monsignor led the way, and each new pair of doors was opened by a set of uniformed flunkies. Members of the Swiss Guard kept giving the salute—not for me, but for Cardinal Spellman.

I suppose I was something of an old hand at the big occasion. I had stood alone on stage in front of some of the greatest audiences in the world. I had mixed with the mighty and influential, but when at last we stepped into the Papal apartments, my heart was going like a power-hammer.

Pope Pius was sitting at a desk. He got up and came over to greet Spellman, who knelt and kissed the ring on the papal finger—the Ring of the Fisherman.

I was then introduced, and sought to repeat the Cardinal's performance without showing too much nervousness.

I was impressed with the height of Pius. And the eyes—dark, piercing, powerful eyes. He was very much the aristocrat. He had the aristocrat's graciousness. He gestured to us to sit. Spelly told him something about my career and thereafter the talk was of music and recording and travel.

I cannot claim it was one of my best performances. I continued to be overawed. I was grateful to Pius the way he brought me into the conversation. Otherwise I'm afraid I would have sat dumb and left the speaking to Spelly.

We were there for all of 15 minutes. There was no question of being told to leave. The Cardinal rose first as if reacting to some invisible signal, and of course I followed suit. Even in the business of saying good-bye, the poise and polish of Pius were exquisite.

Spelly escorted me to the little street that runs behind the Sacristy of St. Peter's. I thanked him and suggested I'd like to walk back on my own. I was walking on air. I wanted to savour the experience as long as I could.

The Cardinal did me another great favour—he came to one of my concerts in New York. Of course, there wasn't one empty seat, and when he appeared the entire audience stood to attention.

Halfway through, I asked them: " Is there anything you'd like me to sing for you?"

There were answering shouts of: " When Irish eyes are smiling!"

I told them I didn't know the words. The real truth is I didn't like the song.

Throughout America I found the average taste in Irish songs was appalling. Always they wanted the " Galway Bays " and the blarney rhyming with Killarney.

Sometimes I took a great delight in announcing: "Would you like me to sing, ' When Irish eyes are smiling '?"

And there would be a great, mass howl of " Yes-s-s-s!"

I'd wait for the noise to die and say quietly: " Well, I'm not going to!"

Then I'd explain that what they were going to hear were the real folk songs of Ireland, not the synthetic shillelagh-and-shamrock rubbish from Hollywood.

This appetite for the spurious music was not unusual abroad. I met up with it in Australia, New Zealand and Canada as well. Inevitably in Australia there would be shouts from the audience: " Give us ' Granny's Hielan' Hame!' " or some such phoney ballad.

The Scot in America was a different proposition. I found him well informed about the genuine folk song of his native land. His nostalgia was for the real Mackay. He seemed to sense the shoddiness of the haggis-hashing, Tin Pan Alley substitutes.

Nor were there so many blatantly professional Scots as there were blatantly professional Irishmen. It pays to be Irish—especially in New York or Chicago or Boston. It opens doors in business. It sometimes gives you a start on the other guy, when it comes to going after a job.

So these cities are cluttered with emerald-eyed phoneys who lay on thick what they think is the brogue, and sprinkle their conversation with frequent Irishisms — I'm after telling you, begorrah, they do!

Sometimes we say of a Catholic that he's more Catholic than the Pope. But preserve me from the Scot who is more Scottish than the Scots, or the Irishman, in inverted commas, who pretends to be more Irish than the Irish!

Hoots mon and bejabers!

One of the times I passed through Chicago, dear Nate Grose was on the phone: " Is there anyone you'd specially like to meet?"

I'd just finished reading the *Tribune*. And one of its items recorded the arrival in Chicago of Judy Garland. I'd seen her in all the Andy Hardy series. I'd been bowled over by her wistful charm in that wonderful " Wizard of Oz."

" I see Judy Garland's in town," I told him. " Would that be asking too much?"

" Not a bit," said Nate. " I'll ring you back."

The following day about lunchtime he was as good as his word: " This afternoon O.K.?" he said. " Come over to the ranch."

Among all the Western paraphernalia, Judy was sitting on a large black pouffee. She was aged 36. She had still that vivacious, elfin look. She was a bit more plump than I had expected.

This was one of the curses of Judy's career—the nervous eating followed by the constant battle to take off surplus tissue. Even as a teenager, she was bound like a mummy in plaster bandage in an attempt to conceal her extra inches.

I found her charming—gay, quick-witted and prone to chuckle infectiously.

We talked of course of singing, and she began to sing a song that was going the rounds. I had a pleasant surprise when it turned out to be the revival of a number we used to sing in the Glasgow parish halls in that ill-fated, infamous minstrel troupe.

" You've got the words wrong," I said.

She looked at me in surprise.

" This is the way we used to sing it," I told her:

> " She's the sweetest rose of colour this darkie ever knew,
>> Her eyes are bright as diamonds and they sparkle like the dew:
>> You may talk about your fairest love or sing of your Rosalie,
>> But the yellow Rose of Texas beats the Belles of Tennessee."

She had the words off pat before she left—my words. The next time we met was in the Waldorf Astoria. She ran across the foyer and threw her arms round my neck. She'd just made a come-back in " A Star is Born." Everything seemed right for her again.

She was really a star. She was playing a part all the time —acting out the role of the happy, carefree extrovert. Whereas now we know that her life was never far removed from heartache, and tragedy was its end.

When I sailed home in 1955, the *Queen Mary* was on her winter schedule. For the first time I sensed that Cunard might be in trouble.

Their great ship was losing the place. The shadow of the aeroplane was dark across her expensive decks.

When I walked into her dining-room there were more empty tables than full. Yehudi Menuhin was one of her passengers. Throughout the whole voyage he never once budged from his cabin. Maybe he wasn't a sailor.

Another ominously deserted sector was the lounge, where I went to hear the news on the radio. One other passenger sat there. It was Viscount Montgomery.

He was the first to break the ice in that brusque, efficient manner of his. Of all the chance meetings in my wanderings around the world, this one thrilled me.

As an avid reader of war histories, I was face to face with one who made history.

Monty didn't miss the carnage of World War I. He was then a young officer. He saw at first hand the thousands of lives that were wasted by the aristocratic clowns who masqueraded as generals: the chinless idiots with their polished boots in the security of their chateaux behind the lines, who persistently sacrificed whole regiments to gain a few useless yards of mud.

Luckily for us, Montgomery was spared. Luckily for us, he remembered. He became the general to whom human life was sacred, who never made a move until victory was almost assured. Who scorned the safety of behind-the-lines and was up there in front with his men and the danger.

That's how he got their affection and respect—and his picture hung on walls all over the country, in such unexpected places as the poverty-stricken hovels I used to know in Glasgow.

His shipboard routine was a walk before dinner, and he asked me to join him. I walked the deck of the *Queen Mary* with this great soldier, and he turned out to be what I had expected: a delightful companion; an intelligent listener; a forthright debater. And he could quote his Bible with accuracy.

My enthusiasm for the noble art landed me once in a spot of bother at New York. A friend put me up for the day between planes, and I remember lying in his apartment dreaming of the Clyde and the joy it would be to be out there on the grey water even in a howling gale of rain.

I had just come from Australia's winter, and now it was summer in New York. Even the Amazonian jungle cannot be more oppressive than New York in this climatic mood. Air becomes a solid thing, pressing down on you like a hot, moist blanket and seeming to squeeze the sweat out of every pore.

All day I lay on top of the bed, sipping soft drinks and perspiring like a punctured water-bottle.

My plane was due to pull out that evening. I suppose it was a daft move, but I was determined to fit in a boxing match before I left.

The heavies in particular have always been my passion. Jack Dempsey was my boyhood hero, and mine was the good fortune of meeting him in person the last time I passed through New York.

This time it was to be another of the greats—Joe Louis, somewhat past his best maybe, but in a contest that promised to be exciting—against the almost as notable Jersey Joe Walcott.

Pugilistic promotions cannot be timed right down to the minute like football matches. This one ran late, and I left myself exactly one hour to get to La Guardia airport.

The taximan was splendid. He exerted all his skill and local know-how to get me there on time. But after ten minutes I couldn't resist a persistent fear that we weren't going to make it.

The plane was still there all right. I could see it out on the tarmac. But everyone except MacEwan was already on board—and I had all the formalities of air travel yet to go through.

Now I was suddenly chilled—with something akin to panic. The plane took off, and all I could keep on saying to myself was: "What am I going to do?"

It wasn't long after the war. Planes were still scarce. The next plane for the U.K. with a vacant seat could well be two or three weeks hence.

My forlorn look of having been dropped in the middle of the Sahara prompted a stranger to ask: "What's the trouble, Father?"

He wore a straw-basher—and a Roman collar. He was an American priest, a jolly, sallow, extrovert man.

"I've just missed my plane," I said. And immediately I was back in "the club" that I've referred to before.

"What ya gonna do?"

"I'll have to try ringing up a friend," I said.

" You've got yer friend right here," he said. " Come on—you're stayin' with me!"

I sent a telegram to St. Andrew's Cathedral, and for three days at the New York presbytery I lived very pleasantly indeed.

I was fascinated by a machine which the American Church used for counting the collections.

This aspect of the life of a priest was one of the bugbears of Monday mornings. In Glasgow it was mostly ha'pennies, pennies and threepennies — with some sixpences and shillings.

Every week we had the tedious job of sorting out this great mass of coins into separate bundles and counting each denomination by hand.

The American technique was to shovel the lot into this clever device that not only dispatched each coin to an appropriate collecting bag, but registered a total in dollars and cents.

When I got back, I was determined to introduce this bit of labour-saving equipment to Glasgow. I wrote to New York and sent out samples of our British coins.

Eventually, I had to face up to the depressing fact that the cost of a special machine for our kind of money was going to be out of the question.

At St. Andrew's Cathedral of a Monday morning they would have to go on manually counting their blessings—if that's the right way to put it!

Once Oscar met me in London. Dear Oscar never let me down—every time I came home from abroad he was there to greet me with rail reservations, sleeper booking and any other little special needs taken care of.

This time he said: " We want more records. Your old friend, Phil Green, is all set to do the backings."

By this time my record run was about 25 years—and every recording I made enjoyed a considerable export market. As a Scot, I was in a unique position. I was the only one singing to Scots abroad. I had a big share of Irish nostalgia as well. It was a virtual monopoly that remained intact till round about 1955.

" What about new numbers?" asked Oscar. " Remember the one you told us about—the one McCormack sang?"

" Mary Shaw?"

The name brought back a magical evening with Count John in the Albert Hall. I'd never heard the song before, and I went round afterwards and asked John who wrote it.

" God, Sydney!" he said, " I can't remember."

Thereafter it was almost like a love affair. "Mary Shaw" just would not get out of my head.

I was well known to every music publisher in the land, but none of them could help me.

Inevitably the infatuation cooled. " Mary " slipped into the background, and I went on with my daily task of parochial duties and visiting my parishioners.

One lovely, loyal, old dear in a wee cottage went into the scullery to put on the pot, and I spent the waiting minutes studying the books on some shelves by the fireplace.

Unexpectedly, I found a volume of songs, and when I opened it at random, what was the first thing I saw right at the top of the page in old-fashioned script—" Mary Shaw "!

I tried to contain my excitement. " I've been looking at your books," I called to the scullery. " There's one here I'd like to borrow."

She poked her head round the door: " Certainly, Father —keep it, Father." And almost wistfully, as if the song had gone out of her modest life: " It's no' ony use tae me now."

I sent down the copy to Phil. He liked it except for the length. " Mary Shaw " was too short—it wouldn't fill out the three minutes of one side of the old 78 kind of disc. It needed another verse.

The afternoon of the day I was due to leave for the London studios, I went to the rehearsal rooms of Paterson's in Buchanan Street, Glasgow, and Barbara Lane of the

B.B.C. played piano for my warming-up scales and exercises.

When I stepped out into the street again, I had a shirt to buy before catching the train to London.

"Mary Shaw" was at me once more. I wanted so much to capture this one on wax. "I wish I'd told Joe," I said to myself. "Joe could have written that extra verse beautifully."

Joe Corrie was the one I had in mind, the miner-poet and playwright, who later died without making a great deal of money, in a council house in Fife. Poor old Joe—a grossly under-rated Scottish littérateur, dead now maybe, but certainly not gone beyond recall, so long's his poems are still around.

Thirty yards along Buchanan Street I couldn't believe my eyes. Walking towards me, head slightly down as if pondering a difficult couplet, was Joe himself! Out of all the thousands in this great old city!

I stopped right in his path. "Joe!" I said, "Joe—you're the one person in the whole world I wanted to meet at this precise moment!"

He didn't share my excitement.

"I've a train to catch in about an hour," he said.

"So have I," I told him. "But that's plenty of time!"

And I explained about the verse for "Mary Shaw."

I practically dragged him back to the Cathedral. I put him in a room by himself and laid out paper and pencil: "Joe, you can do it," I urged. "You can make me the most grateful of men!"

And I dashed off again to buy my shirt. I was back in just over half an hour. No sign of Joe. The room was deserted. But one sheet of the paper I'd left was filled with his irregular handwriting.

This is what he'd written—the extra verse that was vital to my record:

> "Oft I have heard the blackbird gay
> At the peak o' evenfa',

> Singing from a hert o' love,
> Surely 'twas for Mary Shaw:
> And the flooers that fell asleepin'
> When the dew began to fa'
> Were adreamin' o' the beauty
> O' my bonnie Mary Shaw.
> Mild and modest, bonnie lassie,
> Een sae fu' o' love an' a',
> Innocent and sweet wee lassie,
> Oh, I love you, Mary Shaw."

Oh, I loved you, too, Joe Corrie—and never more than that late afternoon on a street in downtown Glasgow.

I was a seasoned recording artiste. I knew a fair share of the tricks of the trade. But I never ceased to be willing to learn—especially from Oscar.

He was so much more than a recording manager. I stayed regularly at his home. We ate together and we talked together. I found his reminiscence priceless. Oscar had recorded all the greats—Caruso, Gigli, McCormack, Schipa, Galli-Curci.

One day at the studios he said: " Tauber's next door—come and see him in action—it's fascinating."

To most people the extent of Richard Tauber's repertoire was: " You are my heart's delight," snatches of " Old Chelsea," and that sort of thing. They were aware of only the latter years of Tauber.

But at his peak he was one of the giants. In his sensitive handling of Mozart songs he was the world's master. His " Il mio tesoro " is near perfection—second only to John's.

From that introduction by Oscar I came to know him as a lovable man as well as tenor-extraordinary. I made a point of seeing his London shows and sometimes thereafter with Oscar we would make a threesome for dinner.

Not that Richard was always available after a performance. He was frequently otherwise engaged. His heart's delight was a late-night appointment in some luxury hostelry with a glamorous lady.

He liked to live at that sort of pace. He revelled in the good things of life and spent a fortune in their pursuit.

As it turned out, the money he might have saved from a lucrative career, he never needed. He died early enough to escape the indignities of a very old age.

The world lost a magnificent artiste and showman. I lost a good friend.

In the corner of my study there is something that serves as a little memorial—his Viennese walking stick. It is fragile and graceful and silver at the top—not unlike his wonderful tenor.

CHAPTER

3 1

For one of my concerts on the 1956 U.S. tour, two thousand people crammed the magnificent ballroom of the Waldorf Astoria. Mary Garden, the opera singer, was there—and, of course, Lily, John's widow.

I remember there was also a remarkable speed-cop called Officer McCafferty. He came up to me afterwards and said in a brogue that sounded newly-imported from County Kerry:

"I managed to get in, Father! And I can tell you—I listened to every single song—every single song, Father! And you didn't sing a wrong note, Father—not a wrong note! I know, Father—I was listenin'!"

Everyone stood up when I walked in and made my way to the grand piano. I held up my hand for them all to sit down, and I happened to spot a little patch of red to the right of the third front row. It was a bishop's zucchetto.

"This must be the first time in history that a bishop has stood for a priest!" I said.

Everybody laughed, and again we were off to a good-humoured start.

"I'm going to sing you some Celtic music," I told them. "I hope it will fire a wee spark in your hearts."

The following morning a critic wrote: "A wee spark! So beautiful was the music and so sweet the singing that the wee spark in every heart burst into a great flame."

It seems that I had told them that they could choose to forget me altogether—what mattered was that they should remember the songs.

A critic said: "We were haunted by both the singer and the songs.

"It's seldom enough in offerings of nationalistic music that one encounters a singer with a voice to do it justice.

"This voice was a big and opulent tenor with quite an astonishing range."

They were kind to me, the Americans—very kind indeed.

Time devoted its whole music section to this concert: "Father MacEwan sang the centuries-old songs of plaintive and merry love of the sea and the rocky Hebrides, while mink-jacketed matrons and soberly-dressed tycoons were immediately reduced to tears."

Maybe a bit of an exaggeration—I wouldn't like to say. But it was nicely put—a colourful piece of language.

There was someone at that New York concert I didn't know about. He'd travelled 200 miles to get there, then got bogged down in the treacle of New York traffic.

And at the Waldorf they tried to keep him out: "Sorry," they said, "you've left it late—there isn't a single seat in the place."

It was one of those singular little coincidences that give life its savour, which saved him from all that travel in vain. One of the Waldorf's girls happened to be a Scot: "Here, that's Robert Wilson," she whispered. "We must try to get him in somehow."

Dear Robert made it, and he came round to see me after the recital.

Meeting him so far from home was like a salt-filled breeze off Loch Fyne.

"Did you get a good seat?" I asked.

"I'm afraid I had to stand—right at the back," he said.

"I was lucky at that—I'd left it late."

It was typical of one of the most delightfully modest men it has ever been my fortune to know.

Firstly, that he should bother to break off from one of his White Heather Club tours and come all that way to see an old friend. Then be content, despite his fame, to stand at the back of the hall.

I recall the first time I heard him sing, away back in the early days of the war when I was studying at Bearsden.

He turned up in an ENSA concert party along with Will Fyffe. I'd never seen or heard of the man—he had not even yet made a record.

The song that sticks in my mind was " Afton Water." I thought it was magnificent. I sat entranced through every note.

Round about 1945 I was staying with Joe Corrie at Mauchline, Ayrshire. It was Joe who said: " Robert Wilson's in the show at Ayr—I suppose you've met?"

I told him we hadn't, and that night we went to the Gaiety Theatre and I got my first introduction to Robert. I discovered that the tenor which had captivated my ear was contained in a personality that was equally charming.

Despite all the ballyhoo, despite all the big names and the posh receptions, despite the constant VIP treatment—high up in my most treasured memories of America is that reunion with Robert in New York.

He turned up at a time of great nostalgia, for I'd just said hullo to another two friends who brought with them a bitter-sweet memory of the Glasgow days of long ago.

Remember that terrible minstrel troupe in Glasgow and the faithful lassies who remained our unflinching support through all the catcalls and backstage disasters?

The bonniest were a couple of girls called Peggy Cassidy and Winnie O'Donnell. And this was them now in the Waldorf Astoria—more prosperous, more sophisticated, more self-assured, but still as gay and lovely as ever—at the age of 43.

There were wealthy and eminent American guests all assembled in an ante-room to greet me after the show. As soon as I decently could, I slipped away to join my unexpected companions from the days of old.

We made for the Oriel Society rooms, where Lily McCormack was waiting. What a time of reminiscence the five of us had together! It was one of those precious occasions that could have gone on all night.

But I felt a tap on my shoulder: "Come on, Father MacEwan—bed-time!" someone said. It was one of my American management team. As I say, the Americans were extremely kind. They even ensured me the ration of sleep that a tenor needs nightly to be in good voice!

I remember I was leaving Carnegie Hall one evening after listening to a recital by Victoria de los Angeles. In the foyer a little man stopped me and introduced himself as Sol Hurok.

He wanted to take me on and arrange my next American tour. I had to tell him that I was pretty happy with the management I had already.

At that time Mr. Hurok was reckoned to be the biggest impresario in the whole of the United States.

Before I sailed away from New York, I had a game of tennis—on a quiet private court with not one spectator.

I mention this minor sporting occasion because of its significance to the role of John McCormack as a prophet.

Almost twenty years before to the day, over afternoon tea at a country-house in England, he had predicted that I would make the grade as an international tenor.

Simultaneously, he had also forecast that his protégé, Fulton Sheen, would rise to great heights in the Church.

Fulton that day was my tennis opponent—taking time off from his onerous duties as Auxiliary Bishop of New York and one of America's most successful broadcasters of religion.

"We're dining tonight with Fritz Kreisler," he told me. "He likes your singing and wants to talk music."

"It should be quite an occasion," I said, remembering the fiddle I had under the bed back home in Lochgilphead. "Two great violinists under one roof!"

Kreisler was a friend of the McCormacks. John made many records with the violin obbligato played by Kreisler. He used to say they were among his best. The challenge of having to match the sheer perfection of Kreisler's tone brought out his very best.

Kreisler to me was the greatest—I could pick him out on the radio every time he played. The same still applies when one of his records is played. There is just no mistaking that beautiful, rich, fat, mellow sound.

I was therefore delighted at the prospect of this date with the master himself. And it turned out to be a memorable evening.

The Kreislers were old. Like the minstrels of old, he had hung up his harp. The celebrated Fritz was now a quiet, gentle, pacific man.

But age sat lightly on Mrs. K. She was gay and vivacious and kept joking about their marriage and how she had had so many other eligible suitors — including a European prince.

We talked music. The wine flowed. And largely due to the gaiety of Mrs. K., the party was one of those pleasant occasions when time has wings and night slips into morning almost unobserved.

I still had one ambition unfulfilled. Could I see the maestro's fiddles? Could I have the pleasure of touching the precious instruments from which all that magic music flowed?

Mrs. K. was delighted. She took me into the study and opened up two worn, faded cases. In one was a Stradivarius. The other contained a Guarnerius. I ran my fingers over the strings of the Strad and did the same to the other.

I have to report that both the Kreisler fiddles were very much out of tune! He hadn't played for eight years—perfection was now impossible for the aged master and he chose to stop.

One thing spoiled that evening out. After dinner I had this excruciating pain across my chest. I tried to tell myself it was something I'd eaten. But all the time, I must admit, there was the nagging suspicion that perhaps I'd overdone things a bit, that the strain of such a full concert schedule had caught up with me at last.

I went straight to Cameron-MacDonald when I got back home. His father, a former Moderator of the Church of Scotland, had been a good friend of mine. His examination was extremely thorough. I felt I could almost put the words of his verdict into his mouth: " It's your heart."

But he smiled encouragingly and said: " I'm afraid you're extremely healthy. It *must* have been something you ate."

Preaching at the Memorial Service for Sir Compton Mackenzie.

(Photograph by courtesy of the *Glasgow Observer*.)

The world première of Sung Mass of St. Francis —Sydney MacEwan, celebrant.

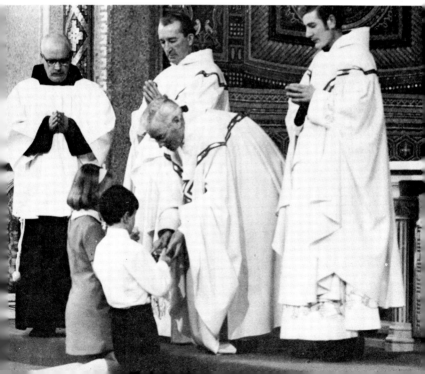

With Mother and Annie Cleary at Highland Games, 1967.

St. Columba's Church, Kingussie,

CHAPTER

32

I got back to my Lochgilphead routine—my stained, black, corded jacket and the trousers that were always alleged to be needing pressing.

I walked out again in the wind and the rain and among the snowdrops up at Kilmory.

The sky went pink across Loch Gilp and I thought: "It's going to be fine again."

There was something about those sunsets that you could never achieve with neon on Broadway. And the cry of the gulls, like hungry babies, was basic and real—not man-made and synthetic like the scream of New York's motor tyres and strident whine of speed cops' sirens.

I never altered my diet. I ate as I'd done before. And that pain in my chest never once returned. It remained somewhere among the skyscrapers 3,000 miles across the western sea.

"Maybe it was my heart after all," I thought. "Maybe it was aching to get back home."

One of my parishioners in Lochgilphead said: "Well, Father, that was some tour you had of America!"

I was rather taken aback: "How'd you hear about that?" I asked.

"It was in the papers," she said. "I think it was the *Daily Express* had a great screed about you."

She turned up later with a copy of the paper, and sure enough, there was quite a glowing resumé that described me perhaps not with complete accuracy as "the sturdy little Highlander with the silvery mane!"

I was so intrigued that I wrote to the editor and asked if he could tell me the source of the report.

Back came the reply: "It was sent by Robert Wilson."

Robert had forwarded the U.S. press cuttings by air-mail to Scotland. It was typical of a man who worked himself into an early grave—largely because of his concern for others.

Before I went to America on the 1956 tour, I told Oscar Preuss that I'd been offered another contract with the Gramophone Company — now E.M.I. — with whom I worked for twenty-two years. He asked its terms.

"Not bad," he said thoughtfully. "But I think I could get you something better—with Columbia America."

He came up with a remarkable deal—five per cent on all retail sales. A twentieth on every record sold over the counter.

By this time Oscar was officially retired. But he sold Columbia America a brilliant idea—that I should record a Mass in Rome.

I decided one good turn deserved another. I told the Columbia executives: "Oscar has been my recording manager since the day I began. He's out of it now, but could I have him as my manager for this Mass?"

They were delighted to oblige. I decided to push my luck a bit further.

"When we go to Rome, would it be possible for him to take his wife as well?"

"Why not? Great idea!"

I thought to myself—these Americans are terrific. Wonder if I can try just one more little shove.

"One thing Oscar's always wanted and that's to see Capri," I said. "All right if we popped down there for a look-round?"

Again the suggestion was greeted with enthusiasm. And this, remember, was all at their expense!

Columbia America was like that—most generous, most accommodating. Every time I travelled down to record in

London, they put a chauffeur-driven Daimler entirely at my disposal.

There was always a bowl of fruit and a bottle of whisky in my hotel bedroom. They never forgot a Christmas—as well as the traditional greetings card, there were always six bottles of Scotch.

If I got a card from the Gramophone Company, that was really quite a Christmas!

Like many an inspired piece of thinking, the Rome idea turned out to be less simple than it seemed. I was given a choir of seminarians and the recording equipment was to be set up in the great church of Santa Susannah in Rome.

We ran into trouble right away. The traffic noise was hopeless. Rome has been ruined by the motor-car—just that bit more so than most other cities.

There is only one noisier place I know, and that is Tokyo.

Anyhow, recording in Santa Susannah during normal working hours was very definitely out of the question. We decided to try siesta time. But there is no siesta for the infernal internal combustion engine.

Eventually, we had to check with a device for measuring decibels every hour of the night from midnight onwards to find out the time of greatest peace and quiet.

I think we started on the Mass in Rome about three o'clock in the morning.

Nobody's usually at their best at such an unearthly hour, but the record was a winner. Columbia did the thing in style. With the disc went a booklet filled with pictures in colour by eminent photographers of great church buildings throughout the world. A history of the Mass was written specially for the occasion by my old friend, Fulton, now Archbishop Sheen.

Sales in America were tremendous. But the record was never issued in Britain. Phillips, the British subsidiary of Columbia America, decided that for the U.K. market, it would have priced itself out.

The record is now a collector's piece—for the Mass sung in Latin has gone forever.

Back in London, I stayed a night with Oscar, and we reminisced about the Roman journey. Before I left, he said casually: " By the way, Sydney, I'm going into hospital tomorrow. Nothing serious—just for a check-up."

I went back to Scotland—and I never saw dear Oscar again. It was only a matter of weeks till the phone call from London. Oscar was dead.

My slight consolation was that his very last recording assignment should have been with me. I hope that's the way he would have wished it.

CHAPTER

33

The hydro camps moved away from Argyll, and my little wooden church went with them. Every Sunday, however, I still travelled up to Inveraray to say Mass in the wee local hall.

Then one night I got word that the hall had been gutted by fire. In the compact, little, white-washed town, there was no other suitable place. So far as the faithful of Inveraray were concerned, we were homeless.

I mentioned my predicament to my good friend, the local Episcopalian minister.

" Would there be any chance of our using your church?" I asked.

This was long before Vatican II—long before the prolonged wave of ecumenical fervour had swept across the country.

"I don't see why not, but I'll have to consult the Bishop," he said.

And his verdict was: " The Bishop thinks it's a splendid idea."

So far, so good. But I still had to consult our own Church authorities.

Bishop McGill was most enthusiastic. But he came back with the instruction to delay the move meantime. " I've consulted a Canon lawyer," he explained, " and he's of the opinion that we'll have to get permission from Rome."

I got my way. Rome approved. In that lovely little Episcopalian church in Inveraray, I should imagine I was the very first in the whole of the country to say Mass within a non-Catholic place of worship.

To replace the little white bungalow at the edge of the town, I had a new house built beside St. Margaret's—in the same stout, grey stone as the church itself. I gave £3,000 towards the cost—a lot in those days.

It was money I spent readily. I got from its spending a great deal of pleasure. I felt like a father who was grateful to God for being so blessed as to be able to afford to give his own family a lift along the road.

St. Margaret's was my family—St. Margaret's and its faithful folk who accorded me the only return I could wish for—their loyal and lasting friendship.

About this time I had another experience of misfortune being turned to good account.

All those years—those glorious, varied, rewarding years —my mother had been with me. Latterly she was my domestic guardian. I was able to pursue my spiritual vocation by virtue of her attention to the more mundane but still essential things of life, like cream on my porridge and a bed with clean sheets.

But now she was eighty—a spry, alert, intelligent eighty, but an age nonetheless to be relieved of responsibility and allowed to relax and relish lazily the memories of a lifetime well spent.

She had no fear of dying. We used to joke in fact about the final curtain: " Never mind, mother," I would say, " we'll give you a great send-off. You'll get the full treatment—Requiem Mass and all!"

Death called first at another door. From Annie Cleary— our close and lifelong friend—we got word that her husband had died. Suddenly, Annie was alone. Overnight she was disabled by that handicap that escapes the attention given to the blind and the maimed—the disablement of widowhood.

We offered her the solace of a home—by inviting her as my housekeeper at Lochgilphead.

Annie is with me still. Over the years she may not have achieved the impossible by making me daily polish my shoes or do something about those uncreased trousers. But she has tended me constantly and tended me well.

Perhaps even more important — Annie is a sunshine person. She aerosols my house with good nature.

Housekeepers in any shape or form are hard to come by these days. Housekeepers like Annie are as rare as butterflies in winter.

I took my mother abroad a lot. But after her eightieth milestone, I thought, there may be no harm in a change of bed, but the business of aeroplanes and sudden temperatures of 80 degrees was perhaps no longer to be recommended.

So we chose to holiday in Dunoon—that lovely Clyde resort that loomed so large in my childhood.

The second day we were there, my brother phoned: "Keep it under your hat, Sydney—you're going to be on 'This Is Your Life.' I thought I'd let you know."

This programme, run by Eamonn Andrews, was once the pride and joy of the British Broadcasting Corporation. It turned the spotlight on people whose lives were alleged to be that bit outstanding by way of achievement or courage or triumph over adversity or devotion to duty.

Its prime appeal was supposed to be that of surprise.

The technique was to inveigle the unsuspecting victim to London, where eventually Mr. Andrews proceeded to turn back the pages of life before his guest's shocked and incredulous eyes—and the usual battery of high-wattage lamps and mobile cameras.

I had good fun for the next few weeks maintaining the Great Pretence. There were B.B.C. photographers up taking shots of the village, and people stopped me on the street and said: "I wonder what they're up to?"

"It'll be one of those travel things," I said, hoping that my expression would not disclose that I wasn't a very good liar.

They were even buzzing around the mental hospital, doing interviews with the staff and discovering that I was one of the hospital's ministering angels—which was really a great exaggeration.

Even Bishop McGill was in on the plot. He told me one day: "Sydney, our man on the B.B.C. Religious Board can't make it for the next meeting in London. You know the ropes—I wonder if you'd go down in his place."

This was really a testing moment. When he mentioned the date, it needed all my will-power to suppress a quiet smile.

Dear old mother had to go down as well. She was at the stage of not being able to realise what was going on. All that she could tell me was that she was off to London with my brother to visit somebody or other.

I suppose it was lucky for the B.B.C. that, because of her age, she didn't have to live with the deceit. She just didn't understand.

Funnily enough, it was mother in all her innocence who almost blew the gaff completely.

They had her off with an earlier train than mine, so that we wouldn't meet. The B.B.C.'s concern was that I shoudn't be around London's Euston Station when she was met by their reception committee.

Unfortunately, mother's train was an hour late. And I understand that there were a number of nail-biting types at Euston, growing more and more convinced with the passing of the vital moments that the very worst would happen and our two trains would come in together at one and the same time.

They were saved the embarrassment by five minutes. The B.B.C.'s Catholic representative, Father Agnellus Andrew, met me at the platform and drove me to the Catholic Radio and T.V. Centre at Hatch End, where the religious conference was supposed to be taking place.

The whole charade began to amuse me more. I was chuckling inwardly. I lost count of the number of times I was tempted to say: " Wouldn't it be funny if I was on this ' This Is Your Life ' thing?"

Eventually Eamonn Andrews turned up at Hatch End with his inevitable book and that dramatic greeting of his: " Sydney MacEwan, this is your life!"

I was grateful for my brother's tip-off. It ensured that in front of the millions I was at least half-decently dressed!

It was bad enough being constantly labelled " The Singing Priest." To have added to this the nation-wide reputation of the priest with the baggy breeks would have been rather unfortunate.

But I was left wondering—how often has the secret of " This Is Your Life " really been preserved intact?

Could all the wives of those subjects who were husbands, for instance, have survived the agony of going around with sealed lips for weeks and even months?

I was part of this series, when despite its critics, it seemed to me to have an element of quality and dignity about it. It also achieved an essential versatility. Its characters were from all walks of life and some had brought to the world so much goodness and self-sacrifice that this mass exhibition of their virtuous example would certainly do no harm.

More recently as far as I can gather, the " secret dossiers " of Eamonn have tended to concentrate on various personalities of the show-business world.

I love stage people, but " This Is Your Life " has thereby got itself into something of a decorative rut. It also frequently runs the risk of developing into a mutual admiration society.

I was far from happy with what was alleged to be My Life.

Lily, Countess McCormack, was in it—and Robert Wilson and my brother, and my right-hand man at Lochgilphead, Peter Ciarella.

So far, so good. All splendid folk whose friendship I cherished.

But there was also a policeman who was supposed to have brought me up my haggis from the Glasgow Constabulary's Burns Supper. There were Sheila Craig, widow of Hector McNeil, and the playwright, Roger MacDougall, whose only link was that we were contemporaries at university. Actually, I'd never met them again since.

They were presented as vital cogs in the wheel of my fortune, when the only real connection was that we each took part in the long, long ago, in one of those " College Pudding " entertainments at Glasgow University.

My Life had no Mannix, no Spellman, no De Valera or Arthur Caldwell. Not even the B.B.C.'s Andrew Stewart or Auntie Kathleen Garscadden, to whom I had been very close in the early days.

The whole thing came over as a trivial little cameo concerned with the life of someone who had certain experiences similar to my own. But that was as far as it went. I certainly never recognised it as my life. I hardly sensed it was dealing with me.

I remember as we walked towards the stage, Eamonn whispered somewhat apologetically: " Canon, you may be disappointed with this."

I'm afraid I was—especially when it wasn't even a surprise.

He was accurate with his mode of address. I had received my Canon status at the age of 46, well ahead of a number of priests who were my senior. I was aware of no jealousy, however—of no grumblings at my having jumped the gun.

I took the award as a tribute to what I had been able to do for the diocese, not strictly an honouring of myself. That way I preferred it.

CHAPTER

34

My lifetime's love affair with Scotland had been, I should imagine, like all love affairs—there was not sunshine all the way.

It was an early January day, and my lovely land was in one of her foulest moods. The wind that came in from the sea was armed with sleet. It seemed to cut right through to the bone and sought even to penetrate the headstones of the graveyard.

It was a funeral I could not miss. He was not a Catholic, but he was a friend—an admirable friend for years, and no weather could keep me from walking with him this last bit of his journey.

But everyone I knew who stood with me in the sleet that day was thereafter stricken with a bronchial cold—one of those persistent attacks that worked its depressing devilry for weeks.

I was therefore really out of sorts with this particular Scottish winter when I spotted the advert in the *Sunday Times*. Normally it would probably have been ignored.

It was listed under the heading of "Property for Sale," and made the offer of houses in Sunny Spain. With the cold and the weather remaining unfriendly, I was indiscreet enough to write off immediately.

I offered to buy on the spot. No surveyor's report. No question of price. I was so desperate to stake a claim in the sun.

The advertisers were obviously of the highest integrity.
"We prefer our clients to know what they are buying,"

was what they wrote back. " We would therefore invite you to join the party which we are flying out to inspect the properties . . ."

The date was unsuitable. I couldn't get away. I tried to forget about the deal, but the mood of restlessness refused to disperse.

Come the summer of 1964, and the rhodies up at Kilmory, I was still of a mind to have my place in Spain.

I flew out myself and bought a house in Malaga on the Costa Del Sol—lovely Malaga, the cathedral town with sun-browned people and its markets bulging with sun-ripened fruit. I now had a warm haven for the times when I fell out with my dear but sometimes climatically temperamental Lochgilphead.

Little did I realise that the seventeen-year romance was virtually at its end.

Lochgilphead was small, but I had no great ecclesiastical ambitions. It came therefore as a shock when the Bishop announced: " I'm sending you to Rothesay."

There was so much I was going to miss, above all, my beautiful church and the dear friends I had made there. No more fascinating nights with George Malcolm of Poltalloch—Chief of Clan Malcolm and one of the kindest of men.

His house is on the north side of Crinan and stands like a watchdog guarding the Sound of Jura.

This ancient place was once a Campbell stronghold.

And its fascination stands not in historic stones alone. The Castle of Duntrune is a haunted house. I had George Malcolm's word for it—and he is a man I trust.

A notorious Irish rover of the seventeenth century was known as Macdonnel Coll Ciotach—or Macdonnel the Left-handed One.

He set out from Ireland for the Mull of Kintyre and pillaged every Campbell property that crossed his marauder's path.

At Castle Sween in North Knapdale, he sailed out for Loch Crinan. This time his target was the Castle of Duntrune.

A wily fox, this Ulster reiver. He was aware of the old, old Scottish tradition that a piper was welcome in any home. So he had his piper go on ahead to spy out the land at Duntrune.

The musical secret agent was not impressed with what he saw. The castle was strongly fortified. Its access was by way of a narrow staircase, which one man could block on his own.

The piper decided to warn his chief to call off any direct assault. But Campbell for all his love of the pipes suspected this Ulster-spoken stranger. He had him locked in one of the upper turrets. But forgot to remove his pipes.

The piper still got his warning through—by playing a specially pre-arranged tune that winged its way out to the raiding ship.

The tune is still played in the places of the West, and its name is " Colla mo rhun "—" the piper's warning to his master."

It was a costly piece of subterfuge. The Campbells observed the ship turn about and linked its manoeuvre with the bagpipes in the attic room.

Coll Ciotach's piper paid for his cunning with his life. But not before the Campbells had wreaked their revenge on the very fingers that had played the trick—by lopping off each hand at the wrist.

" That's a pretty gruesome legend," I said to George when he told me the tale.

" I'm not so sure about the legend bit," he said.

" It's about sixty years since my grandfather decided to do some alterations. He arranged for the lifting of one of the stone floors and underneath there was a human skeleton —a skeleton without hands!"

I've seen the cavity under the floor where the piper's remains were found.

" What about the ghost?" I asked George.

" Not so much a ghost as ghostly music," he said. " We used to be plagued with mysterious bagpiping that apparently came from nowhere.

" Then it was decided to give the piper's remains a decent Christian burial. We got an Episcopalian minister to do the ceremony, and he also attempted to lay the spirit with the rite of the bell, book and candle."

So I never actually heard the ghost piper of Duntrune. But George has told me that his house still has what he describes as " manifestations."

Sometimes things go bump in the night. Well-secured pictures drop off walls for no apparent reason. There are knockings on doors and nobody's there.

George has a theory that the piper's spirit is still abroad because the burial he got was a Protestant one. And the piper from Ulster was a Catholic man.

I wonder.

Once I'd got over the initial shock of leaving Argyll, I tried to warm to the prospect of Rothesay. At least I'd be back to my beloved Clyde. I'd be back again with my steamers and in sight of the places I knew as a child.

St. Andrew's, Rothesay, was a beautiful church, created out of strong, red sandstone by courtesy of the wealthy fourth Marquis of Bute.

My mother by now was fading. Dear Annie Cleary was a priceless help in those final, fragile weeks. She tended her like her own flesh and blood. She cooked all the things she loved—for one of the myths of growing old is that the appetite starts to fade.

Mother, despite her 89 years, was never an absentee from breakfast—not until that morning when Annie went up to find out why she was late.

Annie came down again and said simply: "Your mother won't waken."

The doctor arrived promptly and ordered mother to hospital. I gave her the last sacraments. And in hospital she was able to open her eyes.

" Is this the end, Sydney?" she asked.

She'd never been in hospital in her life before. I held her cool hand and told her the truth : " I don't know, mother."

" Och, well," she whispered, " my bags are packed— I'm ready."

She had another week for sleeping. No pain. No sickness. Just an old, old lady winding down after a lifetime that had been almost as blessed as my own.

" Your mother has passed away," the phone call came from the hospital at a quarter to four in the morning. I knew the euphemistic wording for once was accurate—she had passed on leisurely from a life in which I think she had served her Master well.

She had spoken to children of the Christian life for all of forty years. For more years still she'd sewn and knitted to help clothe the bairns of the threadbare days.

There were many Govan youngsters who went to their first Communion in white, because of mother's skilled and devoted hands.

And now that she was dead, she was due for all the honours. She was ready for the great send-off that we had often joked about.

Alas, it never happened. We took her to Glasgow, to St. Kentigern's, and she was buried very quietly in the little family plot of earth.

Mother died in Holy Week. It is the week when Requiem Mass is banned. That is the law of the Church.

Rothesay after the death of my mother continued to be like a place of continual penance.

As a little boy I was stricken with measles, as happens to most little boys. It was an illness that grannies knew all about. You darkened the windows and kept the light off the eyes and gave out warnings about scratching the spots.

Now we know that it wasn't as simple as that. From my boyhood measles, I was left with a permanent ear infection.

Sometimes it would be dormant for years, then the flare-up would go on for two or three months. It was a condition known as *otitis media.* We called it a running ear.

My left ear throughout all my singing days had hearing of only fifty per cent.

In my tranquil days in Argyll, my ear trouble rarely erupted.

We men are probably allergic to admitting any emotional reaction to the death of an elderly parent. But soon after my bereavement, my *otitis media* started up more violently than ever before. The doctor described a complication known as *labyrinthitis.*

If that sounds alarming, it was!

Sometimes the world seemed to revolve around my head. I daren't drive a car. The attacks would sometimes vary and give the frightening impression of a constant, recurring series of somersaults—as if I were tied to a mill-wheel.

They told me I had Menière's disease. There was no escape by going to bed. One slight turn of the head and the bedroom would begin to whirl until you were physically sick.

I had no curate at Rothesay. I was stuck in this large parish entirely on my own—for a fit man even, a formidable task.

Bishop McGill was completely understanding. I told him the doctor's verdict—the flare-up might last a year or even two. There was no cure, but thereafter I might look forward to a period of normality.

" You have this house in Spain," the Bishop said. " Why not get away for a spell? Shut yourself off from all the stresses and strains and you'll most likely get better the quicker.

" My advice is Spain. And if you want to come back to this part of the world, there will be a quiet little parish somewhere for you."

I parted from Rothesay with no regrets. There were hardly any Clyde steamers left.

I looked forward to Spain. I even had the feeling that I might not ever come back.

For five months I soaked in the comforting sun.

Between Malaga and Torremelinos there were about 2,000 British families who'd decided to settle in Spain. After some weeks, I said Mass every Sunday in Malaga's lovely old cathedral. One Sunday I got the surprise of my life. Who should be among the faithful but my old friend, Phil Green!

To find Phil in Spain at all was unexpected enough. But for him to be there in a Catholic church—this I just could not comprehend.

Phil is a brilliant musician. He it was who made the arrangements and conducted the backing orchestra for most of my records.

Phil was a Londoner who'd been carrying on a love affair with Ireland for years. And Phil was a Jew.

The unforeseen pleasure of our meeting was mutual.

"What on earth are you doing here?" he said.

"More to the point," I told him, "what on earth are *you* doing here—and at Mass in our cathedral?"

Phil's enchantment with Ireland had gone as deep as his soul. He'd been converted to Catholicism.

We had so much to talk about that we met thereafter every day. One morning Phil jumped up from his chair on the balcony of my home.

"You know what?" he said excitedly, "I'm going to write a new Mass."

It was entirely in English. Its music was sometimes gay and explosive and filled with haunting, Irish-sounding melody. It proclaimed the glad tidings with drums and the clash of cymbals and a great, rolling sound of massed, mellow strings.

Ten years ago it would have sounded like sacrilege.

But R.C.A. liked it so much that they invited me down to take the part of the priest. They drafted in a Trinity Chorale composed of the cream of George Mitchell's Singers and, to express his musical revolution, Phil was given a magnificent orchestra of hand-picked musicians.

Cardinal Heenan blessed the project by writing the introduction to the glossy, coloured sleeve, and the royalties were given to his Choir School.

" I hesitate to use the word ' exciting,' " he said, " but I can think of no other to describe this Mass."

In its first week the record sold out in places as far apart as Glasgow and New York.

It was heard by the organisers of the Cork Film Festival, who broke with tradition completely by opening the festival with Phil's St. Patrick's Mass done live in St. Francis' Church. The local Franciscan Chorale was augmented by the Mitchell Singers, flown over specially for the occasion.

Three thousand people crammed every inch of seating space. And something happened at the end of that service that I have never before experienced. The great congregation stood up and clapped.

I feel that my old pal, Phil Green, has employed his great musicianship to do our Church a notable service. Indeed, I have the feeling that the Lord smiled on that chance meeting in Malaga as benevolently as the sun of Spain.

My doctors had given strict instructions to keep my ear entirely from contact with water. Even the act of washing my hair was considered a hazard, and I had to plug the ear with cotton wool every time the shampoo bottle came out.

But my condition improved slowly. I had access to a drug that controlled the infection.

Bathing in the sea was, of course, banned as well. But I began to feel so fit, it was torture to sit on the beach and watch that great, gleaming stretch of blue swimming material and not do anything about it.

314

The medicos to this day are not aware that now and again I broke the rules and went for a swim. The point is that there weren't any ill effects.

As one radiant, purposeless day grew out of another, the sheer incessancy of sunshine began to pall. Once again I was straining at the lead.

It was something of which I was aware every time I left my native land—that I was bound to Scotland with a permanent, unseen umbilical cord.

I had seen a bull-fight once before, and my reaction was one of bored nausea. But my housekeeper was insistent. How could she tell her friends about Spain with no mention of handsome matadors and the excitement of the bloody ring?

So with her I went reluctantly. Throughout the performance I sat and read James Bond.

I know my indifference gave offence to the patrons on my left and right, but I am incurably anti-bull-fighting.

I love sport. I also love animals. I am against a so-called sport that introduces publicly a living creature with the full intention of ensuring that before the show is over, it will be dead.

What makes the whole business even more degrading is that for our amusement, the animal will not die before it has been cruelly tormented and tortured out of its wits.

Man's other noble friend, the horse, is brought into the act of wickedness also. These bull-fighting horses are lovely beasts. Most of them have led an honest, inoffensive life of service carrying tourists round the handsome and historical places of Spain.

Now their latter-day lot is to be forced into an arena along with an increasingly frenzied bull, and with no means whatever of escape.

They cannot even indicate their terror by whinnying or screaming. Before they're forced into the bull-fighting business their vocal cords are severed.

It is argued that the matador is the bravest of men, that the whole point of the exercise is his demonstration of great human skill and courage—it is an art. For me it's hateful and degrading.

I am going to suggest, however, that in this bull-baiting business the British are not without guilt.

The new breed of Spaniard, if not allergic to bull-fighting, is certainly less interested. The modern sport of Spain is football. It's the kicking of a ball, not the harrying of a bull, that now thrills the Spanish people.

In Spain they are soccer-mad, and all that keeps the hateful bull-fight alive is the morbid curiosity of the tourist.

If the millions who flock to the Costa-this and the Costa-that for a fortnight's sun treatment, would only boycott the whole ugly business, the bull-fighting industry would wither overnight. And a very good riddance.

Bull-fighting in England was abolished in 1835 and is said to have been far more cruel than the Spanish ceremony—in England the poor bull had no defensive horns—they were sawn off and his nostrils were tightly plugged with pepper.

I will not say it was bull-fighting that sent me back to Scotland.

Rather was it this same old nostalgia for a glimpse of snow on the mountains and the cry of the curlew, and a dram when the air has knives in it, and all the sights and smells and sounds of a country that is at once fierce and friendly and never boring. I wrote to Argyll's new Bishop: " So far as my health is concerned, I should get the all-clear any day now. I want to get back to work."

His reply was that there would be no parish changes until June. He suggested that I should relax and enjoy myself for another three months and then he would have something for me.

I liked Spain the more after that—I enjoyed my pleasant Spanish flat because I knew that it wasn't for always.

One thing I shall never forget was Malaga's Holy Week celebrations.

By this time we had already had Vatican II with its instruction to cast out various statuary from our churches. That directive, it seemed, had never reached Spain!

In every church I visited in Malaga there would be as many as eight different representations of the Madonna—each adorned more lavishly than the other—in fine silks and satins, some of them embellished with what looked like jewels, but turned out to be only bits of coloured glass.

When Holy Week came I was made to realise the significance of those large collections of various religious imagery. The churches were being used for storage space—for the paraphernalia of the great processions.

Some of the giant figures in the Holy Week parades needed as many as a hundred bearers. They were mounted on platforms with the men underneath.

In front of each was a sort of sergeant-major who gave his instructions by ringing a bell. It was all very slow and obviously exhausting. Every thirty yards or so, the bell would clang and the effigy was lowered while its carriers took a rest.

The significance of the ceremony used to be one of penance. And each night of the week was given over to various categories or professions.

The statue-bearing might be undertaken on one occasion by the doctors, then the lawyers—or engineers or students or gipsies. But things had changed.

The processions I saw may have had in them one or two doctors or lawyers or students, but I discovered that the " acts of penance " were now being done by professionals!

They were most of them husky labourers from the docklands. And far from performing a sacred rite, they were in it for the money!

Holy Week for them was something of a bonanza—a time for going on bonus.

No doubt by way of threatening to strike, they had had their conditions of service adjusted to include refreshment at many a stop.

Their supporting of the great statues came so close to being a drunken and sometimes hilarious escapade, that Cardinal Herrera at one time had to issue the threat of banning the processions altogether.

Each float had its following of representatives of various Brotherhoods. Their outfits reminded me of the Ku Klux Klan, except that they were in brilliant reds, purples, yellows, blues and white.

Some of them brought along their youngsters—rigged out also in the same sort of uniforms. There were those who looked no more than six or seven years old.

Police bands followed military bands. The Spanish Foreign Legion added their bit of colour to the scene. Candles burned all over the place.

Along the route, the café proprietors were rubbing their hands, as their busy waiters moved in and out among the congested tables on the sidewalk. The trade for wine and brandy was never so brisk.

I'd been brought up to look upon Holy Week as a time of penance and prayer. I loved its solemnity. I loved its sadness.

The trooping round the Seven Churches on Holy Thursday. The Seven Last Words on the Cross. The darkness of the Tenebrae. The Stations of the Cross at three o'clock. The liturgy of Good Friday. The Mass of the Presanctified.

It was all very wonderful. It was all very real. I think I preferred Holy Week to Christmas—and that's saying something.

Certainly the Malaga event was much more spectacular. The staging was superb. There was a grandiose operatic quality about the whole proceedings, but I couldn't help feeling that I was sitting in on a religious circus. One felt this show was for the tourists.

CHAPTER

35

I have lived to see much change in my Church. But I get the impression it will be as a zephyr compared to the whirlwinds that now threaten to uproot so many dogmas and attitudes that at one time seemed so sacrosanct.

Shortly before that " This Is Your Life " debacle, we had the Second Vatican Council. In London I listened to Bishops from all over the world, and their constant talk was of the dangers of schisms in the Church.

They were warnings that fell strangely on my ears. Schisms? In my own little religious world I'm afraid I felt completely cosy and secure. Yet here was obviously evidence of great unrest and near-rebellion in the greater worldwide organisation.

Pope John had sensed it and wisely decided that what festered under the surface should be permitted to emerge into the healing open air—so we were told anyway.

Great documents of recommendation have come out of Vatican II, and the tragedy is that today they have been read by only the few.

And among the few there is understandable frustration that so little of the suggested change has so far come to pass. Ours is a sage and very old Church, stretching right back to the very beginning of the Christian faith. It will not alter overnight like a pop music chart. That any change should be slow and gradual is probably not without good reason.

But the progressives did triumph at that Vatican Council, and the most obvious evidence of their agitation is at liturgical level and the language used at Mass.

I have said before that my affection is deep for ancient things and the customs and practices that sometimes don't show up all that favourably in the hard light of logic and modern practicality.

The sheer majesty of the old Tridentine Rite is something that I cherish. But I will be the first to admit that its language was foreign and therefore frequently meaningless.

This lack of significance was particularly apparent when the place of worship was large and the Mass for those faithful at the back of the church came over as a rhythmic holy mutter.

There were also priests who mouthed the unfamiliar syllables at such a pace that even with the help of their missals, the faithful were left completely behind.

Of this I am sure—when the unexpected happened at Vatican II and the day was overwhelmingly won by the advocates of change to Mass in the vernacular—the Holy Spirit was at work.

Certainly the English version of the Mass is painfully pedestrian. At no time does it yet achieve the overtones of the old, established liturgical language. The Latin Mass was indeed a thing of beauty.

And no one will deny the power for the inspiration of creative man that the Mass in Latin has provided through the centuries. The Latin Mass was an art form. Every great composer felt he had to write a Mass.

The Latin text has been the inspiration of a host stretching far across the horizon of artists, poets, philosophers, musicians, sculptors and architects.

As well as to churchmen and formal Christians, the Mass belongs to a universal culture. In a materialistic and technocratic civilisation that is increasingly threatening our lives and minds and spirits, it might therefore seem inhuman to deprive Man of such a worthy, grandiose inspiration.

Perhaps in time the Mass in the vernacular will evolve into a similar source of aesthetic power.

But meantime, surely, there is room in our Church for both the vernacular to enrich the spiritual experience of millions of individuals, and the ancient, traditional Latin for occasions of ceremony and especial celebration.

And so I came back to Scotland—to a Speyside that is still magnificent and handsome and challenging despite the tremendous post-war change, that has brought to the mountains the people of the city, and turned the road to the Highlands into a non-stop, noisy highway that is increasingly an accessory to human slaughter.

All, all is change. Myself I am changed. At an age when I should have arrived, I find that I am still travelling. At an age when knowledge and the experience of three score years and more should have hammered into some kind of certain permanency my thoughts and philosophy, I find myself more confused than at the start.

I am a puzzled priest and a bewildered one.

My parish is in the centre of a great holiday area. My house at Kingussie is something of a transit camp—a sort of staging post where people call and people talk.

Nuns, priests and bishops. Bare-legged Benedictines in khaki shorts on their way to camp with their boys. Holy men in T-shirts and polo-necks, with a compass on their wrist and a breviary in their knapsack.

Sometimes we talk far into the night. Always there is questioning, always debate. This is the age of the great, big query mark.

Men in religious orders ask, if priests are in such short supply, why should their time be spent in teaching the sons of the rich in expensive and undemocratic public schools?

Nuns tell me they must still nurse the sick in hospitals exclusive to the wealthy, and run boarding houses. Can this be, in this day and age, their most urgent apostolate?

But is this sort of thing what nuns are made for? Can this be called vocation? Nuns ask me these things. Nuns ask these things of other nuns. Nuns ask their own consciences also.

Questions, questions, questions. All the great and golden certainties are suddenly in the melting pot. Why celibacy, the Pill, collegiality, appointment of Bishops—why Papal Nuncios, Structures of the Church—why auricular confession? Questions, questions, questions. Frustration that many of the reforms of Vatican II are so slow in becoming a reality. For others the period of change has been alarming and breath-taking.

Their Church that from time immemorial was so solid and secure now seems almost to tumble about their ears. They are bewildered by a situation in which almost everything that Luther and the Reformers craved is virtually now being granted by Rome.

Loyal priests and people who have travelled the road without question, the traditional road of Faith, find themselves presented with a theology that seems to savour more of Luther than St. Paul or Thomas Aquinas.

What twenty years ago was condemned as wrong now gets the award of right. So many certainties now seem no longer so certain. The house that was held together by a blind, patient and unquestioning faith now gapes to the winds of questioning and argument.

This little story of my puny life is a light-hearted journey, and I'm no theologian. I suppose I should feel depressed. The Church I grew up in, I loved with a passionate devotion—it was my sheet anchor—the certain Rock. Frankly, I think I would really have wished it to remain that way; but now that we are having the Revolution, I am not blind to its merits, above all the greater honesty and freedom in the Church.

I am thrilled at the extent, more than ever before in my lifetime, of enthusiasm for talking about Christ, the Scriptures, the Church, among priests and laity. The Church is very much alive, and the new-found freedom allows us to talk so honestly without the nagging fear of other days, of delation.

For the Barque of Peter the prevailing seas are stormy. Some things have been lost overboard, and to ensure her safety other things may have to go. But what hasn't altered is my absolute certainty that eventually she will come safely home. The Church will survive every crisis because the Master will be with her all days, even to the consummation of the world.

My life has been full and the rewards have been rich. Have I any regrets? Yes, that I didn't always live up to my high vocation; but my Faith has never wavered in the One I hear now strangely described as Super Star.

APPENDIX

A SELECTION OF RECORDINGS COVERING
A SPAN OF 39 YEARS
1934 ——————— 1973

Bonnie Earl of Moray.
Maiden of Morven.
Island Moon.
Turn ye to me.
O gin I were a Baron's heir.
Jeanie with the light brown
hair.
Ho ro, my nut-brown maiden.
Panis angelicus.
O Sanctissima.
My Master hath a garden.
Christ in His garden.
O men from the fields.
To Jesus' Heart all burning.
Mother of mercy.
Jesus, my Lord, my God, my
all.
Bring flowers of the rarest.
The Holy Child.
Pater Noster.
We long to see Thee so.
The Rosary.
Song of the passing soul.
Ave Verum.
Be still, my soul.
Pange Lingua.
When the children say their
prayers.
The Christ Child's Lullaby.
Charm me asleep.
A Prayer to Our Lady.

Beautiful dreamer.
Gentle Annie.
Sweetly she sleeps my Alice
fair.
The Kashmiri song.
Trusting eyes.
Love is mine.
Plaisir d'amour.
Silent worship.
Where'er you walk.
O del mio amato ben'.
Sento nel cuore.
La maison grise.
Stornellatrice.
Pietà Signor.
Bonnie Strathyre.
The green bushes.
O Bothwell bank.
I know my love.
I saw from the beach.
A perfect day.
Silver threads among the
gold.
An Eriskay love lilt.
Coronach.
Scotland the brave.
Killarney in the Spring.
Duna.
The rowan tree.
She moved through the fair.
The lark in the clear air.

Salve Regina.
Salve Mater.
Ave Maris Stella.
Eja Deo accinamus.
The youth of the heart.
A Tiree love song.
Uist tramping song.
The young May moon.
Terence's farewell to Kathleen.
Home, sweet home.
Pleading.
Little Boy Blue.
The village that nobody knows.
Westering home.
Bonnie George Campbell.
Durisdeer.
Kitty of Coleraine.
In Praise of Islay.
Lewis bridal song.
The stuttering lovers.
The old house.
Who is Sylvia?
Warum?
Violetta.
Maire's wedding.
Song of the seals.
Till I return.
Love's old sweet song.
The harp that once thru' Tara's halls.
Afton Water.
The Rose of Tralee.
Believe me if all those endearing young charms.
When the kye come hame.
Misty islands of the Highlands.
Galway Bay.
Oft in the stilly night.

Silent, oh Moyle.
The last rose of Summer.
Somewhere a voice is calling.
I love my love in the morning.
I'm a sentimental one.
Ye banks and braes o' bonnie Doon.
Loch Lomond.
Johnnie Cope.
Will ye no' come back again?
Hail, glorious St. Patrick.
Down by the Sally Gardens.
My ain folk.
Skye boat song.
Mother Machree.
In summertime on Bredon.
Una Waun.
My Laggan love.
Ireland my home.
The foggy dew.
The dawning of the day.
Since first I saw your face.
I hear you calling me.
Rose of Killarney.
The road to the Isles.
My Nancy.
Mary Shaw.
The bonnie lass o' Ballochmyle.
O Bethlehem.
As I sit here.
Macushla.
The peat fire flame.
Maighdeanan na h'airidh.
I know where I'm going.
The Spanish lady.
On the banks of Allan Water.
Tog orm mo phiob.
Mhnathan a ghlinne so.
The meeting of the waters.
Mowing the barley.

The short cut to the Rosses.
A fairy story by the fire.
Kitty my love.
Phil the fluter.
Just for today.
All in the April evening.
Bonnie Mary of Argyll.
Bonnie wee thing.

Kelly the boy from Killann.
Land of my heart.
The Lord is my Shepherd.
Adoro Te devote.
The fairy tree.
O quam amabilis.

ALBUMS OR L.P.s

1934 ——————— 1973

Memories of Scotland
(6 vols.).
Memories of Ireland (6 vols.).
An Evening with Sydney
MacEwan.
Sacred Songs.
A Recital by Fr. Sydney
MacEwan.
Songs of the Shamrock.
Songs of the Thistle.
Songs of the Gael.
Songs of Scotland and
Ireland.
Presenting Fr. Sydney
MacEwan.
Peat Fire Flame.

Songs by Fr. Sydney
MacEwan.
The Emerald Isle.
Hebridean Songs (2 vols.).
The Spirit of Christmas.
A Garland to the Blessed
Virgin.
The Lord is my Shepherd.
Christmas Carols.
Memories.
St. Patrick's Mass.
The Latin Mass (recorded in
Rome).
Let me bring love (Mass of
St. Francis).